SUCCESS IN YOUR
ALLOTMENT

SUCCESS IN YOUR ALLOTMENT

GROWING YOUR OWN VEGETABLES, HERBS, FRUIT AND FLOWERS

WITH OVER 530 PRACTICAL PHOTOGRAPHS AND ILLUSTRATIONS

CHRISTINE AND MICHAEL LAVELLE

southwater

This edition is published by Southwater
an imprint of Anness Publishing Ltd
Blaby Road, Wigston
Leicestershire LE18 4SE

Email: info@anness.com
Web: www.southwaterbooks.com;
www.annesspublishing.com

If you like the images in this book and would
like to investigate using them for publishing,
promotions or advertising, please visit
our website www.practicalpictures.com
for more information.

© Anness Publishing Ltd 2011

Publisher: Joanna Lorenz
Senior Editor: Felicity Forster
Designer: Lisa Tai
Jacket Design: Nigel Partridge
Illustrator: Liz Pepperell
Photographers: Peter Anderson and
    Colin Leftley
Production Controller: Bessie Bai

ETHICAL TRADING POLICY
At Anness Publishing we believe that
business should be conducted in an ethical
and ecologically sustainable way, with
respect for the environment and a proper
regard to the replacement of the natural
resources we employ.

As a publisher, we use a lot of wood pulp
in high-quality paper for printing, and that
wood commonly comes from spruce trees.
We are therefore currently growing more
than 750,000 trees in three Scottish forest
plantations: Berrymoss (130 hectares/
320 acres), West Touxhill (125 hectares/
305 acres) and Deveron Forest (75 hectares/
185 acres). The forests we manage contain
more than 3.5 times the number of trees
employed each year in making paper for
the books we manufacture.

Because of this ongoing ecological
investment programme, you, as our
customer, can have the pleasure and
reassurance of knowing that a tree is
being cultivated on your behalf to naturally
replace the materials used to make the
book you are holding.

Our forestry programme is run in
accordance with the UK Woodland
Assurance Scheme (UKWAS) and will be
certified by the internationally recognized
Forest Stewardship Council (FSC). The FSC
is a non-government organization dedicated
to promoting responsible management of
the world's forests. Certification ensures
forests are managed in an environmentally
sustainable and socially responsible way. For
further information about this scheme, go to
www.annesspublishing.com/trees.

A CIP catalogue record for this book
is available from the British Library.

Previously published as part of a larger
volume, *The Practical Step-by-Step
Book of Allotment Gardening.*

PUBLISHER'S NOTE
Although the advice and information in this
book are believed to be accurate and true
at the time of going to press, neither the
authors nor the publisher can accept any
legal responsibility or liability for any errors
or omissions that may be made nor for any
inaccuracies nor for any harm or injury that
comes about from following instructions or
advice in this book.

CONTENTS

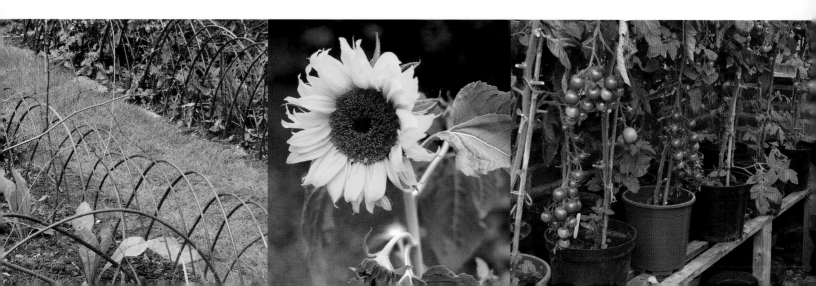

INTRODUCTION

The aim of this book is to show how anyone can become a successful allotment gardener. Whether you are an experienced gardener or not, an allotment can easily become a productive and absorbing hobby that can involve your whole family. Time spent on an allotment provides a vital link with nature and an opportunity to escape the troubles of modern living. To most people they are places to grow fresh food, but they can also have a value as little green oases or even mini nature reserves.

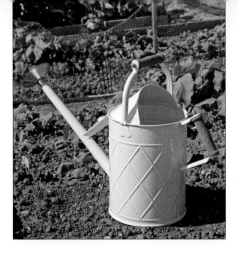

Above: *Watering is just one example of a task that, while straightforward, must still be done correctly in order to ensure success.*

The start of the 21st century has seen a huge rise in the popularity of home-grown foods. Many turn to this because of concerns for their family's wellbeing following successive food scares, although it is arguably the individual empowerment that growing food gives that ultimately proves the biggest draw. Many home-growers also believe that the food they grow is not only inherently healthier, but also tastier and, without a doubt, fresher.

Growing your own food, although an attractive idea, does require certain skills. This comprehensive book is intended as an essential guide to show you how to do this. It aims to try to demystify this area of

gardening, and is structured in a simple, down-to-earth way, with easy-to-follow explanations throughout. The language used is largely non-technical, although the techniques described are based upon sound scientific ideas. Explanations of underlying principles are followed by clear advice on how best to lay out, build, plan, plant and maintain plots for home-growing. While ideally suited to beginners, the book should also prove useful for those with more gardening experience who want to expand and transfer their skills to an allotment site.

The text is lavishly supported with illustrations and photographs and, wherever possible, growing techniques and systems are described. Projects are accompanied by straightforward step-by-step instructions showing how jobs should be done, and

many important tips and useful 'how-to' guides bring all the ideas to life. Plans and instructions are included to help you to understand how to blend the functionality of the growing space with other needs, such as providing a outdoor play space for children.

Starting with an explanation of what allotments are, the text outlines the main principles and natural cycles that exist both on a global scale and within your own plot. It aims to show how an allotment should ideally work in harmony with nature's rhythms and reveals how you can manage your cropping to take best advantage of these. Understanding the soil is fundamental

Below: *In time, your allotment will develop its own character that is as much about you as the plants that you choose to grow there.*

Below: *Planning crops, such as lettuce, is very important if you want to ensure a steady supply through the season.*

Left: *The framework and layout of your allotment is a key aspect of successful growing, and needs careful planning.*

and diseases. There are tables listing the most common problems you are likely to encounter, with advice on prevention and treatments, from using protective mesh coverings to introducing beneficial predators and companion plants.

The final chapter, a month-by-month calendar of care, helps you plan your plot for the year and provides an at-a-glance guide to the main tasks you need to do.

The book isn't just about the practice of growing crops, however, and considerable emphasis is placed upon getting out there and enjoying time on your plot. Tending plants, rather than being a chore, can easily become a time for you and your family to relax and experience closeness to nature within your own 'safe' space.

Whether you see your allotment as an outdoor living space, a wildlife haven or as a place to grow food for your table, the application of careful planning, sound crop selection and tried-and-tested gardening techniques outlined in this book can help you to transform your plot into a highly productive space. Ultimately, an allotment can offer you a healthy place in which to spend time, a great opportunity to meet fellow gardeners and a relaxing and sociable way to garden.

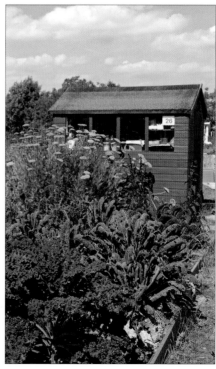

to creating a successful allotment, and this is described simply and concisely to ensure that you can prepare the ground properly.

Once these basics are explained, the section dealing with planning your crops gives detailed advice on how to assess your own wants and needs so that you can go on to create an effective and workable plan for a yearly cropping schedule.

This is followed by a section on how to grow the crops themselves. Practical, effective horticultural practices are combined with simple, commonsense advice on harvesting and storing a range of crops;

helpful hints on choosing tools, equipment and materials; and advice on how to decide whether you need structures such as sheds or glasshouses. The importance of environmentally friendly practices features throughout the text, although alternatives are also discussed and compared.

A section on plant health explains why your plants sometimes get sick and what you can do to minimize the impact of pests

Right: *Sheds provide both storage and shelter from the elements, making them an invaluable addition if you have the space.*

ALLOTMENT BASICS

Obtaining an allotment can be a time-consuming process. It helps, however, to know a little about the area, the specific site, the rules and regulations governing the allotment, and what you want to achieve so you can be specific about your requirements. Once you have a plot, you will need to make a number of decisions about what you can do with it and how you are going to set it out. This chapter aims to help you with your planning by providing information about how how to set realistic goals, different layout options, and additional considerations such as permanent structures, and buying tools and equipment.

Left: *The sight of an allotment at the height of the growing season is enticing, but is ultimately the product of much hard work.*

Above: *Flowers such as these sunflowers make a colourful addition to the plot and can be used as cut blooms for the home.*

Above: *Time spent protecting your crops is worthwhile, and means you will reap the rewards later with a bumper harvest.*

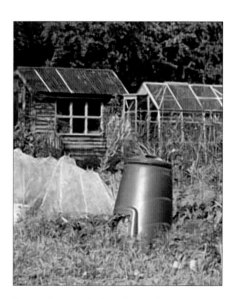

Above: *Larger allotments may have room for a glasshouse and shed, but you should always allow space for a composting area.*

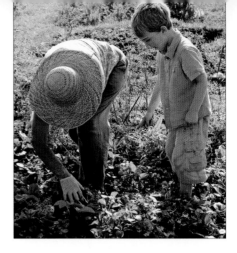

Above: *Allotments have always been a place where generations meet, sharing both time and experiences in a natural setting.*

THE HISTORY OF ALLOTMENTS

Allotments and community gardens are a familiar sight in a modern urban setting. They originated as a result of social concerns about the plight of the poor and needy, as well as to provide a source of vital food production during wartime, but for many gardeners today the emphasis has shifted and they now represent a place where city-dwellers can get back to nature and grow tasty and healthy food while mixing with like-minded individuals.

WHAT IS AN ALLOTMENT?

Essentially an allotment is an area or 'parcel' of land allotted to a tenant, who undertakes to tend and cultivate the area, usually in return for a small rent being paid. The word 'allotment' was first coined in England In the late 1500s, under Elizabeth I, as the name for the plots of land attached to tenant cottages that were given as compensation for the loss of common lands. Similar land allocation schemes exist in other countries; they follow a similar framework, although their names can vary. In North America, Australia and New Zealand, for instance, the term 'community garden' is used, whereas across much of Europe they tend to be described as community, family, social or work gardens.

WHY WERE ALLOTMENTS NEEDED?

Since ancient times, people have shared pieces of land around their village in order to eke out an existence by growing crops and grazing livestock. As populations have grown, and particularly as industry and agriculture have developed, the need for increased efficiency has meant that there has been ever more pressure on traditional 'shared' approaches to food production. As a consequence, many common areas have disappeared, and people's link with the land and the food it provides severed.

Land Enclosure, as it came to be called, occurred in many parts of the world during the 18th and 19th centuries. While this did increase efficiency in agriculture and food

supply to the burgeoning urban centres, it benefited only a relatively small minority of landowners; the majority of people became disenfranchised and were forced to seek work in the growing urban centres as they lost access to the land. In response to this, certain influential members of the ruling elite of the time made moves to provide land in the form of allotments, principally for the poor and unemployed so that they could grow their own produce.

Over time the popularity of allotments persisted, but it was during the two world wars of the 20th century that they were most appreciated, providing food security during times of shortage. After World War II, however, there was a decline in interest as eating and growing fresh food was eclipsed by the arrival of convenience food, a trend that escalated through the second half of the 20th century. This was reversed only at the very end of the century, as concerns over food quality and a feeling of alienation from nature led to a new demand for allotments, which is as yet unabated.

WHERE DO YOU FIND THEM?

Allotments and community gardens are often concentrated in areas of high-density living, mostly in urban centres, although some are to be found in more rural settings. What they all usually have in common is a group of local residents who no longer have a direct connection to the land. Allotments can be very diverse, often as varied as the surrounding communities of gardeners that use them. Some are nurtured communally and their produce shared among all participants, whereas others contain individual plots for personal use.

Left: *In the mid-20th century allotments fulfilled a vital social need, as successive wars caused food shortages for families.*

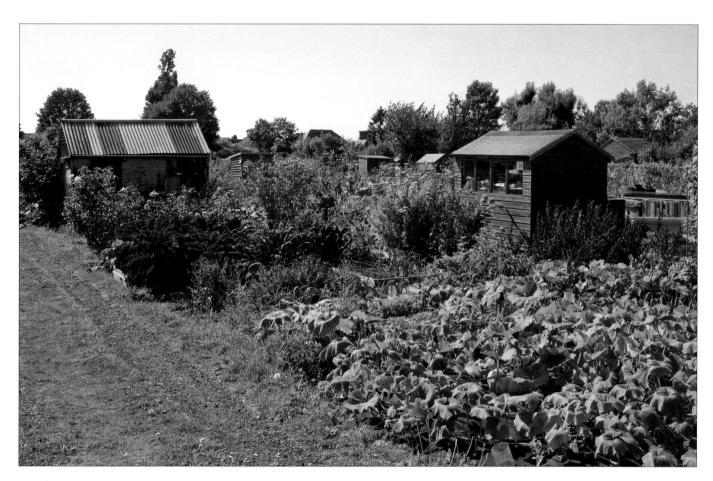

Above: *Allotments are typically moderately sized plots, tended by one owner, and contain a range of edible produce.*

Allotments and community gardens can also vary depending upon where in the world they are found. In the UK and the rest of Europe they tend to be characterized by collections of individual plots, each measuring hundreds of square metres. In North America, while community gardens do include the so-called 'victory garden' areas that consist of numerous small plots, they also encompass 'greening projects', which transform man-made communal areas into green spaces that can be used for growing, keeping livestock or simply as pleasant recreation zones.

THE BENFITS OF ALLOTMENTS

In the hectic modern world, allotments can enhance the quality of urban life, providing a meaningful leisure activity and enabling people to try their hand at sowing, growing, cultivating and harvesting vegetables. In addition, they may also be a place where children and adolescents can play, communicate and discover the natural world. Some are used by disadvantaged groups, such as the unemployed, those with disabilities or immigrant families, offering them the chance to meet like-minded individuals and to help build confidence and a sense of communal living.

As most allotments are characterized by either a collective space or numerous land parcels in one place, tenants quickly develop a sense of cohesion and belonging, involving not only the social interaction of gardening but also contributions to growers' associations, competing in shows or events, and the shared responsibility of having to abide by an agreed constitution and bylaws. This involvement entitles people to certain democratic rights within their communities, and with this comes a sense of empowerment and purpose.

Ultimately, then, the exact nature of an allotment or community garden will vary according to its location and the needs of the surrounding community. For the purposes of this book, an allotment will be viewed as a single 'parcel' of land that is accessible for an individual or family, and, while the communal aspects of allotment gardening are extremely important, it is the mechanics of how to actually grow things on the plot that will be the main focus here.

Above: *Community gardens in urban areas enable tenants to experience growing food, despite often having very modest plots.*

WHY GROW ON AN ALLOTMENT?

An allotment is far more than simply a place in which you can grow your own food. Indeed, many people recognize that having a plot is actually a lifestyle choice. While producing healthy fresh fruit and vegetables may be the central activity, the site also provides opportunities for fresh air and exercise, fun for the whole family and the chance to join an established community of people with similar interests.

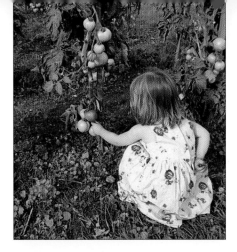

Above: *Seeing where vegetables come from helps children to connect more readily with nature in a way that is great fun for them.*

FRESH, HEALTHY FOOD

In recent years people have become much more interested in growing their own fruit, vegetables and herbs. In itself, this may not seem particularly remarkable, but it represents a dramatic reversal of the declining trend in this area that marked most of the late 20th century. One of the reasons for the shift was concerns about the quality of food from supermarkets following numerous food 'scares' in the 1980s and 1990s and new information about pesticide residues, both of which raised the profile of organic foods. This, coupled with a growing awareness of

Below: *Harvesting your own produce is the greatest pleasure of allotment growing and serves as a fitting reward for your hard work.*

food miles and wasteful packaging, meant that many became increasingly sceptical about the food they were buying. A greater public demand for more details about where food came from and how it was grown arose, and with it there was a corresponding surge in grow-your-own tendencies, as this it not only assures the safety and quality of the food, but also cuts out the need for transport and packaging.

The problem for a lot of people, though, is that many modern households do not have gardens, and those that do either don't have enough room to grow crops or they are poorly situated. Allotments are an ideal solution for people in this situation, offering them the chance to grow enough fresh food to feed the whole family in some cases.

Below: *The whole family will enjoy eating the fresh and tasty food they have grown themselves, and the shopping bill will also go down.*

An allotment of around 250m² (2688ft²) can produce enough vegetables to keep a family of four or five going for most of the year. Not only that, but clever planning will result in a wonderful array of fresh produce, from expensive delicacies such as artichokes, asparagus or French (green) beans, to traditional staples such as cabbages, carrots and potatoes.

HEALTHY OUTDOOR LIVING

Although food production is usually the prime motivation for most allotment-growers, the lure and benefits of fresh air and gentle exercise are also extremely important. In many ways, an allotment could be likened to an outdoor gym, enabling people to take exercise while being in touch with the natural world around them. All in all, an allotment is good for both mental as well as physical well-being, and has the added bonus of being much cheaper than joining a gym.

An allotment also allows people with little or no land around their own property to have a plot of land 'to call their own.'

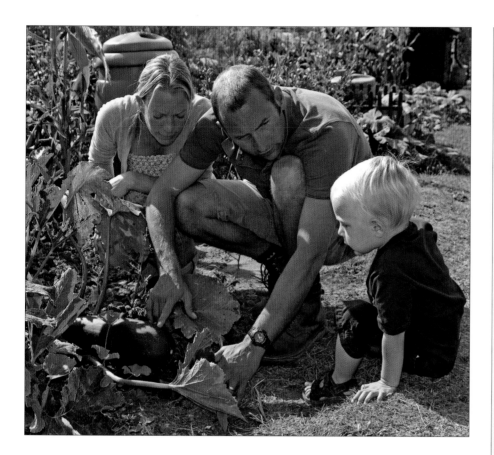

Above: *Allotments offer a hobby that can involve the whole family and help promote a healthy way of living.*

This in itself can be an extremely important motivation, enabling people to gain fulfilment within their leisure time and achieve a sense of ownership and personal space.

SOMETHING THE WHOLE FAMILY CAN DO

Allotments can be a personal, and solitary, hobby, where growers go to escape from it all and spend a little time on their own. Increasingly though, they are places where the whole family will go. Even a modest-sized plot can be a wonderful place to encourage children to learn about nature and growing food. At its most basic level it shows them where food really comes from – that it is grown, involves effort and is not merely a pre-packaged product on a supermarket shelf. It also introduces them to a wider variety of foods than they may otherwise have encountered, and involving them in the whole process, from seed packet to dinner table, can be a great way to get them to eat their five-a-day. The excitement and anticipation involved in growing the food is often the best motivation there is to encourage healthy eating.

HELPING PRESERVE THE ENVIRONMENT

While many of us feel that we would like to help protect the environment, modern living often leaves us feeling helpless in the face of the challenges of reducing our carbon footprints. An allotment is a form of empowerment in this respect, giving you the ability to grow food that limits the use of fertilizers and pesticides, transportation, packaging and waste. A well-managed allotment that takes full advantage of recycling and composting techniques is an environmental benefit in itself, which, if managed properly, can help not just to minimize harm to nature and wildlife, but can even become a mini nature reserve.

A LIFESTYLE CHOICE

Growing food on an allotment will change your life in a variety of ways. At its simplest it will reduce your weekly shopping bill and provide fresher food which almost invariably tastes better than that bought from stores. It is also a great chance to meet new people, often from all walks of life, and share both their and your own experiences. It is perhaps this communal aspect of an allotment that is ultimately the most life-changing benefit and, in many cases, proves the greatest inspiration.

BENEFITS OF GROWING ON AN ALLOTMENT

Below are just a few of the positive benefits that allotment gardening may bring to you, your family and your local area and environment.

- It is a good way to keep fit, in the fresh air, without having to expend very much money.
- Provides an excellent opportunity to make new friends.
- You will produce your own food, which will be tastier and cheaper than that available in most stores.
- Crops can have higher nutrient values than commercially grown ones, as well as inevitably being much fresher.
- The monthly shopping bill should be greatly reduced if you plan the crops carefully so there is something on offer all year.
- Growing your own food gives a sense of achievment and satisfaction that can bolster the spirits.
- It will provide cheap entertainment for all the family and an opportunity for everyone to learn new skills.
- Offers the space for novice and experienced gardeners to expand their horizons and try their hand at growing crops that they may not have room for in their home gardens, as well as potentially being introduced to more exotic species by neighbouring plot holders.
- Children and young people will have a safe space in which to play and learn more about the natural world as well as gaining an understanding of where food comes from.
- An allotment is a community and can help people to feel more involved with their local area.
- The allotment site will provide a habitat for insects, birds and animals, enriching the local environment and helping biodiversity.
- A well-tended allotment is attractive and will improve the look and overall atmosphere, especially in urban areas.
- Compost heaps offer an easy way to reduce household waste, while lateral thinking and recycling of wood and other materials engenders a sense of thriftiness and sustainability.

OBTAINING AN ALLOTMENT

A well-tended allotment site can be quite a spectacle; one that can excite and inspire you to obtain and tend a plot of your own. While the prospect of the allotment lifestyle is appealing, it is very important that you find out how to apply for one and make certain that you get one that is right for your needs. Remember that an allotment can be a real commitment that will require time and effort for it to be as productive as possible.

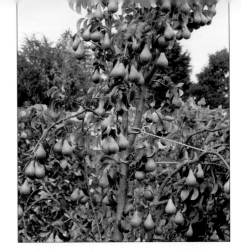

Above: *Fresh home-grown crops are a major incentive for getting an allotment, but are the result of commitment and hard work.*

FINDING AN ALLOTMENT

Obtaining an allotment is usually a relatively simple process, once you have the details of where to apply and who to contact. Who this is often depends upon the ownership of the site. Allotments and community gardens vary around the world and their ownership might well be influenced by where you live. In Britain for instance, the majority are owned by local authorities and applications are lodged with a local council. Others elsewhere may be owned by private associations or even private landlords, and it is well worth visiting an allotment area near you to familiarize yourself with the site in question and find out more about who you would need to contact.

Some community gardens limit their membership to residents within a particular catchment area or even an individual housing project, and membership may be relatively short term. In other places, however, plots might remain with a particular tenant for years, even decades, meaning that applying for a plot might simply get you on to a waiting list, which can be as much as 20 years! Either way, it will pay for you to do your homework, and you may discover you need to apply to several to stand a chance of getting a site. Contacting local allotment or produce associations can be extremely useful as they will often be able to put you in touch with the right people.

BE REALISTIC ABOUT YOUR OWN ABILITIES

While enthusiasm is an essential prerequisite of allotment gardening, it is essential that you temper this with a degree of realism about what you will be able to achieve. You need to remember that established plots are the product of a sustained level of effort by the tenant. In short, what you get out of a plot will depend upon what you put into it.

The biggest obstacle for many new allotment tenants can be over-ambition. If you are applying for a new plot, you would be well advised to pause for a moment, examine your motives and consider what will be involved in taking it on. Try not to be put off by the difficulties you foresee however, as the object of the exercise is not to stifle your ambition but merely to be objective. Once you have a clear idea of your own capabilities then you are ready to make your application, as you'll be clearer about what sort of plot best suits your needs and can make your application accordingly.

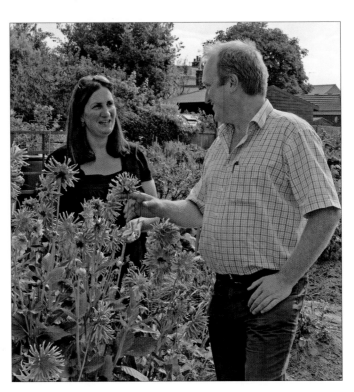

Far left: *If you are unsure how to get an allotment, you can always phone a local allotment or produce association for help, or look on the Internet.*

Left: *When you are considering getting an allotment, it is always worth talking to other plot holders first to find out if it is for you. They will be able to tell you how much effort, time and money is really required, as well as providing inspiration and advice.*

Right: *You will need certain tools in order to establish and maintain an allotment site, and these should be factored in when calculating the cost of having a plot.*

Below: *Allotment and community gardens have committees or site representatives that are usually more than willing to help new growers get started. They may also be able to tell you if a plot is likely to become available.*

CONSIDER THE TIME AN ALLOTMENT WILL NEED

While the idea of time spent on an allotment can be enticing, you need to remember that it is a year-round commitment that will often involve your being there in all weathers. Crops need regular attention and fitting this around the rest of your life can occasionally be a struggle for even the most committed allotment-growers.

The best way to approach this is to remember that a little bit of time as often as other commitments will allow is usually better than sporadic bouts of feverish activity. It isn't something that you can be half-hearted about though: a successful allotment is the product of regular attention and, perhaps most importantly, time devoted to crops just when it is needed.

GO AND TALK TO PLOT HOLDERS

The idea of approaching more experienced plot holders may seem daunting, particularly when you are new to allotment growing. In reality, however, the majority of

allotment holders are very friendly and approachable. People that tend plots are essentially gardeners, and as a rule they will enjoy meeting people who share their interest and be more than willing to answer questions and pass on their pearls of horticultural wisdom and encouragement.

Plot owners can usually offer invaluable practical advice about whether the site in question may suit your particular needs, what type the soil is, which crops can be grown there, and the rules and obligations that apply to plot holders and how these affect them. They may also give insider information on whether plots are likely to become vacant for rent. Often they will offer to take you on a tour of their own patch and tell you how they went about creating a productive plot.

Talking and meeting tenants can also be the best way to understand the sense of community that exists on a site, which in turn can bolster your enthusiasm if your application results in your being put on a long waiting list.

WEIGH UP ALL THE POTENTIAL COSTS CAREFULLY

While one of your objectives for growing on an allotment might be for you to save money, you should consider that unless you are lucky enough to inherit a well set out and maintained plot, you may need to invest in some materials in order to make it meet your own needs. Add tools and equipment to this, the cost of seed, fertilizers and a whole host of other sundries such as string, canes, netting etc., and the costs can soon mount up.

The best idea is to plan your plot so that you can set it up gradually, spreading the cost over a period of time, and concentrate on getting the layout right. Don't think that 'throwing money' at projects will guarantee success, and remember that magazines and garden centres are often full of 'must-have' items, which, in truth, you can often do perfectly well without! It is worth investigating local recycling schemes at this point, as you can often get a surprising amount of tools and equipment for free.

UNDERSTANDING YOUR ALLOTMENT

Plants, like all living things, flourish when given the right conditions. Certain plants will only thrive in a hot, sunny and dry garden, for example, while others may need a cool, moist and shady environment to prosper. If you are to have healthy plants, you need to choose those that are best suited to your site and this means understanding exactly what conditions prevail and taking into account a range of environmental factors.

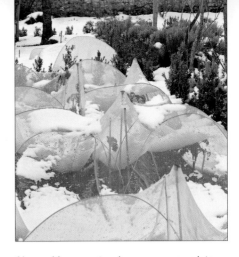

Above: *Young or tender crops appreciate some protection from cold nights and a fleece tunnel is one way of giving this.*

CLIMATE

The climate affects plants in a variety of ways, depending on the plant's location, its stage of maturity, the length of exposure and the intensity of the type of weather. Climate may have a dramatic effect on plant growth and development, especially when extreme weather conditions prevail.

TEMPERATURE

All plant species have their own maximum and minimum temperature tolerances, beyond which the life processes of the plant cease. As a general rule, the maximum temperature that most plants can tolerate is around 35ºC (95ºF), while the minimum is highly variable. The air and soil temperatures are also crucial in influencing dormancy within plants and this, in turn, largely dictates the length of the growing season.

Air temperature is affected by the degree of energy received from the sun. A sheltered site that benefits from the warming effects of the sun may be used for growing plants that are indigenous to warmer climates.

Soil temperature influences a plant's root development and the rate at which water and nutrients can be absorbed. Sandy soils warm up quicker and earlier in the season than clay soils, mainly because they are relatively free-draining and do not hold as much water. Sites that receive a lot of sun, or with a slight incline towards it, will also warm up quicker than shady ones.

WATER

This is the major constituent of all plants. In most allotments, rainfall is the principal source of water for plants and it can be lost through evaporation or surface run-off, although much of it is soaked up by soil particles. This water may then be absorbed by the root hairs of the plant.

Water may also be held in the air and is referred to as humidity. The amount of water vapour in the atmosphere at any one time is referred to as the relative humidity and is measured as a percentage of the saturation point (100 per cent humidity).

Waterlogging refers to the build-up of water that may occur in badly drained soil with poor structure. The roots of plants that are not adapted to these conditions will suffer and probably die through asphyxiation.

LIGHT LEVELS

Sunlight enables photosynthesis (the method by which plant food is made) to occur. As a result, it is vital to new growth as well as sustaining existing growth. Seasonal changes in light levels may also trigger different stages in the plants' development.

AIR CIRCULATION

Even moderate winds can increase a plant's transpiration rate. However, a light wind can also have beneficial effects, providing relief from extreme heat and cooling the foliage. It will also 'change the air' around the plant, and thus help to alleviate a stagnant atmosphere that could promote disease.

ASSESSING THE CLIMATE

Climatic information for your local area is generally available. Weather forecasts are an obvious source, but long-term records are a good option. From these you can find out about average rainfall, snow, frosty days, wind direction and monthly temperatures.

Left: *Seasonal crops growing on an allotment need watering in dry times, and there is no better source than collected rainwater.*

MICROCLIMATES IN AN ALLOTMENT

Even a small plot can contain a variety of microclimates, ranging from cool, shady corners to hot, dry areas. A proper assessment of the growing conditions allows you to choose the right plants for the right place.

Apples and pears ripen well in a sunny part of the allotment.

Potatoes will thrive in a warm, sheltered site.

Most herbs require open, sunny spots.

Position the greenhouse in an east-west orientation so that it catches maximum solar radiation.

Sour cherries (eg. 'Morello') will grow well in shady locations.

Compost bins need to be in a sunny location to keep them warm, otherwise the organic material will take longer to break down.

Exposed areas tend to be windy, so tall crops such as brassicas may need staking. Avoid growing broad (fava) beans in exposed areas, especially if growing over the winter period.

Cabbages will tolerate exposure.

Light shady areas (behind a fence) are ideal for growing crops such as salad leaves and lettuces. Onions and shallots will also tolerate light shade.

Spinach is best grown in light shade in summer as it reduces the chance of it bolting. It grows well with root crops such as parsnips.

Cool dark areas are ideal places for slugs and snails to congregate. Remove them by hand and dispose of them.

AN ALLOTMENT'S MICROCLIMATE

The prevailing weather conditions in confined or discrete areas are termed the microclimate. For example, there will be a range of environments within a small allotment area that may be very different from those weather conditions prevailing elsewhere in the locality. Observe what is going on in your own plot and keep a careful record of the position and influence of the following features:

Walls, hedges and fences may cause wind turbulence and dryness, depending upon their height and density. They may cause cold air to build up on sloping sites by preventing it from 'draining away" downwards. This can create frost pockets that may have a crucial affect on the type and range of plants that may be grown.

Shadow projections from permanent features, such as buildings, walls, hedges and large trees, may create a range of dense shadows, resulting in dark, dry and often cool conditions that will only suit certain plant species.

Hot spots may occur with aspects that are subject to high and prolonged levels of sunlight. Plants may struggle in the dryness created by such strong sunlight.

Damp areas may be anticipated where the ground is low-lying, especially on very heavy soils. During intense rainfall you should also note the direction of water flow including, where necessary, the route taken by excess surface water, which may in extreme cases be the cause of soil erosion.

Soil type and pH play an important role in the ability of a site to support particular plant species. The relative acidity or alkalinity can affect the availability of certain essential nutrients, leading to either shortage or toxicity in plants not ideally suited to the pH of a soil. It is always better to choose plants suited to the soil type on a plot. Attempts to alter the pH by acidifying or adding lime are rarely satisfactory and neither are long-term solutions.

Existing habitat types on and around the allotment indicate what plants are likely to thrive. Notes should be made on the range of species and the likely wildlife value.

The allotment topography (the shape and aspect of the land) may also affect what you are able to do. If a garden slopes toward the

direction of the midday sun, for instance, it will be warmer than a flat site. Sloping or uneven plots have their own problems, particularly if you wish to site a greenhouse.

RIGHT PLANT, RIGHT PLACE

Once you have assessed your allotment environment, you will be able to choose the right plants for your site. Every location has its own unique set of advantages and limitations, and these take time to evaluate, so trial and error is ultimately the most reliable method.

Right: *A rain gauge allows you to assess soil moisture and helps show when crops might need extra water to maintain their growth.*

THE NATURAL CYCLE

All the crops grown in an allotment are entirely dependent upon a range of natural processes. For example, plants produce their own food using carbon dioxide from the air, water from the soil and energy from the sun in a process known as photosynthesis. The energy in this sugar powers all the growth, development and life-giving processes within the plant. Once the natural cycles are understood, you can learn how to work in harmony with nature's rhythms and cycles.

Above: *Plant leaves are remarkable structures because they are the factories in which a plant makes its food.*

WHAT PLANTS NEED

In natural systems, nitrogen, phosphorus and potassium are repeatedly taken up by the plant, used and returned to the soil when the plant dies, drops its leaves or is eaten by an animal. This process is known as nutrient cycling. Plant nutrients are covered in more depth later. For now we need only look at three of the most important natural cycles: water, carbon and nitrogen.

THE WATER CYCLE

The movement and endless recycling of water between the atmosphere, the surface of the land and under the soil is called the water cycle and is driven by the energy of the sun and the force of gravity.

Water vapour in the atmosphere condenses into clouds, then falls as snow, rain, sleet or hail. This water may be taken up by plants, stored in lakes, enter the soil or flow over the surface of the land in streams and rivers. The sun causes water to evaporate back into the atmosphere, or gravity may pull it down through the pores of the soil to be stored as slow-moving ground water.

Water can also return to the atmosphere indirectly through plants' leaves – a process known as transpiration – and this is highest during periods of high temperatures, wind, dry air and sunshine.

THE CARBON CYCLE

All life on earth is based on carbon, and the chemistry of the carbon atom and its derived substances is called organic chemistry. Carbon has many sources, some living and some dead. When carbon is released into the air, the origin is called a source. All living things release some carbon and are sources, but there are other sources too, including volcanoes and activities such as burning wood and fossil fuels.

When carbon becomes part of a living organism, or is locked up in sediments or rocks, it is said to have entered a sink. The balance between carbon that has been liberated from a source and that entering a sink is important for the health of the planet, and has an effect on the global temperature.

THE NITROGEN CYCLE

Nitrogen is used by living organisms to produce a number of complex organic molecules such as amino acids, proteins and nucleic acids, the 'building blocks' of life. The largest store of nitrogen is in the atmosphere, where it exists as a gas. This store is about one million times larger than the total nitrogen contained in living organisms.

Despite its abundance in the atmosphere, plants can only take up nitrogen in two solid forms: ammonium and nitrate. Most plants fulfil their needs using nitrate from the soil. Ammonium is used less frequently because it is toxic in large concentrations. Most ecosystems have nitrogen stored in living and dead organic matter, which re-enters the cycle via decomposition. Decomposers in the soil, such as bacteria and fungi, chemically modify the nitrogen found in this organic matter.

Almost all of the nitrogen found in any terrestrial ecosystem originally came from the atmosphere and is biochemically converted ('fixed') into a useful form within the soil by specialized bacteria. Members of the bean family (legumes) and some other kinds of plants form relationships with nitrogen-fixing bacteria. In exchange for nitrogen, the bacteria receive food from the plants and special root structures (nodules) that provide protection.

Left: *Understanding how nature's cycles work will help you to take best advantage of the local conditions of your allotment.*

NATURAL CYCLES IN A TYPICAL ALLOTMENT

*Even a modest-sized allotment plot is a perfect example
of what occurs in nature, as elements and nutrients are repeatedly
recycled through both the actions of the grower as well as a range
of other living creatures. This example shows three main cycles.*

*In the food chain, insects and fruits are eaten by birds and
small mammals, which are in turn eaten by larger species
such as hawks and foxes. The carbon and nitrogen cycles
show how these elements are processed by plants.*

FOOD CHAIN — Spiders — Flying insects — Berries — Caterpillars — Sawfly — Hawk — Recycled through composting — CARBON CYCLE: Carbon dioxide — Some carbon returned to atmosphere through respiration — NITROGEN CYCLE: Nitrogen in atmosphere — Fox — Carbon taken in by plants — Hedgehog — Slug — Thrush — Snail — Frog — Ground beetle — Excess nitrates liberated as nitrogen by bacteria — Bacteria fix nitrogen as nitrates, a form that can be used by plants

OXYGEN CYCLE

The oxygen cycle describes the movement
of oxygen within and between its three
main reservoirs – the atmosphere; living
things; and rocks, lakes, rivers and oceans.
The main driving force for this cycle is
plant life and its production of food through
photosynthesis. When plants make food
they release a lot of oxygen, and it is for
this reason alone that the atmosphere on
Earth contains around 21 per cent of it.
All living things breathe in oxygen and use it
to release the energy contained in food. In
this way, the carbon cycle and oxygen cycle
combine and balance.

Nutrient cycles, then, are a matter of
balance, having an important impact upon
our daily lives, and learning to work with them
can improve the health of your allotment.

WHAT ARE ECOSYSTEMS?

Short for ecological systems, ecosystems
are communities of plants and animals that
consist of a given habitat (the place where
an organism lives) and its community (all
the plants and animals that live in it). Any
group of living and non-living things
interacting with each other (including those
found in allotments) can be considered
an ecosystem.

The chemical materials that are
extracted from the environment and
changed into living tissue by plants and
animals are continually recycled within the
ecosystem. These nutrient cycles are at
their most efficient when an ecosystem
has a good diversity of species. Such
diversity tends to make a community
stable and self-perpetuating.

Below: *The presence of animals such
as toads on a plot are an indication
of a stable and balanced ecosystem.*

PLANNING THE PLOT

The prime objective for most allotment-growers will be food production. A good plot plan will outline not only where the crops will go, but also where you need to put all the other things that will help you to achieve this. The shape and structure of the plot can exert a huge influence over what you can and cannot do, meaning that it is important that you get this right from the outset. You also want to avoid the cost, both in terms of time and money, of having to redo something that isn't right.

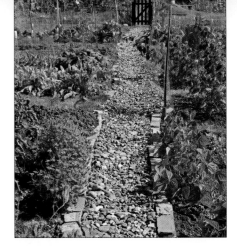

Above: *A network of paths are essential for getting around the plot and help define the layout and overall look of the site.*

SET THE DESIGN OBJECTIVES

The real trick of any successful allotment plan is to start by making two lists. The first list should be a wish list, containing all the things you want to do there. While this will include activities such as growing food, flowers or keeping livestock, remember to add things such as a relaxation or safe area for children's play etc., as these too will influence your design. If the list is not already too long, you can add other, desirable, non-essential features that you might like to include if space permits.

The second list will detail all the things that you will need in order to fulfil the activities you have thus far outlined. It should include the materials required as well as the activities it involves, as these may need additional items to be included in the design that you had not given much thought to until now.

Finally, before you draw up your proposed ground plan, you need to compile an inventory of what is already there. On an established plot there may already be a basic structure on the site that can be used or adapted to suit your needs with little additional effort or cost. If you want to start again, removing the previous layout can add to the time and cost of setting up your plot and will need consideration and planning.

DECIDE THE BASIC LAYOUT

To many, the fact that crops are mostly short term, and as a consequence can be moved around on a regular basis, is part of the essential appeal of an allotment. The yearly planning cycle and changes this regularly brings to the plot make it a dynamic and engaging pastime. While true for the plants however, compost bins, sheds, greenhouses, paths and other structures are necessarily permanent items. This means that you will need to decide where these need to go before you plan where crops will be grown.

You will also need to make early decisions over where certain longer-term crops will be sited. If you want to grow fruit for example, it might need support on wires or trellis, a frame for netting and above all sufficient space. Other crops, such as artichokes, asparagus or rhubarb, require little in the way of structures but are nonetheless permanent, and will require a dedicated space.

Finally, if you want to get around the plot easily, you will need to ensure that you have a network of paths. This is the point when you really start to define how the plot will look and it will give you the chance to apply a bit of creativity. Traditional designs can see the crops laid out in straight rows with

Below: *A composting area is a must for any allotment site. Ideally you will need at least two heaps or bins to ensure a steady supply.*

Below: *Planning your plot in advance is an essential first step to make sure it is both productive and efficient all year round.*

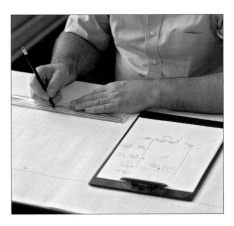

TOP PLOT PLANNING TIPS

Include a composting area – recycling green waste is the easiest way to ensure a good supply of organic soil conditioner.

Include paths and access points – make main paths wide enough to get a wheelbarrow down; paths between rows can be smaller.

Consider whether you need permanent storage – a shed is a great addition to the plot, but is there enough space or do you really need one?

Know where the nearest water source is – if you have to walk a long way to fill a watering can, then planting 'thirsty' crops will mean a lot of effort!

Visit 'model gardens' for inspiration – many gardens have model vegetable patches that can be a great inspiration.

Talk to the adjoining plot holders – they know a great deal about the site as a whole and may even know something about the history of your own patch.

Work out how much time you have – if you can't hoe it, don't sow it!

AN ALLOTMENT PLAN

The vegetable beds shown here have been set out on a four-year crop rotation plan.

Cold frames are used to harden off plants grown in the greenhouse or for sowing seeds such as lettuce outside to bring them on earlier.

Greenhouses are ideal for starting off plants such as runner (green) beans, marrows (large zucchini), cucumbers and squashes

Growing a climber, such as a grape vine, up a shed is a good use of space and will also help keep it cool in the summer.

Sheds house the tools used on an allotment. The implements are best hung up on the walls on secure hooks.

A storage area for canes, posts and pots is essential. This also reduces trip hazards and damage to lawn mowers.

Herb pots outside the greenhouse are attractive as well as functional.

Water butts are a great way to save rainwater that would otherwise be lost.

Tomatoes grown on stakes take up little room and give support to heavy fruiters.

Crops such as blackberries and tayberries can often be grown around the perimeter of the allotment plot, where there is a more protected environment.

Cordon fruit is an excellent way of growing crops such as apples and pears in a small area, especially on allotments where the growing of trees is not allowed.

Use a bay tree as an attractive centrepiece.

A nursery seed bed is used to bring on seedlings, which are lifted and then transplanted to their final location.

Compost heaps are best sited in groups of three. This means that there is always compost at different stages of decomposition and you will have space for fresh material.

After planting asparagus in a permanent bed it cannot be cropped until the third year. This is to allow the plant to establish and become strong before cropping begins.

Fruit cages are essential for growing fruit crops that are often targeted by birds looking to eat the fruits. Blackcurrants, gooseberries and raspberries are just some of the crops that will benefit.

Crop comfrey regularly, then add in layers to the compost heap as it is especially high in potassium.

Ordering manure in the summer and keeping it in bags until the winter will ensure that it is fully broken down when it is required.

square or rectangular beds to accommodate this. There is no reason to stick to this if you prefer not to though, and you can always go for a more ornamental look to suit your own needs or personality.

PUTTING IT DOWN ON PAPER

Creating a plan for an allotment is generally quite a simple affair. Start by drawing up a ground plan of what is there already. The drawing should ideally be to scale and should include notes on the direction of the prevailing winds, sunny or shady spots (noting if these change during the day), always bearing in mind that even the sunniest plot may have shady pockets created by fences hedges or trees.

Identifying your soil type is particularly important when planning the crops, and the existing vegetation often gives you all sorts

of clues as to what will grow well on your patch. Have a look around your neighbours' plots and see what plants are growing successfully there and talk to them about their experiences. Note the position of water mains and any other nearby features.

Once you have drawn up the sketch plan, you can use this to create the design for your allotment. Use some paper to draw a scale outline plan that shows the plot, complete with any features you intend to keep. Place a sheet of tracing paper over this and sketch on your ideas. Start with the basics, such as where your shed, compost bins or other permanent structures will be. Remember that these will need to be accessible, so draw in pathways accordingly.

Once you have the basic structure of the plot set out, you can begin to look at the rest of your wish list. Start with the most

important items and work down the list. Remember to think very carefully about how much space each will realistically need and how much of a particular crop type you are likely to use. How productive a particular variety is should also be borne in mind – some types require a lot of work for little reward. Make sure you separate 'real need' from simple desire when you do this. Cost should also be a consideration here, as there is not much sense in coming up with a complex plan if you don't have enough money to act upon it.

Maintenance is also a key factor during the planning stage. The amount of time, effort and – where some crops are concerned – expertise needed should be thought through before you finalize your plan. The best approach is always to try and fit the maintenance requirements around your own lifestyle and avoid being too ambitious in the early stages.

THE ALLOTMENT FRAMEWORK

Before crops can be planted, the layout of any plot must be defined. Areas earmarked for growing crops, a shed, a composting area or other structure, and the network of paths and boundaries that link it all together must be clearly laid out. Planning which materials will be required, where these will come from and how they will be used is an essential part of the planning process that will pay dividends later if done properly.

Above: *Raised beds are both tidy and easy to maintain, and are a cheap, efficient way to define the framework of your allotment.*

ASSESSING THE SURROUNDINGS

In the vast majority of cases, allotments and community gardens are already set out as part of a planned and orderly framework of individual plots. Each of these will normally have good access – often via a network of paths between individual plots – while the site generally should have a secure boundary, some form of water provision for irrigation, and perhaps other facilities such as storage areas or toilets.

Having said all of this, your own plot, unless you are very fortunate, is unlikely to be structured in the way that you want or need for your own purposes, so you will have to work out a framework that allows you to best use the space. Creating a series of raised beds, for example, may be the first task you need to do.

Before you make any plans for the site, however, establish exactly what will be feasible, given the existing site facilities. Water is usually the most important consideration. If the plot lacks a nearby water source, you may well struggle to grow 'thirsty' plants in dry spells, unless you plan to install water butts or other rainwater capture systems. Equally, any power needed for lights or automated vents on a greenhouse will be difficult to power unless mains electricity is provided. The simplest solution is to work within the site constraints, ideally using simple, reliable technologies whenever and wherever you can.

SELECTING MATERIALS

For most allotment-growers, improving and maintaining the environmental credentials of their plot will be high on the agenda, along with producing high-quality, healthy food. In order to minimize the impact on the wider environment, ensure that the ecological credentials of materials you buy for the allotment are sound. Strive to obtain materials from local sources whenever possible and find out where they come from or how their extraction impacts upon the environment. Timber for posts and fences, mulch material and some types of compost (soil mix) – especially peat-based ones – can all be detrimental to the environment if not carefully sourced.

In addition to the source of the products, it is also worth finding out what chemical treatments the material has undergone during manufacturing. Some timber, for example, is treated with preservative that may leach out into the soil over time. Ask questions before buying.

MAKING A RAISED BED SYSTEM

 1 *Start by levelling the area of ground where you intend to position the raised bed. Use a tape measure to set out the dimensions and mark the corners with pegs or short pieces of cane.*

 2 *Measure and cut the timber using a sharp carpentry saw. If you are using pre-treated timber, you will need to apply a wood preservative to the cut ends to prevent rot occurring on those surfaces.*

 3 *The ends of the sawn wood can be joined by simply nailing them. If the wood is thin or prone to splitting though, a small hole can be drilled and the boards fixed with screws.*

 4 *When placing the frame on the prepared ground, check that all sides are level using a spirit level. This will ensure that water does not run over the sides when you water the bed.*

 5 *Anchor the corners of the frame using 'pegs' made from small pieces of similar treated timber. Drive these down the inside edge of the frame and nail or screw them in place to secure them.*

 6 *Fill the frame with the growing mix. This is normally a mixture of the original topsoil combined with additional compost (soil mix). This ensures that it retains moisture and gives the medium a nutrient boost.*

USING PLANTS TO CREATE A LIVING FRAMEWORK

PLANT SUPPORTS

Any woody plants can be cut down to the ground on a regular basis, and you can collect thin branches in a system called coppicing. On a small site, such as an allotment, limitations on space mean that this must be done every year or two to prevent shrubs from becoming too large.

PLANT SPECIES	CULTIVATION	POTENTIAL USES
Willow *Salix* spp.	Tolerant of wet or heavy soils but very vigorous if not controlled. Usually best cut every year.	Useful for weaving hurdles or making living retaining walls. Can be invasive on small plots; dogwood (*Cornus sanguinea*) is a better choice when space is limited.
Dogwood *Cornus* spp.	Suitable for most soil types. Can sucker aggressively and is usually best cut every year.	After coppicing it produces attractive red, orange or lime green shoots (depending upon the species). Suitable for plant supports or fine weaving work.
Hazel *Corylus avellana*	Suitable for most soils if the drainage is good and the pH is 6.5 or more. May be cut every 2–3 years.	Young straight stems are an excellent choice for wattle work, weaving and bean sticks. Smaller twigs make good pea sticks or bird deterrents.

HEDGES

Low-growing hedges can be used as borders around vegetable beds and are easy to maintain as they can be kept neat by trimming. Do this twice a year, in spring and then again in mid-summer for woody specimens; or once, in spring, for grasses or herbaceous plants.

PLANT SPECIES	CULTIVATION	POTENTIAL USES
Lavender *Lavandula* spp.	Needs a sunny, well-drained position. Prefers alkaline conditions but grows in most soils.	Good for low, informal edges. An excellent companion plant on account of its aromatic foliage. Rich soils promote more leaves but less essential oils.
Rosemary *Rosmarinus officinalis*	Prefers a hot sunny position on slightly alkaline, light, dry soil. Dislikes excessive winter wetness.	Repels carrot fly, making it particularly valuable as an informal edging hedge. Plants are smaller but richer in essential oils when grown on chalky soils.
Miscanthus *Miscanthus* spp.	Grows on most acidic to slightly alkaline soils. Can tolerate drought and occasional wetness.	Can be used to form annual windbreaks. Dry, cut stems can be used as a straw substitute. Choose a dwarf variety such as 'Little Zebra' or 'Little Kitten'.

PATHS

Natural, organic materials used to make paths are more environmentally friendly than hard landscape materials. They often prove more attractive to look at and are much easier to lay than slabs or other hard materials, and generally cost less – an important consideration on a site that you do not own.

PLANT SPECIES	CULTIVATION	POTENTIAL USES
Wood chip	As a rule almost all woody branches can be chipped, provided that they are disease-free.	Excellent material for making paths between beds, it also makes a very effective mulch or soil conditioner if it has been composted for a year or more.
Turf	Grow as a short mown 'lawn'. Make sure that it does not encroach into beds or growing areas.	The easiest way to cover bare earth quickly. It makes good paths but can also be a way of maintaining areas not currently in production until they are needed.

RECYCLED MATERIALS

Wherever possible you should aim to use recycled materials on your plot. The most obvious way to do this is to recycle organic matter such as plant material on a compost heap, although there are other ways that you can use recycled materials that are not produced in your garden. For instance, plastic bottles can be used as mini cloches to protect seedlings and old carpet makes an ideal cover for a compost heap or patch of (as yet) unused ground.

Recycled building materials such as bricks, slabs, timber and railway sleepers often prove extremely useful and can reduce costs considerably, while having environmental benefits.

Gardens that rely heavily upon recycling material produced within their own confines are naturally self-sustaining, and wherever possible you should try to develop this into the framework of the plot. Some external input will always be needed from time to time, but the garden's long-term success will be assured.

LIVING FRAMEWORKS

You can use living material to construct a framework for your allotment. The simplest example of this is probably using grass for stabilizing soil on slopes and pathways, although woody plants are often used to create hedges and delineate boundaries. A little ingenuity and knowledge can provide amazing results. Take a look at the chart above for some simple ideas.

Willow is a prime example of a material that is not only very easy to grow, but can be used in a number of ways. It is fast-growing and roots easily from twigs put into the ground, making it perfect for use as living barriers or even retaining walls for soil. Woven willow (often called wattle) can be used as a building and fencing material.

Below: *Willow is ideal to use as a living framework. It does not rot and is self-sustaining, surviving longer than timber.*

ALLOTMENT STRUCTURES

The excitement of getting a new allotment can, if not tempered by caution, lead to a bout of unabated over-ambition. While structures such as sheds, fruit cages and greenhouses might seem ideal additions to the plot, these can be costly. Before buying or installing any large additions, therefore, consider how much they will get used and whether there are alternatives more suited to your needs, if not your budget. Polythene tunnels and cloches are often perfectly adequate for a small plot.

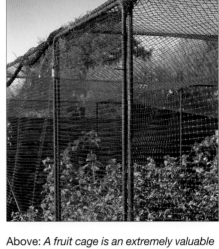

Above: *A fruit cage is an extremely valuable addition to a plot if you intend growing a lot of fruit, but it takes time and effort to build.*

SHEDS

Although a bonus on an allotment, you will need to check in the rules for your site whether you can have a shed or not. Some sites have a no-shed rule, and even where they are allowed, there are often size restrictions. However, many allotment holders can and do build sheds, and occasionally these are quite elaborate structures that double up as a 'home away from home'.

If you are able to erect a shed, the next thing to do is to decide upon how to go about this. They are often available as kit forms ranging from inexpensive (if often flimsy) wooden designs to those made from metal, plastic or vinyl laminates, although the more adventurous might prefer to build one from scratch.

Below: *A shed is arguably the most useful structure on a plot. Its environmental value can easily be enhanced with a green roof.*

Before you rush into buying or designing a shed, think what you will need it for. Essentially you might only need a small lock-up for tools, equipment and other supplies. Having said this, a warm, dry shelter might prove a welcome respite from a sudden shower, or a place to sit and eat lunch. Whatever you chose, make sure that it is something that you can build – an unfinished shed is no use at all – and within your available budget.

GREENHOUSES

Adding a greenhouse to your allotment helps to increase the amount and range of plants you can grow by extending the season. Not every allotment site will allow them, however, and they can be easy targets for vandalism. There are many designs using a variety of materials and the decision to have one or not will depend upon what use you can make of it. Remember that

they need ventilating and unless you can sort out a source of power to enable automation of this, you will need to be able to visit it, usually twice daily, to do this.

If you don't have space or the time to manage a greenhouse, don't despair. Often all that you need are some cloches and perhaps a cold frame in order to gain many of the advantages of a greenhouse.

POLYTHENE TUNNELS

Like greenhouses, polythene tunnels may not be allowed on your allotment, but if they are, they are often a less troublesome alternative to a greenhouse.

Always choose one of the smaller 'domestic tunnels', as these are the ideal size for allotments. Ultimately, a tunnel soon pays for itself, enabling you to protect tender crops and extend the growing season, as well as allowing you to provide a suitable environment to grow more exotic, warmth-loving crops under cover in the summer months.

FRUIT CAGES

Before going ahead with constructing an elaborate cage for your fruit, you should realistically assess how much you need one. Individual bushes or rows of fruit can easily be protected using temporary structures of poles and netting. This is much cheaper than the kits you buy and, unlike a more permanent structure, has the advantage that you can easily remove it once the fruit is harvested so that the birds can get to the plants to pick off any pests.

RELAXATION AND FAMILY

While most allotment tenants take on a plot as a place to grow food, there are many that choose to use the area simply as a recreational space. This may involve growing some crops, perhaps flowers, or in some

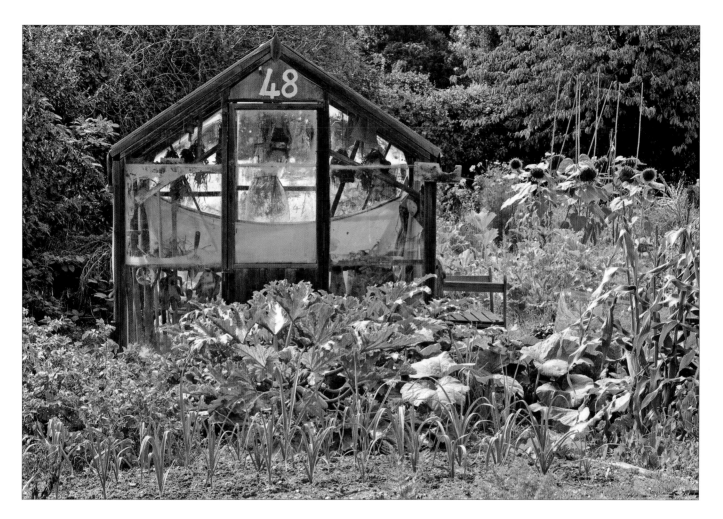

cases using the space as a garden away from home. Obviously, the rules of the site will dictate exactly what can and cannot be done on the allotment (ball games are often not allowed, for instance), but even a moderate-sized plot may have potential and could easily encompass a sitting area. If you have a shed, make sure that you keep a couple of folding chairs in it so you can relax and enjoy the rewards of your labours there and then, or simply put your feet up after a bout of strenuous exercise.

Kids generally love being outdoors, and love to join in. They are never too young to be introduced to gardening, and most enjoy having the chance to play and explore for themselves. For this reason an allotment that consists of neatly growing rows of crops, which might seem like heaven to the parents, offers limited scope to children. Of course the idea of making the plot into a miniature playground would probably be a step too far, but you may be able to devote a little area to a sandpit or a patch of earth for them to dig about in and grow crops, so they can enjoy some real 'messy' fun. If space allows, why not build them a little

shed or den, complete with child-sized tools and other equipment of their own? It will help keep them interested and involved and will provide entertainment in a healthy environment that is free to visit.

Above: *A greenhouse extends the potential range of crops but will need daily attention.*

Below: *Leave space for a table and chairs to turn your plot into an alfresco dining area.*

TOOLS AND EQUIPMENT

When you go into any supplier or look at one of their catalogues, there is a seemingly bewildering array of tools on offer, especially if you are new to allotment-growing. Some of these can be used for a variety of tasks, and this versatility makes them indispensable. Others, however, are geared towards highly specific jobs. Once you've purchased your gardening tools, it is important to look after them to keep them in tip-top condition.

Above: *String lines on spoolers are extremely useful in the allotment, and are used to help form drills and furrows.*

CHOOSING TOOLS

Even if you know what items you want to buy, there is still a huge range of types and brands of tools on offer. There are few absolutes when it comes to choosing which tools will be right for you, but it is essential that they will be durable, functional and comfortable to use. Everyone is different in respect of their strength, build and preferences and it is a good idea to test them in the shop for weight and length of handle so that they suit you.

RIGHT TOOL, RIGHT JOB

Having the correct tool for the job makes work easier and faster and will generally give the best results. Digging, for example, will always be much better with a good-quality spade and fork, and these should always be top of your list when it comes to essential tools as they are used most frequently. They need to be comfortable, but this is easy to judge when buying them. The standard size is a 72cm (29in) handle, and the best way to see whether this is right

Below: *The side of a shed is an ideal place to neatly and safely store materials such as canes and stakes.*

for you is to check whether the top of the handle is around about your hip height. If it is too short, then go for a long-handled one. This is extremely important as using one that is the wrong size for your height can result in back strain. In addition to this, remember that D-handles can be uncomfortable over long periods, but they suit smaller hands better, while a T-handle is much better for larger hands.

Hoes are an essential item for controlling weeds and the best of these are usually forged and have stainless steel heads. Rakes are also indispensable and you should choose one with good solid tines (teeth), mounted on a wooden or metal handle. Finally, a knife, a pair of secateurs (hand pruners), a hand trowel and a wheelbarrow for moving things around the plot should be enough to get you started.

CARE OF TOOLS

Handles of tools often become dirty while you are using them and it is important that you take good care of them in order to extend their useful life. In the case of plastic or other synthetic materials, this usually involves no more than washing them in a little soapy water and drying them thoroughly afterwards.

Many hand tools still use wooden handles though, and these can be kept in tip-top condition with boiled linseed oil. This is simply done by applying the oil with a non-linting rag, allowing the wood to fully absorb the first coat before applying any more. When properly and regularly applied, this prevents the wood from drying out and splintering. On a more regular basis, dirty wooden handles are simply cleaned by removing as much of the soil as possible with a stiff brush. Ideally, clean soil off before you finish working on your plot.

If you need to use water on handles treated with linseed the best way to do this is to gently moisten them with a damp cloth, making sure that you don't soak the wood, as this may cause the grain to lift and the handle to swell. Many modern tools are varnished and a quick scrub can be the best option for them, although even these should not be left in for a soak.

If you regularly oil blades or other metal parts then they should remain rust-free. If any rust does accumulate on the blade,

Below: *Hanging tools up when you have finished with them ensures that you can find them again easily next time.*

remove this with a wire brush and wipe over the cleaned section with an oily rag or brush. Remember that the blades of shears, forks, spades and other tools will soon rust if they are not regularly oiled. If you have bought good-quality tools then it is worth protecting your investment! There is no need to use anything other than general-purpose oil on hand tools but remember that if you have invested in power tools then they may require specialist treatments. Consult the manufacturer's instructions if you are unsure.

SHARPENING TOOLS

Larger blades such as spades and hoes may be sharpened with a fine metal file or, if you have one, a grindstone. Very badly damaged or worn blades may eventually need replacing, if this is an option, or you may have to buy a new tool. If you have any doubts about how to carry out repairs you should consult the manufacturer.

Tools with fine cutting edges, especially knives, secateurs (pruners) and shears, will become blunt with use, and their cutting edges will need regular sharpening. To sharpen blades of knives and secateurs, use a fine sharpening stone prepared with a few drops of general-purpose oil. For a straight-bladed knife, push it forwards and to the side, exerting a little downward pressure. Then turn the knife over and, holding the blade almost flat against the stone, brush it across the surface to take off any rough edges. Use the same method to sharpen secateurs and good-quality forged hoes.

Remember that in very stony and heavy soils, hoes may need sharpening several times per growing season. Sharpen only the outside blade on bypass (parrot-beaked) secateurs and the upper surface of hoes. The job should be finished by wiping the blade with an oily rag.

Above: *Sharpening tools will make them more effective and ultimately save you a lot of effort on the allotment.*

ESSENTIAL TOOLS AND EQUIPMENT

DESCRIPTION AND PURPOSE

Spade	Used to dig or loosen ground or to break up clumps in the soil, a spade has a broad flat blade (called a spit) with a sharp, usually curved, lower edge. The handle should be the same height as your hip.
Fork	A digging fork should have roughly the same dimensions as your spade. It has four strong, sharpened spikes instead of a spit. Forks are used to loosen ground, dig over a plot to lift root vegetables or dig out persistent perennial weed roots.
Swan-necked (English) hoe	The swan-necked hoe is useful for deeper hoeing and cultivating, breaking soil clods and weeding with a chopping action. It is also used to form narrow seed drills with the blade corner, wide seed drills with the whole blade, or drawing up soil ridges around crops.
Dutch hoe	The Dutch hoe's flat, angled, sharp edged blade destroys weeds by cutting them just under the surface. It is particularly useful between rows of young vegetables, ideal for working in fertilizer, and helps maintain a fine, dusty, weed suppressant tilth across patches of bare earth.
Rake	A typical garden rake is a toothed bar fixed transversely to a handle. It is predominantly used for light weeding, loosening, and especially levelling patches of bare soil following cultivation. It can also be used to comb the surface in order to remove stones and debris.
Secateurs	Secateurs or hand pruners are a scissor-like tool, with a 25mm (1in) thick blade that is strong enough to prune hard branches of trees and shrubs. They are available as 'bypass' (two sharp blades that cross each other like scissors), and 'anvil' (one sharp blade cutting on to a flattened base).
Knife	A folding pocket-knife is essential for cutting twine or opening sacks. The ever-popular multi-tool knives often have an assortment of knife blades and other tools.
Hand fork	This hand tool has a pointed, scoop-shaped metal blade and is used for breaking up earth, digging small holes, and especially for planting, weeding, mixing in fertilizer or other additives, and transferring plants to pots.
Dibber (dibble)	Essentially a pointed wooden stick for making holes for planting seeds, seedlings or small bulbs, dibbers come in a variety of designs.
String line	A string that is stretched taut between two pegs or steel pins to make a perfect straight line, this is used to help form drills and furrows for seed sowing. They are easy to make yourself but purpose-made, spooling types are also obtainable.
Seed/planting rule	Essentially a large ruler on to which the correct spacing is marked for planting a range of vegetables or other crops. Some may be notched or marked while others have a hole every 2.5cm (1in) for sowing small seeds.
Watering can	A long nozzled watering can allows water to flow gently and is good for reaching across rows of crops or pots. Ideally, choose one that has handles on both the side and top to ensure easy handling, as well as a detachable spray rose (sprinkler head) for watering seedlings.
Soil riddle	A riddle is usually circular, around 45cm (18in) in diameter, with a rim that holds a steel wire mesh in place. It is typically used to sieve (strain) soil or compost in order to remove stones, twigs, large clods or other debris.
Wheelbarrow	Designed for use by a single person using two handles to the rear, a wheelbarrow is essential for moving bulky or heavy items. One-wheel types are most manoeuvrable in small spaces, on planks or sloping ground, and allow the best control when emptying.
Gloves	Providing a barrier against infection and soil bacteria, gloves are essential for keeping hands safe. Choose a pair that fit snugly on your wrists with no extra room at the fingertips to ensure a good grip. Get tough, pierce-resistant ones for heavy work or impermeable ones if using chemicals.
Twine	Twine is a strong thread or string composed of two or more thin strands or yarns twisted together. A natural fibre that can be composted after use.
Pump sprayer	Sprayers can be used for applying synthetic pesticides, distributing foliar feeds, and misting plants to aid fruit set. Separate sprayers are required for each type of use.

SOIL AND SOIL MANAGEMENT

Soil is the most precious resource in your allotment. Some gardeners inherit well-tended sites, while others may be faced with a rubble-filled mass. However, any soil can be improved through time and effort. If you regard your soil as a living entity, you will see that essential plant nutrients are cycled by a microscopic army of inhabitants and larger worms, insects and grubs. All these creatures need air, moisture and food. Using manure, garden compost and other sources of organic matter is the key to sustaining this soil life and keeping the soil healthy.

Left: The key to developing a successful allotment plot lies for the most part in the careful management of the soil.

Above: *A compost heap needs to be turned periodically to ensure all the plant material decomposes properly.*

Above: *Sieving compost is the best way to remove larger pieces that have not fully rotted down. Return these to the heap.*

Above: *Crops that are grown in rows must be rotated on a regular basis in order to avoid soil-borne pests and diseases.*

TYPES OF SOIL

Soil is probably the most important constituent of any allotment site because it is vital for successful plant growth. Understanding your soil and discovering how it can help you to create a healthy, fertile growing environment for your plants should be a priority. The starting point in this process is to look at the different soil types and find out how they affect the plants you can grow. Once you have analyzed the soil in your own site, then you will be able to create a successful allotment.

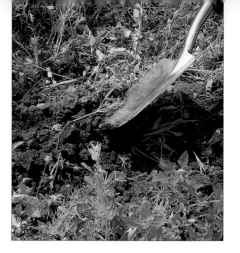

Above: *All soil types benefit greatly from the addition of organic matter such as this green manure.*

WHAT ARE SOILS MADE OF?

Both natural soils and some potting composts (soil mixes) for container-grown plants usually have five main components. These are mineral particles (the inorganic fraction), organic matter (the remains of living organisms), water (the soil solution), air (which fills the spaces between solid particles that are not filled with water) and living organisms. The proportions of these components vary widely according to the soil type, or the growing medium.

The proportions of water, air and organic matter can be readily changed by soil cultivation and other horticultural practices. A good topsoil will continuously supply plant roots with water, air and nutrients. Subsoil (the largely inert soil layer that lies beneath the thin layer of 'living' topsoil) has less organic matter than topsoil. Plant growth will suffer when the proportions of water and air in the medium are out of balance. Too much air will have the same effect upon plant roots as a drought, whereas too much water causes waterlogging. Growth will also suffer if nutrient levels are too low, too high or if there is an imbalance in supply between different nutrients. In addition, soil that is too compacted for roots to grow will also adversely affect growth.

SAND AND SILT

Soils that are sandy and silty originate from river deposits, windblown sediments or from the erosion of sandstone outcrops. Their general properties are that they do not provide or retain plant nutrients; they are not cohesive and therefore possess a weak structure; and in most cases they are free draining.

Silts, unless well structured, will be waterlogged. Sand, on the other hand, is naturally free draining. The structure and texture of sandy soils means that they are only able to hold a very small reserve of water. Organic matter can improve the available water content but the real trick in avoiding drought-stress lies in ensuring that plants root deeply into the soil. Nutrient shortage can also be a problem on sandy soils, which have a tendency to become acidic over time. Liming and the regular addition of organic matter will help alleviate these problems.

Sandy soils do have the advantage of 'warming up' quickly in spring due to their lower water content and are easier to work early in the year. This means that you can grow a wider range of plants in a sandy soil. Planting or transplanting is also easier in the autumn.

Organic material is broken down very quickly in sandy soils due to good aeration and a temperature that favours rapid bacterial action. Many light soils naturally have less than two per cent organic matter and it is vital that organic matter be added regularly to sustain healthy plant growth.

CHOOSING CROPS FOR DIFFERENT SOILS

Soil pH is a measure of acidity. Here are the preferences of some common crops:

Asparagus	6.0–8.0
Basil	5.5–6.5
Beans (runner (green), broad (fava), French (green))	6.0–7.5
Beetroot (beet)	6.0–7.5
Broccoli	6.0–7.0
Brussels sprouts	6.0–7.0
Cabbage	6.0–7.5
Carrot	5.5–7.0
Cauliflower	5.5–7.5
Celery	6.0–7.0
Chicory	5.0–6.8
Courgette (zucchini)	5.5–7.0
Cucumber	5.5–7.0
Garlic	5.5–7.5
Kale	6.0–7.0
Leek	6.0–8.0
Lettuce	6.0–7.0
Marrow (large zucchini)	6.0–7.5
Onion	6.0–7.0
Parsnip	5.5–7.5
Potato	4.5–6.0
Pumpkin	5.5–7.5
Radish	6.0–7.0
Spinach	6.0–7.5
Sweetcorn (corn)	5.5–7.5
Swiss chard	6.0–7.5
Tomato	5.5–7.5
Turnip	5.5–7.0

COMMON TYPES OF SOIL

sand   silt   clay   loam

Sand A free-draining soil that is quick to warm up, but hungry and thirsty.
Silt River deposits can be sticky, but not as sticky as clay. Rich and easy to work.

Clay A heavy soil that is often difficult to work. Slow to warm up, but fairly rich.
Loam A moisture-retentive soil that warms up quickly and works perfectly.

HAND-TEXTURING METHOD FOR ANALYZING SOIL

sandy

silty or loamy sand

loam

clay loam

clay

Finding out what type of soil you have is easy and does not require any specialist equipment. This test is ultimately a matter of judgement and will only give you a relative picture of the sort of soil you have. However, it is surprisingly accurate. Simply take a small amount of soil – about a teaspoonful will do – in the palm of your hand. Moisten with a little water (not too much but enough to make it just workable). Once moistened, try to form the soil into one of the shapes shown above.

• Begin by forming a ball. If it stays together, then proceed to the next shape. If it does not form a ball, then you have a sandy soil.
• If you can flatten the ball without it breaking up, then you have a silty sand or a loamy sand.
• If you can roll the flattened ball into a thick sausage shape, then you have a loam.
• A soil that can be rolled into a thin sausage shape is a clay loam.
• If you can bend the soil into a horseshoe or ring shape, then you have a clay soil.

Above: *Most crops grown on allotments prefer a reasonably well-drained soil with a pH of between 6–6.8.*

CLAY

The particles found in clay are extremely small and are able to interact with, and directly affect, the chemistry of the soil. The individual clay particles are so tiny that they are actually bonded together by electrical charges which produce the characteristic plasticity of this type of soil. Clay is both water retentive and rich in nutrients. It has few pore spaces and those that are there have a tendency to become waterlogged, which results in swelling. Shrinkage occurs when clay is dry. As a result, clays heave (swell outward and upward) when wet and crack when dry. They can also be subject to frost action, which causes an increase in tiny, almost microscopic, airspaces (micro pores). Pure clay soils are rare, although some soils may be very rich in clay. They have the potential to be extremely fertile growing mediums if they are well managed.

LOAMS

These are a mixture of sand, silt and clay that results in a blend of the characteristics of each constituent part. They are usually characterized by their clay content. Heavy loams are about 24–30% clay, whereas light loams contain about 12–18% clay. Heavy loams behave and should be treated like clay soils. Light loams should be treated like sandy soils. Medium loams are potentially the ideal mixture, exhibiting the advantages of both heavy and light soils without many of the disadvantages of either.

HUMUS

This is a stable form of partially decomposed plant material that gives topsoil its characteristically dark colour. Humus has a high nutrient-reserve potential

(2½ x better than clay), retains water, increases the friability (suitability for cultivation) of heavy soils and its darker colour encourages soils to warm up more rapidly.

SOIL PROFILE

A typical soil profile usually consists of three main elements: an upper layer of dark, fertile topsoil; a middle layer of lighter, infertile subsoil; and a lower layer of bedrock, which ranges from a few to hundreds of metres (yards) deep.

Topsoil is the dark layer of soil that contains organic material. Keep as deep as possible, although usually only one spit (spade) deep.

Subsoil is usually lighter in colour and contains little or no organic material or nutrients. It should be broken to one spit depth, but not mixed with the topsoil.

Bedrock is usually below the level of cultivation.

MANAGING YOUR SOIL

Any soil has the potential to be a fertile growing medium in which plants will thrive.

Light/sandy soils
• Maintain levels of organic matter.
• Lime when required. (N.B. It is often easier to select species tolerant of the site conditions in the long term.)
• Fertilize well as light soils are usually infertile. (N.B. Some exotic and native plant species actually thrive under relatively poor nutrient conditions.)
• Irrigate frequently in the first year after planting, less so once deeper roots are established.

Clay soils
• Drainage is essential.
• Maintain lime status.
• Maintain levels of organic matter and fertilize when needed.
• Wise cultivation is needed to conserve winter or summer tilth produced by natural weathering, i.e. cracking due to wetting/drying cycle and breakdown by frost action.

SOIL STRUCTURE

Soils are made up of mineral and rock particles that give them their natural properties. The character of the mineral fraction cannot be changed but the way that these building blocks are organized within the soil can. Creating and maintaining soil structure is a key aspect of maintaining the fertility of the soil and supporting healthy plant growth on an allotment. Even the most difficult soils can be modified to create a fertile growing medium for plants.

Above: *Even 'difficult' soils can be transformed into a good growing medium by hard work and careful cultivation.*

WHAT IS MEANT BY SOIL STRUCTURE?

Soil structure is quite simply the way soils are organized. To use a simple analogy: if we see the soil particles (sand, silt or clay – the mineral fraction) as the building materials – like the bricks and mortar of a house, for instance – then the structure is the architecture. The building materials themselves cannot be altered, but the architecture can vary considerably from home to home. This is the key. It is possible to improve a soil's structure even if the mineral fraction remains unchanged. It is perfectly feasible to have a well-structured clay soil, for instance. It all depends upon how well you manage it.

WHY IS SOIL STRUCTURE IMPORTANT FOR PLANT GROWTH?

In order to survive, plant roots need water, nutrients and air. Plant roots breathe in the soil, taking in oxygen and expelling carbon dioxide. A poorly structured soil may have too little airspace. This can have two negative effects: fresh air (containing oxygen) may not be able to penetrate the soil very easily; and the soil will tend to become waterlogged following rain. Waterlogging will also reduce the air available in the soil.

Below: *A rotavator is a labour-reducing method of breaking up the soil to prepare it for planting. They can often be hired.*

Structure is therefore very important in terms of maintaining the health of plant roots. Plant shoot development is directly linked to root health. A healthy root system ensures healthy shoots and will ultimately result in better growth and crop yields.

HOW DOES SOIL STRUCTURE DEVELOP IN NATURAL SYSTEMS?

Soil structure naturally develops in soils through the effect of weather cycles. Wetting causes soils to swell while drying causes shrinkage. This naturally causes soils to crack. The action of freezing and thawing is also important on clay soils in areas where frosts occur. They form particles known commonly as crumbs. The 'crumb structure' of any soil develops over time and is important in terms of allowing the free passage of water through the soil and air that must be able to move in and out of the soil. In this way soils do not become habitually waterlogged and natural nutrient cycles – oxygen, carbon and nitrogen, for example – are not impeded. Plant roots and soil organisms, such as worms, naturally help to maintain soil structure, as does the natural addition of decaying plant material each autumn.

HOW TO ALTER SOIL STRUCTURE

Humans have learned over time that even an infertile area can be worked – and the structure of the soil improved – by cultivation. This is covered in more detail later but it is essential to understand now that cultivation is a way of rapidly accelerating the natural cycles that promote good structure. Digging and breaking down 'clods' helps to introduce air and creates new pores in the soil. Adding organic matter helps to maintain these pore spaces, retains moisture (in dry soils) and encourages the action of soil-dwelling creatures such as worms. No-dig

Above: *If you need to work on wet soil, work from a plank of wood to ensure the soil is not compacted and its structure destroyed.*

Above: *Dry weather causes soils to crack, which can be a benefit on clay types as it develops their 'crumb structure'.*

Above: *Waterlogging is often the result of poor drainage and can seriously affect plant health as they are deprived of oxygen.*

systems aim to harness this natural cycle more closely, but the goal is the same – a rich, fertile and well-structured soil.

IMPROVING DRAINAGE

Soils that tend to become waterlogged often do so as a result of poor structure and because there is nowhere for the water to go. The vast majority of soils do not actually need (or benefit from) the installation of land drains. Often it is enough to dig over a site because much of the drainage problem may be due to surface compaction. Surface compaction severely reduces the passage of water into the soil and can result in a sticky surface that is prone to 'puddling'.

If you have a sloping site you can dig a 'soak away' drain at the base of the slope and improve the structure of the soil to encourage the rapid dispersal of water following rain. If you have a fairly flat site, then you should consider making a raised bed for growing crops. Raised beds are easier to manage than standard beds and avoid the inconvenience of installing (and maintaining) a drainage system.

IMPROVING SOIL STRUCTURE

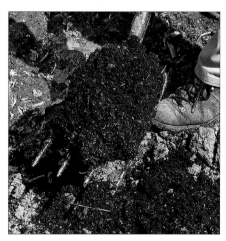

1 *One of the best ways to improve the structure of the soil is to add as much organic material as you can, preferably when the soil is dug. For heavy soils, this is best done in the autumn.*

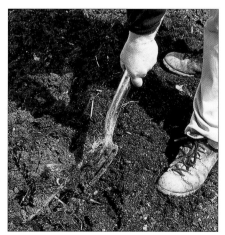

2 *If the soil has already been dug, then well-rotted organic material can be worked into the surface of the soil with a fork. The worms will complete the task of working it down into the soil.*

Above: *A well-prepared soil that is kept free of weeds and dug regularly will result in healthier, more vigorous crops throughout the growing season. A healthier crop will be more resistant to pest and disease attack.*

SOIL CHEMISTRY

While for many of us the word chemistry can be extremely off-putting, the truth of the matter is that everything in life is made up of chemicals. While the pure science of chemistry can be very complex, the chemistry of soil that allotment-growers must master is mercifully simple. A rudimentary knowledge of the chemicals that affect plant growth and how soil chemistry can be controlled and managed is all you need to grow healthy plants in an allotment site.

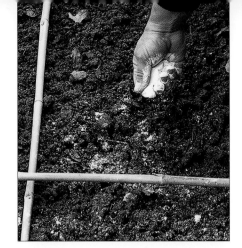

Above: *You can reduce the acidity of the soil by adding lime some weeks before planting. Test the soil first to see how much is needed.*

OXYGEN

The amount of oxygen in a healthy soil controls the type of life it will support. Nearly all organisms need oxygen to survive. Soils without oxygen are described as anaerobic. Most organisms can survive for short periods under anaerobic conditions, but this causes the accumulation of poisons that can become toxic at high concentrations.

A typical soil has about 50 per cent of its pore space filled by air and 50 per cent by water. Only certain bacteria can remain in anaerobic conditions for long periods of time, although some species of bacteria can readily switch from oxygen-rich to oxygen-poor conditions quickly to adapt to local conditions. Microbes use about 70 per cent of the oxygen in the soil and plant roots use the remaining 30 per cent. Under anaerobic conditions, the efficiency of microbes is poor and decomposition rates are much slower.

WATER

Soil water is vital for all soil life. Without it, microbes cannot grow or remain active and many will go into 'hibernation' until water returns. Fungi, on the other hand, are more resistant to water stress than bacteria. With too much water, oxygen levels drop and the lack of air tends to slow down the nutrient cycles driven by microbes. Water is also the medium by which essential nutrients are able to enter the plant.

SOIL pH

The pH scale is an abbreviated form of 'Potential of Hydrogen'. It is a measure of the degree of acidity or alkalinity of a solution as measured on a scale (pH scale) of 0 to 14. The midpoint of 7.0 on the pH scale represents neutrality. A 'neutral' solution is, therefore, neither acid nor alkaline. Numbers below 7.0 indicate acidity; numbers greater than 7.0 indicate alkalinity.

The level of acidity or alkalinity (pH) of a soil can significantly affect the nutrient availability. Many nutrients become 'unavailable' to plants when the soil is either too acid or too alkaline. Microbial activity in soil is also largely controlled by pH. Fungi tend to predominate in acid soils, bacteria in neutral or alkaline soils.

Soil pH is essentially a measure of the acidity of the soil water, although the soil itself is the deciding factor in respect of what this will be.

Most plants prefer or are tolerant of a specific pH range. Some plants, such as the hydrangea, exhibit a different flower colour depending upon the prevailing pH. Most allotment plants, especially vegetables, thrive within a range of 6–7, which happens to be where the majority of nutrients are available. It is best to maintain this pH in order to optimize the availability of nutrients. Many allotment plants, however, are not too fussy about the pH levels, so if you choose plants carefully, it will not usually be necessary to alter the soil acidity.

ACIDIFYING SOIL

Lowering the pH of a naturally limy soil is difficult because the soil often contains a reserve of calcium that is released immediately upon acidification. Lowering the pH involves the use of flowers of sulphur and is only usually successful over a short period of time.

TAKING A pH TEST

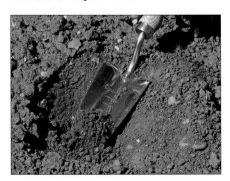

1 *Collect a small sample of soil. Dry it, grind it into a powder and ensure that it is free from stones. Pour the soil into a test tube until it reaches the mark on the side.*

2 *Put a layer of barium sulphate powder into the tube level with the mark. This compound helps the solution to clear rapidly and makes the pH reading clearer.*

3 *Pour in a little of the indicator solution up to the mark shown on the tube. Be careful not to put in too much because this can make the solution dark and difficult to read.*

TAKING A NUTRIENT TEST

1 *Place a small sample of the soil into the test tube up to the mark on the side.*

2 *Add a test solution (in this case one for nitrogen) up to the mark on the test tube.*

3 *Filter the solution to remove any soil particles and leave just a liquid solution.*

4 *Decant the resulting filtered solution into another clear container in preparation for the final stage of the nutrient test.*

5 *Add a small amount of indicator powder. This will react with the solution and enable a colour reading to be taken.*

6 *Shake for about 10 seconds and compare with the chart. Here, the low reading indicates that a nitrogen-rich fertilizer will benefit this soil.*

LIMING SOIL

It is generally easier to raise the soil pH than to lower it. Lime neutralizes soil acidity and is commonly applied as ground limestone, chalk or dolomitic limestone (dolodust). Lime requirement cannot be determined from soil pH because it is influenced by soil texture and organic matter content. Clay and humus act as a 'buffer' because of their complex chemistry. If soil is known to be acidic, regular light application is preferable to heavier, more infrequent, doses.

HIGHLY ALKALINE SOILS

Soils that are too alkaline suffer trace element deficiencies of manganese, copper, iron, zinc and boron. Phosphates are also less available, their maximum availability being between pH 6–7. Disease organisms can be more of a problem in calcium-rich soils, as many disease-causing fungal agents prefer alkaline conditions. Some plants, such as potatoes, prefer to grow on acid soils, while others, such as brassicas, thrive in alkaline soils.

4 *Add distilled water to the mark on the tube and shake the container vigorously for about a minute. Ensure the contents are mixed thoroughly and leave to settle.*

5 *Once sufficiently cleared, compare the colour against those on the chart, choosing the one that most closely matches that of the solution.*

> **GROWTH RESTRICTIONS IN EXTREMES OF pH**
> Many vital nutrients that are essential for healthy plant growth become unavailable in extremes of soil pH.
>
> **Nitrogen deficiency** Most nitrates are released from organic matter and a low soil pH limits the rate of decomposition severely.
>
> **Phosphate deficiency** Phosphate becomes unavailable outside the 6.5–7.5 pH range. Some plants form relationships with soil-borne fungi that release phosphates in acid conditions.
>
> **Trace-element toxicity and deficiency** Trace elements, especially aluminium, iron and manganese, are generally more soluble in acidic conditions. Extreme acidity can lead to excessive quantities of trace elements and to plant death. Other trace elements, such as copper, boron and molybdenum, become less available at low soil pH. Molybdenum deficiency affects legumes, which will not grow in acid soils.

CLEARING THE PLOT

Before you can start growing anything you will need to clear the plot of weeds and any other problems. Take time to check what is there already though, as even a plot that was vacated fairly recently can rapidly become overgrown. As well as hiding the soil that lies below, this weedy mass can often conceal useful structures or even perennial crops left by previous tenants. Have a good look at what you have and always take time to talk to the surrounding plot holders to see what they know about the site.

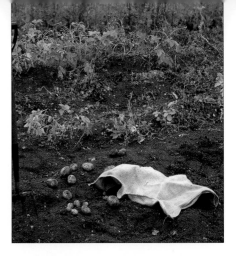

Above: *An overgrown plot, while often daunting at first sight, can contain surprises, which become your first 'windfall' harvest.*

PLANNING AHEAD

Unless you are very fortunate and take over a well-tended plot, the chances are that you will need to clear some or even the entire site. The best way to approach this is to clear a small section at a time. Don't be too ambitious and remember that very overgrown plots might take a year or more to 'tame'. Areas that are not going to be cultivated immediately, but where weeds are more than 15cm (6in) high, will need cutting down though, and the best way of doing this is with a scythe, sickle or – if you have one – a strimmer. On areas with shorter weeds, a rotary mower can be used to keep them in check, until you are able to get around to cultivating them.

USING CHEMICALS

For all but the organic purists, chemicals represent a quick and easy way to control weed growth on the site. Even if you plan to garden without chemicals, applying a systemic herbicide to clear an infestation of deep-rooted perennial weeds can be the only realistic way of getting on top of the problem in the first instance.

If you do decide to use a herbicide spray, however, do so carefully and apply it on a slightly cloudy, preferably cool, still day to remove the chances of it drifting on to neighbouring plots. Always read the manufacturer's instructions and wear suitable clothing, such as gloves and possibly eye protection.

THE NON-CHEMICAL APPROACH

If chemicals are really out of the question for you then you have to work hard to get on top of an overgrown plot. It is important then that you properly assess just how much time, and indeed energy, you can devote to this. Unless you have an army of helpers or a very small plot it is unwise to try to clear a plot in one go and it will often take several visits, plus a lot of hard work, to clear all the weeds away.

HAND DIGGING

Digging over your patch with a digging fork is an ideal way to both break up the soil and remove weed roots. It can be backbreaking work however, and there is always the risk that you will leave some root fragments behind. Many common perennial weeds spread from even a tiny piece of root, even if this becomes dry and shrivelled, and can come back with a vengeance in the months to come even if you have given the area a thorough digging over.

USING MACHINERY

Using a rotavator (rotary cultivator) may seem like a tempting and time-saving option on a larger plot. If you don't have one they can usually be hired, but although they do make quick work of large areas, unless you have already dealt with perennial weeds (ideally using a herbicide), the roots of these will be chopped up and spread around the plot. In effect, you might simply exacerbate an existing problem in your attempts to save time.

MULCHING AND SMOTHERING

Once an area is clear, it is important that you don't have to go back and clear it again before it is time to plant. Mulches are frequently used to suppress or smother weeds as they emerge from the ground

Above: *Hand-removal of deep-rooted perennial weeds involves digging out the roots with a garden fork to avoid regrowth.*

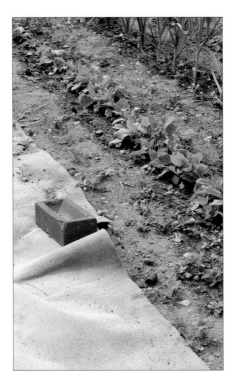

Above: *If areas of ground are to be left unproductive for any length of time, they can be covered over to suppress weeds.*

and the most effective way to do this on bare earth is to use some form of matting. Old, rubber-backed carpet is a modern favourite for this, but a whole variety of materials including plastics and other synthetic fabrics will do. Ideally these should be porous to some degree, as an impermeable layer can actually cause a build-up of toxins in the topsoil if left for a protracted period.

SOLARIZATION

Even if you plan to start growing in the newly cultivated ground quite quickly, it may be wise to try and sterilize the soil. Plots used for previous crops may contain potentially damaging soil pests. Ideally, these can be kept in check by crop rotations, but if you are not sure what was grown in the soil recently, this would necessitate a lengthy period where the land was uncultivated.

Solarizing soil is a simple, green solution for sterilizing the area. It involves laying out a clear plastic sheet, which is buried along its edges, in order to trap the light and heat from the sun underneath it. Make sure that the soil is damp before it is covered or the treatment will be less effective. Over a period of several weeks to a few months, the soil temperature beneath the plastic sheet will become high enough to kill many soil pests, disease spores, weed seeds and roots to a depth of up to 20cm (8in). Although it can be a bit fiddly to set up, it is an environmentally friendly way to clear many problems from the soil and is also extremely cheap.

GREEN MANURES

Once you have cleared a patch, the ground should be ready for final cultivation and for you to start to grow crops. If you are not yet ready to plant anything though, the ground must be covered with something to prevent a re-growth of weeds. Although you could use carpet, it may be an idea to make use of the area and sow a green manure crop. These are fast-growing cover crops that will help suppress weed growth simply by preventing light from reaching the ground. Once you are ready to cultivate the plot these can be dug in to help enrich the soil, prior to planting edible crops.

Right: *Even formerly productive plots can very quickly become weedy and overgrown if left untended during the growing season.*

CLEARING WEEDS FROM THE PLOT

1 *Digging out weeds may be one option on an allotment, but if the site is really overgrown, as this one is, then this will necessitate many hours of backbreaking work and you may want to consider another option.*

2 *Using a chemical weedkiller may be the only answer. Ensure that you follow manufacturer's instructions very carefully when using it and wear appropriate protective clothing.*

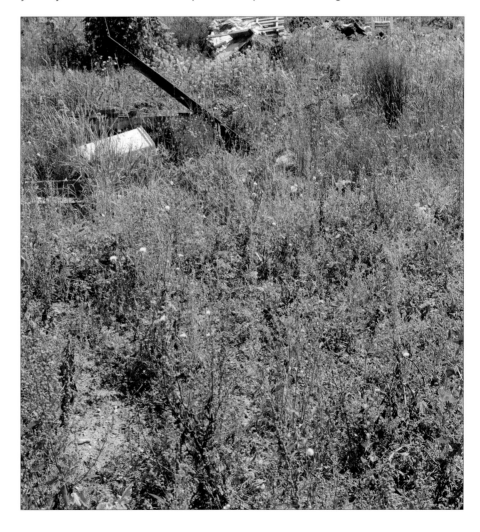

DIGGING AND CULTIVATION

Every allotment-grower's goal should be a healthy soil to support plant growth and development. Digging is one of the commonest ways to create a rich, fertile and ultimately productive soil. It can be hard work at the outset, particularly on sites not cultivated for some time, but the results – in the form of healthier, more productive plants – are worth it. Quite simply, what you get out of your soil will depend upon what you put into it.

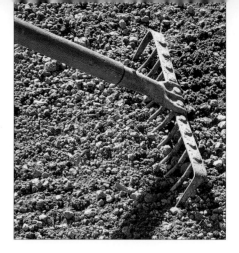

Above: *After a winter exposed to the weather, most soils can be easily broken into a fine tilth with a rake.*

THE BENEFITS OF DIGGING

Winter is the commonest time to dig, but soil can be dug at any time of the year if the conditions are right. Avoid working the soil when it is too dry and impenetrable, or too wet and sticking to your tools and boots. Clay soils may be best dug in mid- to late autumn to allow the action of frost to make the soil more suitable for final cultivation. Lighter soils are best dug in the spring or immediately prior to planting the site. Done properly, digging increases the amount of air space in the soil, which in turn benefits soil-dwelling organisms and plant roots due to the increase in oxygen available. It also lets you add organic matter that will feed these vital denizens of the soil and aid nutrient cycling. Calculate how much organic matter you will need before you start. You should aim to add about 30 per cent of the volume cultivated. A 20m^2 (220ft^2) plot cultivated to one spade's depth will need 2.5 cubic metres (88 cubic feet) of manure or garden compost.

SINGLE DIGGING

This method involves digging down to the depth of one spade (this is called a spit). Single digging suffices on light free-draining soil as long as there is no layer of compacted stones in the topsoil. Much of the procedure is the same as for double digging, but the subsoil is left undisturbed. Mark out the position of the bed. Remove any turf or vegetation from the surface, put to one side and then bury it in the bottom of the bed as you proceed. Work across the bed, digging out a trench that is two spits wide and a single spit deep, and place the soil to one side. Remove stones and perennial weeds as you go. Fork well-rotted manure or compost into the trench. Begin digging a new trench behind the first. Throw the soil forward into the first trench, burying the organic matter. Repeat this process of trenching down the bed until the last trench has been dug. Add organic matter to the base and fill the trench with the soil dug from the first trench.

DOUBLE DIGGING

This is a method for deeply digging the soil, in which the soil is broken up to a depth of approximately 70cm (28in) or more. The method usually involves digging a quantity of soil and setting it aside while aerating and sometimes adding an amendment to the subsoil below, then returning the topsoil. There are several methods of double digging, all of which have their advocates. Two methods for double digging are described here.

First, define the area where the double digging will take place, making an estimate of the area to be dug. Dig a trench, 30cm (12in) wide and a spit deep, across half the width of the bed. Place the excavated soil next to the other half, placing it on to a tarpaulin or similar covering if the surface needs protection.

When the trench is complete, fork the subsoil, rocking it back and forth, to loosen it down to a depth of about 30cm (12in). Then, spread a layer of garden compost

---

SINGLE DIGGING

Single digging is the simplest method of cultivation. It is well suited to light soils or those soils that have been well worked for a number of years. It simply involves digging and inverting the soil to a single spade's depth, leaving the subsoil below undisturbed.

1 *Start by digging a single trench across the width of the plot. Put the soil from the first trench to one side because you will need to use it later in the final trench.*

2 *Put a layer of manure in the bottom of the trench. Dig out the next trench and cover over the manure in the first trench with the earth taken from the second trench.*

3 *Repeat this process of adding manure to each trench and filling in with earth from the next, breaking up the soil as you go and keeping the surface as even as possible.*

4 *Continue down the length of the plot until you reach the final trench. This should be filled in with the earth taken from the first trench, which was set to one side.*

DOUBLE DIGGING, METHOD ONE

Double digging is a good method for compacted, heavy or poor soils that are in need of rejuvenation. It involves a deep cultivation *of both the topsoil and subsoil and is well worth the hard work, producing a wonderful soil in which plants will thrive.*

1 *Dig a wide trench, placing the soil to one side so that it can be used later when filling in the final trench.*

2 *Break up the soil at the bottom of the trench with a fork, adding manure to the soil as you proceed.*

3 *Dig the next trench in the bed, turning the soil over on top of the broken soil in the first trench.*

4 *Continue down the plot, ensuring that subsoil from the lower trench is not mixed with topsoil of the upper.*

DOUBLE DIGGING, METHOD TWO

1 *Keeping soil from each level separate, dig the first trench two spits deep and fork over. Dig the second trench one spit deep.*

2 *Add organic material to the first double trench and dig the lower spit of the second trench into it.*

3 *Dig an upper third trench one spit deep, and place the soil on top of that already placed in the first trench.*

4 *Continue, ensuring that the topsoil and subsoil do not mix. Fill in remaining trenches with soil taken from the first one.*

over the exposed subsoil. Move over one spit's width in the bed, and begin to dig out another trench, moving and inverting the excavated soil into the adjacent trench that was just dug. When you get to the end of the bed replace the soil that was set aside at the outset.

When the digging is finished, level the site prior to planting. More garden compost (approximately 8cm/3in) can be spread over the surface and forked in at this stage.

You do not have to dig the entire plot all at once. Instead, work on small areas, say, one metre (yard) square, whenever you wish. Once you double-dig a bed, it is important not to walk on it. After all, the whole point of double digging is to loosen the topsoil and the subsoil to a sufficient depth so that the roots of the plants can grow unrestricted and water can readily percolate through the soil. Walking on the soil will simply pack it down again.

There is also a second method of digging (shown above) that is less commonly used, which enriches the soil to a greater depth.

SECONDARY CULTIVATION

This normally involves the nourishing of the soil after it has been cultivated by digging and usually entails the addition of some form of organic matter during, or immediately after, its completion. Secondary cultivation also describes light digging used to control weeds or incorporate green manures. The tool generally used for this is a fork. Light forking is often the best method to use in areas with permanent plantings of perennial plants or shrubs.

USING A ROTAVATOR

A rotavator is a useful labour-saving device for breaking down dug clods and creating a fine, free-running 'tilth' that can easily be levelled for planting or seed-bed preparation.

TIPS FOR DIGGING

Digging can be hard work, but simply following the tips given below will help you to avoid strains and injuries.

- Start with a small area, pace yourself and avoid straining your back.
- Use a spade that is right for you and the job. It should be a little higher than hip height when held vertically.
- Do not try to lift more than you can handle. You will dig for longer periods of time by taking smaller amounts.
- As you work, try to establish a rhythm that you can maintain at all times.
- When doing a lot of heavy digging, scrape the blade clean now and then, and, if necessary, use a file to sharpen the end of the spade, following the original bevel of the blade.

SOIL CONDITIONERS

There is quite a range of conditioners available to the allotment-grower for improving the soil. Some are free (if you do not count the time taken in working and transporting them), others are relatively cheap, while those bought by the bag can be quite expensive. The best option is often to begin by using the materials that are closest to hand. Smaller plots or those that are newly established or in poor shape may require soil conditioners to be brought in. This section looks at some of the options.

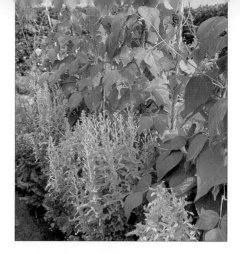

Above: *A well-conditioned soil will pay dividends in terms of enhanced plant growth and development.*

FARMYARD MANURE

This is usually freely available, although these days it comes increasingly from stables rather than farms. It contains a small amount of nutrients although it usually makes the soil more acidic as it decomposes and should always be well rotted before use. It can also contain lots of weed seeds, which often come from the bedding used for the animals. Occasionally there can be problems if the straw used has been sprayed with pesticides, so always be sure of your source. Farmyard manure is usually cheap or occasionally free for the taking.

BURYING GREEN WASTE

If you have space, you can simply open a trench in the soil and bury your green waste 20–30cm (8–12in) deep under the soil. It will take perhaps two to three months during the warm season to break down. Avoid planting crops in the soil above until the material has decomposed properly.

Left: *Spent mushroom compost is an ideal material for improving the structure of many types of soil. Its high pH makes it unsuitable as a mulch around acid-loving plants.*

LEAF MOULD

Many gardeners believe leaf mould to be the finest addition to any soil. The product itself forms naturally under the closed canopy of forest trees. It is, as the name suggests, the rotted product of fallen leaves. It is not particularly rich in nutrients but it has an extremely good ability to condition a soil and encourages natural nutrient cycles in your soil. It is usually made by the gardeners that wish to use it and is rarely sold on. Anyone who has a ready supply of leaves will find this an easy material to make.

Start by gathering up leaves in the autumn and stack in a chicken-wire cage to prevent them being blown back over the site. Do not add any greens or other materials to the pile. The heap will rot down slowly and be ready for use in one to two years. It can be sited in a dark corner where nothing else will grow, but you must ensure that you keep the pile moist all year round. The wire cage can be removed after two months or so and used again the

Left: *Animal manures can provide both nutrients and valuable organic matter when added to your garden soil.*

following autumn. Alternatively, two permanent pits, sited side by side, can be filled (or emptied) in alternate years. Smaller quantities of leaves can be pushed into black plastic sacks with the top closed and with holes pierced by a garden fork around the sides and bottom of the bag to allow some airflow.

SPENT MUSHROOM COMPOST

This is one of the few types of organic matter to have a slightly alkaline effect on the soil. It is a uniform and friable mixture of stable organic materials that is a waste product of the mushroom-growing industry. It is usually quite inexpensive. The composting and growing processes that produce this material bind nutrients to the organic matter, resulting in a substance that holds on to nutrients more readily than fresh or non-composted organic wastes. In addition, the compost has good moisture-holding abilities.

Spent mushroom compost is slightly alkaline, with a pH ranging from 7–8 but generally around 7.3. There are few weed seeds, insects or pathogens because the compost is pasteurized before it is removed from the mushroom house.

BUILDING A LEAF MOULD PIT

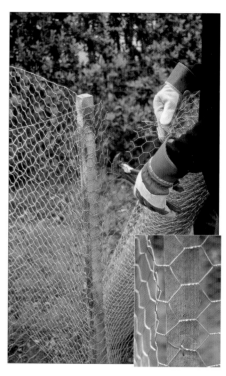

1 *Drive in four 1.5m (5ft) posts to form the four corners of a square on the ground. The posts should be spaced about 1m (3ft) apart and there should be just over 1m left above ground once the posts are driven in.*

2 *Attach chicken wire – a 1m (3ft) wide roll is needed for this – to the stakes using 'U'-shaped fencing staples, hammered in firmly. Pull the wire tight across the length of the roll before attaching it to the next post.*

3 *Once the wire has been securely stapled to the posts all the way around, cut it with wire cutters, folding the sharp ends under the attached mesh so that they cannot cut you or snag any clothing.*

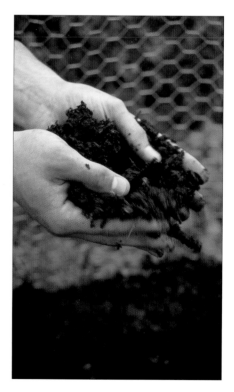

4 *Place fallen leaves into the 'pit' until it is full. Firm the leaves lightly in layers as you go, so that the pit is completely packed with leaves but still contains a little air.*

5 *After a year or two, the leaf mould is ready to use. You could build two pits and rotate their use, as a single pit will not be emptied in time to receive leaves the following autumn.*

6 *In order to gain the maximum benefit, you should apply the finished leaf mould to the soil in your allotment in late winter or early spring, when the soil is moist.*

Left: *Beans and other leguminous plants are an important part of a successful allotment vegetable garden, 'fixing' their own nitrogen and so naturally helping to raise levels of soil fertility.*

The addition of spent compost to garden soil can result in a higher pH, increased nutrient-holding capacity and better soil structure. The main disadvantage occurs when the compost is first mixed with soil, as bacteria convert the proteins in the compost to ammonia, which can be toxic to young plants. Try to ensure the source of your compost is an organic mushroom grower.

VEGETABLE INDUSTRIAL WASTE

Some by-products of the food industry, such as spent hop waste and cocoa shells, can be beneficial as soil conditioners in the allotment garden. They are useful in terms of their ability to improve soil structure. However, their smell, which may be described as rancid ale or beer with hops, or sickly cocoa, is often enough to put people off. They are sometimes marketed commercially although they may be available as a local by-product of industry. Whatever product you use, it should be well rotted before it is used as a soil conditioner.

WORM COMPOST

Kitchen waste can be composted with worms both indoors and outdoors, although these two locations have their limitations and advantages.

The materials that are being composted are consumed by the worms and then excreted as worm casts. This process binds the nutrients consumed into a form that can be used by plants and reduces the volume of the original materials. These worm casts are covered with slow-dissolving, semi-permeable mucus that acts as a time-release mechanism for the nutritional content of the worm casts and also gives the finished compost good water-retentive qualities.

Above: *Brandling or tiger worms readily reduce vegetable matter into a useful compost material within a wormery.*

A WORMERY

Worms are an effective way to break down kitchen waste such as vegetable scraps. They will eventually eat their bedding as well as the kitchen waste. The resulting worm casts are a nutrient-rich soil conditioner.

Decomposing waste (strong manure, leaf mould, shredded newspaper, old garden compost)

Planks of wood to separate compost from gravel

Drainage holes

Damp newspaper

New kitchen waste

20cm (8in) bedding material

15cm (6in) gravel

Worm colonies can be built in a similar way to a cold pile compost heap, with materials added as they become available. Excessive heat and frequent pile turning are not needed. Too much heat will actually kill the worms. Alternatively, a purpose-built wormery can be used. Both methods require materials to be placed in a shaded, cool and moist location. The worm colony must not become heated by the microbial action that takes place in normal composting. If the colony does get hot, it may cause the loss of the worms if they do not have cooler areas to which they can escape.

For an indoor worm colony, the wormery (a sealed, ventilated box with a close-fitting lid) is filled with bedding materials (usually damp shredded newspaper or similar) and the worms are added. Vegetable waste from the kitchen is placed on top or a few inches under the bedding where the worms can find and devour it. Eventually, the worms eat their bedding as well as the vegetable scraps. The finished worm castings can be removed and used. New bedding and kitchen scraps are then placed

in the container and the worms returned to make a new batch of compost. Many purchased wormeries have the facility to collect the liquid by-product of the worms' activities, which makes an excellent liquid plant food.

It is advisable to check the pH level of the wormery every now and then. Thin, white, thread-like cotton worms are usually

Above: *Leafy crops benefit from the addition of organic matter because it encourages nitrogen-fixing bacteria to do their all-important work in the soil.*

an indication that the pH is too low. Adding some calcified seaweed can help to counter this acidity, as can a regular addition of eggshells.

Above: *Organic matter buried under a layer of soil will allow it to break down gradually. A trench 30cm (12in) deep can easily accommodate a layer of well-rotted material 8–10cm (4–5in) thick. This will break down, enriching the soil over time, and is the most commonly used method to add organic matter when digging a plot.*

BENEFITS OF ADDING ORGANIC MATTER

Using organic matter as a mulch or soil conditioner will help to warm up the soil earlier in the spring. This in turn will allow for the earlier planting of some types of plant.

- Organic matter inoculates the soil with vast numbers of beneficial microbes and provides the food source that soil-dwelling microbes need to live. These microbes are able to extract nutrients from the mineral part of the soil and eventually pass the nutrients on to plants.
- Adding organic matter to your soil improves the way in which water interacts with the soil and improves the overall soil structure. All soils can benefit from the regular addition of organic matter.

To sandy soils
- Organic matter acts as a sponge to help retain water that would otherwise drain down below the reach of plant roots. This has the benefit of protecting plants against drought.

To clay soils
- Organic matter helps to increase the air space within the soil, making it drain more quickly. This ensures that the soil does not become waterlogged or dry out into a brick-like substance.

MAKING GARDEN COMPOST

Every allotment should have at least one compost heap, where plot and kitchen waste can be broken down by microbes and other soil-dwelling creatures to produce a good medium-fertility soil improver. Making compost is not difficult and is an excellent way to recycle waste. Many growers take great pride in their home-produced compost and all sites can benefit from this sustainable approach to soil improvement.

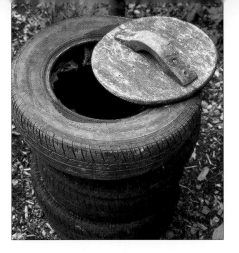

Above: *Even a stack of old car tyres can be recycled and used to make a cheap but effective compost heap.*

THE SITE

A position in full sun will give the compost heap additional heat, allowing the contents to decompose more rapidly. If time is not a key factor, partial shade or even full shade will do. Compost is easily made in a

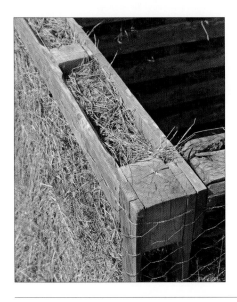

freestanding pile in a sunny or partially shaded area in the allotment. Alternatively, a simple structure can be used to contain the pile. A variety of materials can be used to make these structures, including wood, bricks, pallets, a wire cage or even a stack of used tyres. Whichever method you use, you must provide good drainage. An average heap should be around a cubic metre (10 cu. ft). It can be much larger, but any smaller and it will not be as effective.

When adding waste materials to the heap, the items should be as small as you can make them. The more surface area that is exposed, the quicker it will decompose. A chipper or shredder is a big help. Many gardeners are keen advocates of adding a small amount of good topsoil in order to introduce microorganisms that will kick-start the process of decomposition.

Left: *A wall made from a pallet, filled with straw and held in place with chicken wire, allows air to circulate, aiding decomposition.*

Compost heaps in containers can be built up with successive layers of 'green' and 'brown' materials, separating these with thin layers of topsoil.

Sifting the pile is the final stage of the process, with any large pieces of residue being returned back to the new heap.

COMPOST INGREDIENTS

The potential ingredients for your compost heap will be either 'brown' or 'green'. Browns are dry and dead plant materials, such as straw, hay, dry brown weeds, autumn leaves, nutshells, shredded paper, pine needles, tough plant stems and wood chips or sawdust. Because they tend to be dry, browns often need to be moistened before they are put into a compost system.

Greens are fresh (and often green) plant materials, such as green weeds from the plot, fruit and vegetable scraps, green leaves, grass clippings, tea bags, coffee grounds, seaweed, eggshells, fish scraps, green manures and fresh horse manure.

MAKING A HOT PILE COMPOST HEAP

1 *Starting with an empty compost bin, place a layer of 'browns' – straw, old leaves and chipped wood are ideal – in the base of the bin. If the bin is positioned over bare soil, include some fine twiggy material to help to circulate air to the base of the pile.*

2 *Add a layer of brown compost materials, such as autumn leaves, plant stems and wood chips, which should be approximately 15cm (6in) deep, and ensure that it is of an even thickness. The material should be lightly firmed in.*

3 *Add a new layer of 'greens' to the compost bin. Most plant material can be used for this, although you should avoid too much fibrous or woody material such as plant stems. Never include weed seeds if possible.*

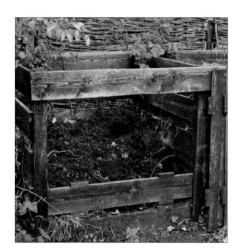

Above: *An enclosed compost heap should ideally have one side that opens in order to make it easy to empty the finished material.*

Compared with browns, greens contain more nitrogen. Nitrogen is a critical element in amino acids and proteins, and can be thought of as a protein source for the billions of multiplying microbes.

A good mix of browns and greens is the best nutritional balance for microbes. This mix also improves the aeration and level of water in the pile.

THE 'COLD PILE' METHOD

Make a pile of 'browns', such as autumn leaves, moisten them well and then slowly incorporate 'greens' such as kitchen waste or lawn clippings over the next year (this method can take a full year to finish the compost). If it gets very cold in winter, cover the heap with cardboard or old carpet and peel this back to stir in any greens. In this type of composting, there are never enough high-nitrogen greens to get the pile really hot. Turn the pile a minimum of once a month if you have not recently added any greens, thereby breaking up the decaying mass and making it friable. If you do use this method, be sure you always have at least as many browns as added greens, as too many greens will just create a slimy, smelly mess. Some compost heaps (those with lots of greens added) may reach very high temperatures, some even reaching 70°C (158°F), thereby killing weed seeds. Cold piles, on the other hand, do not and it is best not to add any weed wastes that will contain seeds. If you do, you could risk spreading weed seeds across your allotment in their own growing mix when you come to use the compost.

THE 'HOT PILE' METHOD

Wet the ground under the pile and add twigs or other un-shredded browns to provide some aeration at the base. Layer the rest of your materials, alternating green and brown layers of about 15cm (6in) thickness, and add water as you go. Topsoil can also be added as a 2cm (¾in) layer between each cycle of green and brown materials. Finish the pile with a layer of browns. Cover the pile with a lid or piece of carpet to keep out rain and conserve heat. Check to see that your pile becomes hot within a few days. Turn the pile to decrease composting time. This action allows all the material to be exposed to the hot centre, thereby increasing aeration. Do this once a week in the warmer season, and once a month in cooler periods. The pile's heat should peak every time you turn it, although the peak temperature will be lower with each turn. Always make sure that the pile remains moist, but avoid over-wetting, as this will limit the amount of air circulation and ultimately reduce the speed and efficiency of the process.

COMPOSTING MATERIALS

Many items can be composted into valuable soil conditioners. Whether because of toxins, plant or human diseases or weed problems, some things should never be used.

Good compost materials
Animal manure
Fallen leaves
Grass/lawn clippings
Hay and straw from organic farms
Kitchen waste
Prunings
Sawdust
Shredded browns
Soot and charcoal
Spent hops or cocoa shells
Spent mushroom compost
Weeds and other allotment wastes

What not to compost
Chemically treated wood products
Diseased plants
Human and pet waste
Meat, bones and fatty food wastes
Pernicious weeds

---

4 *Continue adding greens until you have a layer about 15cm (6in) thick, the same depth as the browns below. Lawn clippings should be placed in layers of about 10cm (4in) or mixed with other green waste to avoid the layer becoming slimy and airless.*

5 *Kitchen refuse, such as vegetable waste, can also be added and is usually classed as a 'green'. You can include a thin layer of soil to add microorganisms before the next layer of 'browns'. Continue layering until the bin is full, then water and cover.*

6 *After two to three months, you should have well-rotted garden compost, which, due to the heat of the pile, will be largely free from weed seeds, pests and diseases. Once the bin has been emptied, it can be refilled in the same way.*

GREEN MANURES

Sometimes referred to as 'cover crops', green manures are plants that are grown to benefit the soil rather than for consumption or display. Green manures replace and hold nutrients, improve the structure of the soil and increase its organic material content. They also smother the soil and so prevent weed growth. Green manures also 'fix' atmospheric nitrogen. They are easy to grow and can be used to improve the soil when manures are not readily available.

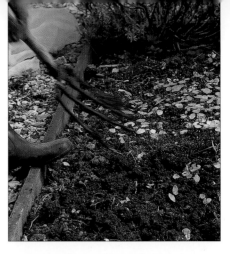

Above: *Growing a green manure is an easy and effective way in which to add some organic matter to the soil.*

BENEFITS OF GREEN MANURES

At any time of year, but especially in winter, the soil loses nutrients if it is bare for six weeks or more. Green manures help to counteract this and maintain a more even soil temperature and moisture content. Many green manures grow deep roots to tap resources unavailable to some crops. Others produce a fibrous root system to help build structure in the soil, while many have flowers that attract pollinating insects.

TYPES OF GREEN MANURE

Some green manures are nitrogen-fixers, using bacteria that colonize the nodules on their roots. These microbes take nitrogen out of the air and convert it into a form that plants can use. Green manures are usually divided into two groups: legumes and non-legumes. Leguminous manures include clover, peas, broad (fava) beans and alfalfa. Despite their nitrogen-fixing abilities, legumes have slow autumn growth and add less organic content. They can also be less winter hardy.

Winter rye is the most commonly grown non-leguminous cover crop, but oats, wheat, oilseed rape and buckwheat are also used. Although they do not add nitrogen to the soil, they help maintain levels and have the additional advantage over legumes of growing faster through the autumn, thereby giving better weed suppression. They also tend to break down more slowly than legumes and add more organic matter to the soil. You may wish to use a combination of green manures in order to balance the benefits of the different types.

DEEP-ROOTED GREEN MANURES

The roots of certain green manure 'crops' work through the soil, holding it together as they grow. Once dug in, however, they help to make it crumbly and friable as they rot. Some green manures have very deep roots that reach down into the subsoil and can harvest nutrients that are unavailable to other allotment plants. In this respect they are a form of biological double digging.

PLANTING GREEN MANURES

Winter green manures should be planted early enough to give about four weeks of growth before cold weather stops their growth. Spring or summer crops must be given sufficient time to develop before they are dug in. After preparing the soil, plant large-seeded cover crops in shallow, closely spaced furrows. Smaller seeds can be broadcast over the surface and covered with a light raking, watering if needed until they germinate. Dig the crop in once it is ready, allowing at least three weeks before you intend to plant to give time for the material to rot down. It is best not to allow green manures to go to seed as they all have the potential to become weeds.

Gardens are traditionally dug over and manured in autumn, then left bare over winter. Many nutrients can be lost during this time due to the leaching action of rain. A hardy green manure sown in the autumn can be dug in the following spring, yielding nutrients to a newly sown or planted crop.

USING GREEN MANURES

1 *Sow the seed evenly across the area where you plan to grow the green manure. Either broadcast the seed or sow larger seed thinly in shallow drills and close rows.*

2 *Lightly rake in the seed so that it is covered and will germinate quickly. Water the area thoroughly if there is no rain due or if it does not rain for the following 48 hours.*

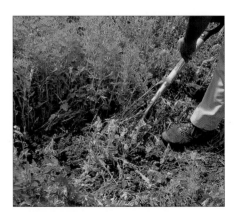

3 *Once the seed germinates, allow it to grow a little before digging it into the soil. Never let green manure crops set seed or they will become a weed in later crops on the site.*

TYPES OF GREEN MANURE

GREEN MANURE FOR GROWING OVER WINTER

These species can withstand moderate to hard frost for a long period and can be cut down in the spring, prior to cultivation. The shorter types can also be used as catch (cover) crops around winter vegetables or biennial crops for harvest in the early spring.

GREEN MANURE	SOWING TIME AND METHOD	HEIGHT	WINTER HARDY?	NITROGEN-FIXING ABILITY	TERMS OF GROWTH	DIGGING IN	OTHER NOTES
Alfalfa *Medicago sativa*	Early spring to mid-summer; broadcast at 3g ($^1/_{10}$oz) per square metre (yard).	100–150cm (3–5ft)	Yes	Yes but poor	Perennial. Grow for several months or more than one season.	Any time. Medium effort if young. Hard if left for more than one season.	Very deep rooting. Will grow on most soils. Dislikes acid or waterlogged soils, but drought resistant.
Asilke clover *Trifolium hybridum*	Mid-spring to late summer; broadcast at 3g ($^1/_{10}$oz) per square metre (yard).	30cm (12in)	Yes	Yes	Several months	Any time. Medium effort.	Will withstand wetter soils than other clovers but more prone to drought. Shallow rooted.
Essex or red merviot clover *Trifolium pratense*	Mid-spring to late summer; broadcast at 3g ($^1/_{10}$oz) per square metre (yard).	40cm (16in)	Yes	Yes	Several months	Any time. Easy, little effort.	Prefers good loamy soil. Can be mown or cut several times per season and used for compost.
Grazing rye *Secale cereale*	Late summer to late autumn; broadcast at 30g (1oz) per square metre (yard) or thinly in rows 20cm (8in) apart.	30–60cm (12–24in)	Yes	No	Autumn to spring	Before flowering. Hard work.	Grows in most soils. Keep watered during germination, else yield is poor. Sow thickly to smother weeds.
Phacelia *Phacelia tanacetifolium*	Early spring to early autumn; broadcast at 3g ($^1/_{10}$oz) per square metre (yard) or thinly in rows 20cm (8in) apart.	60–90cm (12–36in)	Yes	No	2 months in summer; 5–6 months over winter	Before flowering. Easy, little effort.	Grows in most soils. Quick to grow in summer. If left, will produce mauve flowers that bees love.
Trefoil *Medicago lupulina*	Early spring to late summer; broadcast at 3g ($^1/_{10}$oz) per square metre (yard).	30–60cm (12–24in)	Yes	Yes	Several months to a year	Any time. Medium effort.	Will grow in most soils but dislikes acid. Can be used for undersowing. Dense foliage.

GREEN MANURE FOR WARM-SEASON GROWING

Plants for use in the spring and summer have to be quick-growing in order to cover the ground and yield benefit within a short period of time. They are generally slightly tender, although lower-growing species can be used as a catch crop around other seasonal crops.

GREEN MANURE	SOWING TIME AND METHOD	HEIGHT	WINTER HARDY?	NITROGEN-FIXING ABILITY	TERMS OF GROWTH	DIGGING IN	OTHER NOTES
Bitter lupin *Lupinus angustifolius*	Early spring to early summer 4cm (1$^1/_2$in) deep; 3cm (1$^1/_4$in) apart; in rows 15cm (6in) apart.	50cm (20in)	Mild winters	Yes	2–3 months	Before flowering. Easy, little effort.	Prefers light slightly acidic soil. Foliage not very dense. Deep rooted.
Buckwheat *Fagopyrum esculentum*	Early spring to late summer; broadcast at 10g ($^1/_3$oz) per square metre (yard) or thinly in shallow rows 20cm (8in) apart.	80cm (32in)	No	No	2–3 months	Before or during flowering. Easy, no effort.	Grows on poor soils. If allowed to flower, attracts hoverflies to aid pollination of crops.
Crimson clover *Trifolium incarnatum*	Early spring to late summer; broadcast at 3g ($^1/_{10}$oz) per square metre (yard).	30–60cm (12–24in)	Mild winters only	Yes	2–3 months or over winter	Before flowering. Medium effort.	Prefers sandy loam soil but will tolerate heavy clay. Large red flowers attract bees.
Fenugreek *Trigonella foenum-graecum*	Early spring to late summer; broadcast at 5g ($^1/_5$oz) per square metre (yard) or thinly in 15cm (6in) shallow rows.	30–60cm (12–24in)	Mild winters	No	2–3 months	Any time before flowering. Easy, little effort.	Prefers good drainage but will tolerate heavy or light soil.

NO-DIG GARDENING

As the name suggests, no-dig gardening is a method of growing plants without cultivating the ground they occupy. While this may seem unnatural to some confirmed tillers of the soil, it is actually the most natural method available. No-dig gardening mimics the natural cycle; after all, plants have grown on the Earth's surface for over 400 million years without people digging the soil for them. This approach also has the advantage of being less labour-intensive.

Above: *Adding organic matter to the soil surface encourages worms and other organisms that cycle nutrients naturally.*

ESTABLISHING A NATURAL CYCLE

Essentially no-dig gardening relies upon natural soil processes combined with the action of soil organisms to produce a good soil structure and natural nutrient cycles. There are numerous ways that this can be done, but all rely upon inputs from the top down. A thick top-dressing of organic matter is placed on the surface to be absorbed by the soil itself. Less laborious than digging, the no-dig method does need planning and careful input in order to be successful, although a properly prepared no-dig bed will be every bit as effective as a conventionally cultivated one.

WHAT ARE THE BENEFITS?

Assuming weeds can be controlled, most vegetable crops can be grown with reduced tillage. The key features of a no-dig vegetable-growing system are to keep the soil covered with organic mulch as much of the time as possible and to keep off the soil. The beds are left permanently in place, and there is no cultivation.

Plants grown without tillage use water more efficiently, the water-holding capacity of the soil increases, and water loss from run-off and evaporation is reduced. For crops grown without irrigation in drought-prone soils, this more efficient use of water can translate into higher yields.

In addition, the organic matter in soil and populations of beneficial insects are maintained, as are earthworm populations and microbial activity. Soil and nutrients are less likely to be lost from the ground, less time is required to prepare the soil for planting, and, since there is less bare soil, there will be fewer opportunities for weeds to get established. The mulch of organic matter also helps to keep weeds down.

WHAT ARE THE PROBLEMS?

Potential problems associated with the no-dig method are compaction, flooding and poor drainage. However, if the water-holding capacity of a soil improves, no-till systems may produce higher yields. Soil temperatures under organic mulch can be several degrees lower than bare soil or soil under a plastic mulch. Although the lower temperature can be an advantage, especially in the summer when soil temperatures under plastic can be excessive, it can delay crop development.

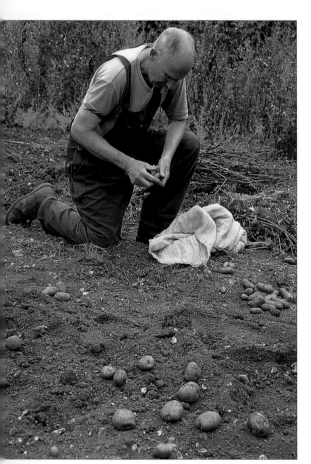

Left: *Many allotment gardeners grow crops such as potatoes quite successfully without ever resorting to digging.*

ADVANTAGES AND DISADVANTAGES OF NO-DIG SYSTEMS

Although no-dig beds may require a little longer to establish initially than cultivated plots, they do offer considerable labour-saving benefits to the allotment gardener. They also suffer very few disadvantages when these are weighed against the considerable advantages.

Advantages
- Plants use water more efficiently.
- Better water-holding capacity of the soil.
- Reduced water loss from run-off and evaporation.
- Higher crop yields in areas prone to drought.
- Organic matter in the soil and soil organisms are maintained at higher levels.
- The lower temperature can be an advantage, especially in summer when soil temperatures under plastic can be excessive.
- Soil and nutrients are more easily maintained.
- Less time is required to prepare the soil for planting.
- Fewer weeds become established due to the mulch of organic matter and the lack of bare soil.

Disadvantages
- Soil can become compacted or poorly drained if it is not properly managed.
- Soil temperatures under a mulch can be several degrees lower than bare soil, which can delay the development of crops.

MAKING A NO-DIG BED

A bed system which includes permanent paths is essential if digging is to be eliminated from gardening tasks. Planning the area so that all parts of the bed can be reached from the paths means that you can grow your crops closer together (you do not need to leave extra space for access) and you will be able to harvest more from a smaller area.

Mark out the beds on the ground or build simple raised beds with wooden sides. Alternatively, those wishing to make a more permanent edge could consider a low brick wall. By raising the bed it is possible to create a deep bed of good-quality soil that will warm up more quickly than the surrounding soil. A raised bed also means you do not have to bend down so far to carry out routine tasks and the method is tailor-made for disabled gardeners. Raised edging is also useful for attaching supporting hoops, crop covers and cloches. Edges such as these are also ideal for providing barriers for pests. Devices

such as water traps or copper paper are easily attached to them to prevent slugs and snails from entering the bed.

Beds should be no more than 1.2m (4ft) wide and paths at least 30cm (12in) wide with every other path double this width to allow for easy wheelbarrow access. Individual beds should be no longer than 3.5m (12ft), otherwise you will waste a lot of time walking around them. The beds can

Above: *Edging your beds with hoops of bent twigs provides barriers for pests.*

be of any design, from a simple series of parallel rectangles to a more complex pattern of interlocking shapes. Whatever design you choose, follow the same recommended bed and path widths, remembering that narrow angles and very small beds are more difficult to construct.

PLANTING POTATOES IN A NO-DIG BED

1 *Place a thick layer of well-rotted manure or garden compost on the bed to be planted. This should be quite deep – at least 15–20cm (6–8in) – as it will quickly decompose during the growing season. Early planting is possible by manuring in winter and covering with plastic sheeting to warm the soil. The potatoes are planted directly into this and may be more closely spaced than those planted in soil, perhaps as close as 30cm (12in) apart.*

2 *Apply a generous mulch of straw once the bed is planted to give cover to the tubers and to suppress weed growth on the manure or compost. Spread a second layer of composted organic material over the straw. Add another layer of straw and composted material. Water the bed well. Once the potato plants begin to emerge, more straw can be laid down on to the bed, as the material put down earlier in the season will begin to compost down.*

3 *As the potato stems grow, mulch heavily in order to ensure that no light reaches the developing tubers. The potato crop will mature at the same rate as potatoes grown in ordinary soil. The no-dig system is possibly the best method for heavy clay soils that are prone to waterlogging. Potatoes grown in this way are also easy to harvest as there is no digging and the potatoes are cleaner once they are ready for harvesting.*

PLANNING THE CROPS

Successful cropping requires an understanding of how crops grow, what they need, when they mature, and the systems and structures you will need to put in place to ensure a good harvest. Each crop has its individual preferences, although many share similar requirements, which means they can readily be grown in the same setting. Knowing the requirements of your fruit and vegetables allows you to choose which ones are right for you, plan an appropriate alloment structure and layout, and work out what needs doing in order to get a successful result.

Left: *Allotment sites can provide a summer spectacle as well as a wealth of fresh, home-grown food for your table.*

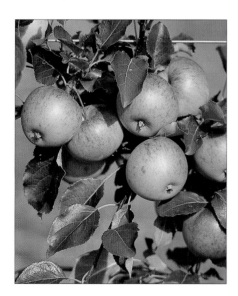

Above: *Fruit such as pears and apples grown on an allotment are one of the most welcome delights of autumn.*

Above: *Planting companion flowers on your allotment helps to keep your vegetables healthy by attracting beneficial insects.*

Above: *A greenhouse on the plot not only helps you raise earlier crops but also allows you to greatly increase the range you grow.*

STARTING YOUR PLAN

Taking on an allotment can be quite time-consuming and it is important not to let things slip during the busy times of the year or your crops will suffer and the yield will be lower. Ideally you should get down there as often as possible, but in reality it is best to pace yourself and apply the little and often principle. Choose what you want to grow wisely, according to your needs, tastes and lifestyle, and plan ahead to ensure a steady harvest of useful produce over the course of the year.

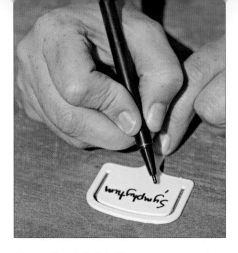

Above: *Carefully labelling crops means that you know what is growing where and lends a sense of care and order to your plot.*

MAKE A PERSONAL SCHEDULE

When you take on a new allotment, it is possible that you might be 'making' extra time to get out there. If this is taking you away from other things, it is likely that other matters in your life might become neglected. If there is a chance that time will be an issue, the crops you grow will need to reflect this. An allotment featuring a range of more permanent crops, such as fruit, rhubarb, asparagus or artichokes will prove less time-consuming during the summer months, although it will be less productive on a yearly basis.

Below: *Cloches and low tunnels can increase the range of early crops that can be grown on an allotment.*

It is a good idea is to spend some of the time that you are there taking a look at what other plot-holders are doing. See what crops are successful and what works well for them. Remember that the social angle is often a good way to learn how to get the best from your plot and, as a result, needs to be a part of your schedule.

SET SOME TARGETS

Once you have an idea of how much time you can commit to your allotment, you will need some goals to aim for. While there is no reason not to be ambitious, you need to temper this with a little realism. If your main objective is to grow some fresh vegetables for your kitchen table, then you need to have a harvest by date for the first crop.

Always keep this in mind through the time leading up to this. You could always make a little event of the first crops being cooked; after all, you've worked hard to get to that stage. Don't stop there though, as you'll quickly find targets and achievements to be a great motivator, particularly when you have to go out in chilly winter weather to tend your patch.

DECIDE WHAT TO GROW

A visit to a local seed supplier will usually leave you facing a bewildering array of seed packets. Not only are there many vegetable types but there is also a huge number of varieties for some of them. The descriptions point to bumper harvests of mouth-watering vegetables and it is easy to become confused.

As with any shopping trip, the secret of success when obtaining the right crops is to have a list. Start this by writing down all the things you regularly eat. Chances are, this list will be quite long and will quickly fill up the growing space available to you.

PLANT ACCORDING TO YOUR REQUIREMENTS

Remember that liking something is not the same as wanting to eat a lot of it. Gluts are common on allotments and this is usually because people overestimate how much of one thing they need. In contrast, crops that you are likely to use a lot of can easily run short if you don't plant enough of them.

A quick look around your neighbours' plots will reveal subtle differences in what they are growing. This probably reflects personal tastes on their part and, in time, your plot will be similarly distinguished with your own preferences.

SPREAD YOUR HARVEST OVER THE YEAR

Even if your plot is packed with crops that you will definitely want to eat, the chances are that they could all come at once. If you haven't got somewhere or a way of storing them, this can lead to waste, so it is a good idea to grow several varieties of one crop, choosing a range that matures over a period

Above: *Time spent planning your plot is an essential part of the yearly schedule. Make notes concerning both success and failures.*

Above: *Careful planning and preparation will be rewarded with a successful allotment packed with your favourite crops.*

of time. You can also stagger a few sowings or plantings to spread out the season of each of these, meaning that the food stays on your plot for as long as possible and is always harvested fresh to your table. Sharing and swapping produce with your allotment neighbours is a great way to make the most of each other's gluts, and friends and family will normally welcome free food!

You will also need to learn to fit in with the rhythms of nature. Some crops have a definite season and, although this can be extended artificially using cloches, polythene tunnels, cold frames and greenhouses, there are nonetheless limits as to when it will be available. Remember that this is part of the fun of an allotment; seasonal, tasty, fresh food, that is enjoyed at its best, rather than the same vegetables all year round.

DON'T BE AFRAID TO BREAK THE RULES

Probably the best thing about growing your own produce is that you can always experiment with something new. This might be trying to grow a wacky variety or an exotic crop that is more reminiscent of tropical climes, or trying to stretch the season for something well beyond the norm. It can also be an opportunity to try out new techniques in a constrained, controlled environment.

The collective knowledge of the plot-holders around you often outstrips the best books and, what's more, it is specific to your own site. Ask questions, read up on the subject but always make sure that you exercise the basic freedom to just try something new if you want to. If it works, then you will gain a tremendous sense of achievement. If it fails, it doesn't matter. It was fun trying and probably taught you a thing or two along the way without costing you very much other than a little bit of time.

CHOOSING CROP VARIETIES

There is a seemingly endless array of seeds available to the allotment gardener. Each supplier makes claims that their variety is better than all those that went before and any others currently available. Others claim to have older varieties saved from extinction. Personal preference usually dictates the best varieties for you, but an understanding of what you can expect from the seed in a packet can be very useful.

Above: *Onions come in a range of attractive colours and can be grown for their ornamental value as well as for eating.*

WHAT ARE HYBRIDS?

Often when we purchase seed, we respond more readily to the picture on the front of the packet. We may not notice whether it is marked with the terms 'F1' or 'hybrid'. A hybrid is the result of a cross between one variety with pollen from another specific variety. The breeder chooses parent varieties that will produce first generation offspring (F1 hybrids) with known characteristics. The crossing is done in a very controlled manner so that no pollen from another variety is able to pollinate the flowers. As a result, all of the plants that are grown from the hybrid seed will be genetically identical.

Hybrids may be bred to be more widely adapted to environmental stresses such as heat, cold, disease or drought than non-hybrids. They tend to have more uniform characteristics, making crops more predictable in their qualities. They also have 'hybrid vigour' and may grow faster or be more disease-resistant than either of the parents. They may also give better yields than open-pollinated varieties. They will not breed true, however, meaning that seed collected will not produce plants that are the same as the parent (F1 hybrids). For this reason, seed cannot be saved from F1 hybrid plants by the allotment gardener. Seed for hybrid varieties must be purchased year after year from seed companies or nurseries instead, unless you want to take a gamble and grow an array of offspring.

WHAT ARE OPEN-POLLINATED VARIETIES?

Open-pollinated varieties are traditional varieties that have (in some cases) been grown and selected for desirable traits such as taste, yield or disease-resistance for many years. They often grow well in allotment sites as many were originally selected under organic conditions. These plants can mutate and adapt to the local ecosystem, as the seed is often collected and re-used by the allotment gardener.

If a seed packet is labelled 'heirloom', 'open-pollinated' or has no special markings, then it is most likely a standard or traditional variety. The majority of lettuce, bean and pea varieties for domestic use are open-pollinated, while most cabbages, broccoli, tomatoes, cucumbers, melons and Brussels sprouts are hybrids.

Left: *Unusual crop varieties can often be grown from seed that you have collected yourself each year. This is a striking variety of kohl rabi.*

Right: *Allowing a few of your crops to flower will provide you with valuable seed for growing next year's crop.*

Hybrid seeds can dominate the seed market, but open-pollinated varieties are more or less stabilized in their characteristics, remaining fairly consistent and producing seed that will grow into plants that are more or less like the parent plants. They are a little less uniform than hybrids, but the allotment gardener can safely and confidently collect seed and grow plants from them that will be essentially the same as the original plants. Open-pollinated varieties either self-pollinate or are pollinated by wind or insects and they usually produce viable seed.

There have been various claims that open-pollinated varieties do not taste as good as hybrids. It is also claimed that they are smaller and not as uniform and, in many cases, this may be true. However, where matters of taste in varieties are concerned, the only real answer is to try them and see for yourself.

Right: *Old varieties of tomato tend to have varying sizes of tastier fruits. They grow even better among companion flowers.*

WHAT ARE HEIRLOOM VARIETIES?

In the 1970s the European Community brought in regulations to encourage the breeding of new vegetable cultivars and the standardization of older ones. This resulted in a list of approved cultivars being drawn up and it became illegal to sell any cultivar that was not included on this list. It is very expensive to have a single cultivar tested in order to then register it on the list. This meant that many old cultivars were put in grave danger of being lost forever, as the funds to test each variety were not available. It was due to this legislation that the Henry Doubleday Research Association (HDRA), an organic garden organization in England which was established to promote organic issues, founded the Heritage Seed Library (HSL). This seed library ensures that old or 'heirloom varieties' are kept safe for posterity by distributing their seed. Although HDRA grow some of the seeds themselves, they also employ contract growers and seed guardians to make up the bulk of the seeds that are supplied.

Each year a catalogue is sent to HSL members from which they can select up to six varieties free of charge. This distribution set-up overcomes the clause of selling only approved cultivars. This service is also available to members in the United States.

The best heirloom cultivars can be traced back 50 years or longer. Many of these early varieties have been lost already, making those that remain all the more precious. A number of these cultivars have been collected and saved by families and ethnic groups dating back many years. This practice protected the genetic make-up that made each variety successful within a given environment. These base characteristics have become invaluable and the genetic strains of these vegetables are the backbone of modern disease- and drought-resistant hybrids. It is this that makes the collection and preservation of these cultivars so important.

Left: *Many of the heirloom varieties have been selected for the way they perform in local conditions, rather than for crop size, taste or uniformity.*

CROP ROTATION

This is the practice of grouping and growing related plants together and rotating them around different areas of land in a regimented fashion from year to year. Rotating your crops in this way has many advantages, including helping to prevent pest and disease problems from arising in the first place. This method of gardening is fundamental to successful growing. It has been practised for thousands of years and developed into a system that is easy to follow and implement on an allotment.

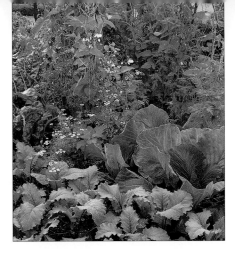

Above: *The secret to achieving a thriving and healthy vegetable area is to rotate the crops on a regular basis.*

WHY ARE CROPS ROTATED?

Continuous cropping in the same area puts both plants and soil at risk. It not only allows large numbers of soil-borne pests and diseases to build up, but, because crops require the same nutrients from the soil year after year, the practice can deplete nutrient levels. A poor infertile soil produces weak unhealthy plants, which, in turn, will be more prone to pest and disease attacks. All these problems amount to reduced yields and even complete crop failure.

When crops are rotated, the groups are divided up into closely related plants that are prone to similar pests and diseases. For example, carrots, parsnips, beetroot (beets) and potatoes are members of one group and prone to carrot fly, whereas cabbage, kale, broccoli and Brussels sprouts, which are members of another group, can be prone to clubroot and cabbage root fly. If the groups are grown in different areas on a rotational basis, it can help to prevent the establishment of soil-borne pests and diseases.

Combined with regular additions of compost and manure, crop rotation will make the soil richer, replace certain

Above: *Brassica crops, such as these red cabbages and Brussels sprouts, should be grouped together in your allotment.*

BENEFITS OF CROP ROTATION

There are many benefits to be gained from rotating your crops regularly.

- Prevents the build-up of soil pests and diseases.
- Helps to prevent nutrient depletion from heavy-feeding crops.
- Rotated crops produce higher yields.
- Results in a healthier soil.

---

nutrients and help prevent pH imbalances that can result from repeated crops of the same type of vegetable.

MAKING A ROTATIONAL PLAN

The basic rules of crop rotation are simple. If you are planning a four-year crop rotation, the plants you have selected are split up into five groups. Group one contains the legumes (peas and beans); group two contains the brassicas (cabbages, Brussels sprouts, broccoli, kale etc); group three contains the onion family and others (onions, lettuce, garlic, sweetcorn [corn] etc); group four includes root crops (potatoes, parsnips, carrots, beetroot [beets] etc); and finally, group five houses permanent crops such as asparagus and rhubarb.

The vegetable plot is then divided into five sections. The permanent crops are given a specific area and are not moved or included in the rotational cycle. The remaining four groups are allocated an area in which to grow. Every year each group is moved on to the next plot, making it four years before the crops are grown on the same area of land again; hence the term crop rotation.

If space is limited, crops can be grown on a three-year rotation – they are split into three groups and divided up as before, except group three is incorporated into group one.

There is no need to grow each crop in every year of a cycle. Remember that it is the vegetable groups that dictate the cropping cycle according to their soil needs and any associated problems. Rotating the crops helps provide the correct soil requirements for certain crops. For example, cabbages and the rest of the group grow well in soil that has been manured the previous autumn, whereas carrots and other root crops (not including potatoes) do not. Where carrots are to be grown, then the plot will need to be dug deeply in readiness for them.

It is important that you plan where the crops are to be every year, so that you know their position for the following year. A comprehensive cropping plan can help you to maximize the yield on a year-round basis by working out successional sowings and intercropping and catch cropping.

COMMON DIFFICULTIES

When planning the cycle, you may encounter certain problems. Careful planning will show that potatoes often take up more space in a vegetable bed than any other crop and finding enough room to grow them in their allocated area may prove difficult.

If space is proving a problem, consider some of the following strategies. Keep brassicas together as a group and never plant them in the same ground two years running. Keep potatoes together every year; if you have planned a lot of potatoes, move all the other members from group four into group three. Also bear in mind that some root crops, such as potatoes, are manure-friendly, while others, like parsnips, are not. Finally, alternating shallow-rooted plants such as cabbages or lettuce with deep-rooted plants like tomatoes or squash will allow the plants' roots to do much of the soil loosening that would otherwise have to be done by hand.

THREE-YEAR CROP ROTATION

Plot 1 – Peas; broad (fava) beans; French (green) beans; runner (green) beans; bulb onions; leeks; sweetcorn (corn); marrows (large zucchini); squashes and pumpkins; lettuce.

Plot 2 – Potatoes; parsnips; beetroot (beets); carrots; salsify; scorzonera; tomatoes.

Plot 3 – Cabbages; Brussels sprouts; calabrese (Italian sprouting broccoli); broccoli; kale; swede (rutabaga or yellow turnips); turnips; kohl rabi; radishes.

Plot 4 (permanent) – Rhubarb; asparagus; perennial herbs; globe artichokes; Jerusalem artichokes; sea kale.

FOUR-YEAR CROP ROTATION

Plot 1 – Peas; broad (fava) beans; French (green) beans; runner (green) beans.

Plot 2 – Cabbages; Brussels sprouts; calabrese (Italian sprouting broccoli); broccoli; kale; radishes; swedes (rutabaga or yellow turnips); turnips; kohl rabi.

Plot 3 – Bulb onions; spring onions (scallions); shallots; leeks; garlic; sweetcorn (corn); marrows (large zucchini), squashes and pumpkins; lettuce.

Plot 4 – Potatoes; parsnips; beetroot (beets); carrots; salsify; scorzonera; celery; celeriac (celery root); tomatoes.

Plot 5 (permanent) – Rhubarb; asparagus; perennial herbs; globe artichokes; Jerusalem artichokes; sea kale.

THREE-YEAR CROP ROTATION

Decide on the vegetables you want to grow and divide into the four groups (plots 1–4) shown in the table opposite. Draw a plan to indicate which group of crops goes where, using a different colour for each group. (Remember plot four is for permanent crops.) Move the crops in each group to the next plot the following year.

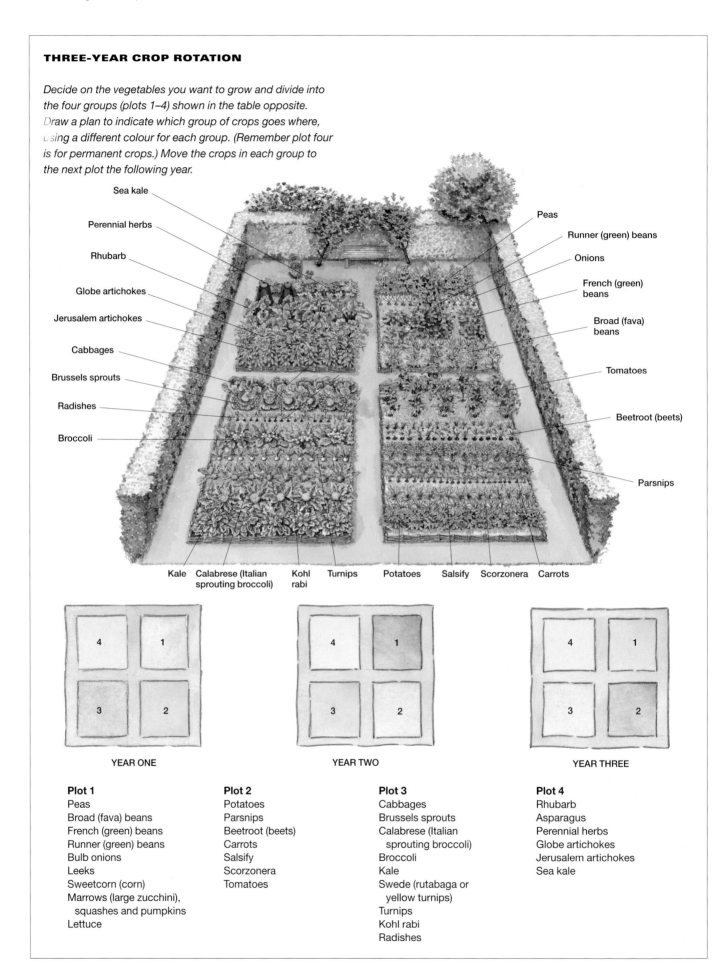

YEAR ONE

YEAR TWO

YEAR THREE

Plot 1
Peas
Broad (fava) beans
French (green) beans
Runner (green) beans
Bulb onions
Leeks
Sweetcorn (corn)
Marrows (large zucchini), squashes and pumpkins
Lettuce

Plot 2
Potatoes
Parsnips
Beetroot (beets)
Carrots
Salsify
Scorzonera
Tomatoes

Plot 3
Cabbages
Brussels sprouts
Calabrese (Italian sprouting broccoli)
Broccoli
Kale
Swede (rutabaga or yellow turnips)
Turnips
Kohl rabi
Radishes

Plot 4
Rhubarb
Asparagus
Perennial herbs
Globe artichokes
Jerusalem artichokes
Sea kale

FOUR-YEAR CROP ROTATION

Divide the vegetables you have decided to grow into the five groups (plots 1–5) shown in the table. Draw a plan to indicate which group of crops goes where, using a different colour for each group. (Remember plot 5 is for the permanent crops.) Next year, move the crops in each group on to the next plot.

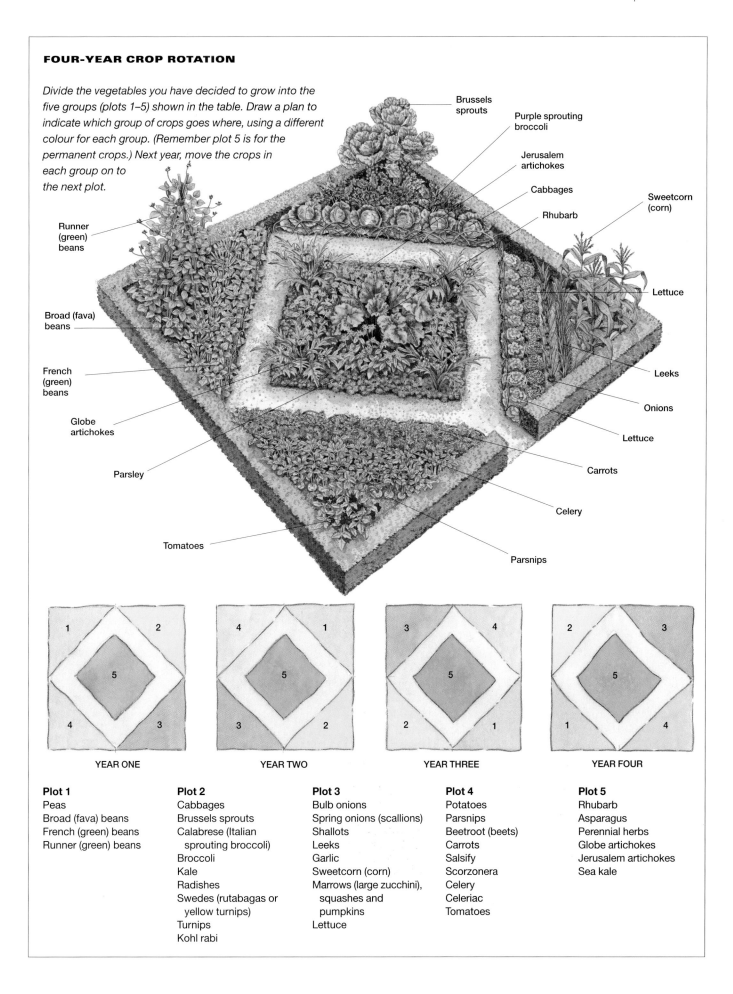

YEAR ONE

YEAR TWO

YEAR THREE

YEAR FOUR

Plot 1
Peas
Broad (fava) beans
French (green) beans
Runner (green) beans

Plot 2
Cabbages
Brussels sprouts
Calabrese (Italian
   sprouting broccoli)
Broccoli
Kale
Radishes
Swedes (rutabagas or
   yellow turnips)
Turnips
Kohl rabi

Plot 3
Bulb onions
Spring onions (scallions)
Shallots
Leeks
Garlic
Sweetcorn (corn)
Marrows (large zucchini,
   squashes and
   pumpkins
Lettuce

Plot 4
Potatoes
Parsnips
Beetroot (beets)
Carrots
Salsify
Scorzonera
Celery
Celeriac
Tomatoes

Plot 5
Rhubarb
Asparagus
Perennial herbs
Globe artichokes
Jerusalem artichokes
Sea kale

COMPANION PLANTING

This is when two or more crops are grown together for the benefit of one or all. The technique creates a colourful landscape, made up of different species, which mirrors nature itself. Plants are grown together for several reasons: for example, they attract beneficial insects and give off odours that may deter or confuse pests. Companion planting is very different from planting large areas of land with only one crop – a monoculture that allows large numbers of pests and diseases to build up rapidly.

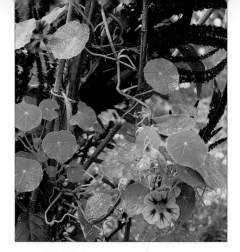

Above: *Nasturtiums (*Tropaeolum majus*) have edible leaves and flowers, as well as being a colourful companion plant.*

HOW COMPANION PLANTING WORKS

Plants have natural affinities with others of their kind. The smell of volatile oils from many plants discourages certain pests, making them excellent companion plants. A good example of this is the well-known relationship between the tomato plant and the French marigold (*Tagetes patula*). The scent of the French marigold is said to deter whitefly from entering the greenhouse and therefore prevents a whitefly attack on the tomato plant.

Plants such as yarrow (*Achillea*) and hyssop (*Hyssopus*) are just a couple of plants from a list of many that attract beneficial insects such as hoverflies. The hoverflies will lay their eggs around these plants and, after hatching, the larval stage of the insect will start to eat adult aphids. So greedy are these larvae that they can eat up to 800 aphids before pupating. Many allotment gardeners grow trays of single-flowered French marigolds to dot around their gardens, both in the vegetable and fruit

> ### BENEFITS OF COMPANION PLANTING
> A mosaic of plants offers many benefits to the allotment, some of which are outlined below.
>
> - Creates a colourful landscape.
> - Plants can attract benefical insects.
> - Plant odour can deter harmful insects.
> - A variety of plants together confuses pests from locating host plants.
> - Plants attract birds that prey on pests.
> - Flowers attract pollinators.

areas, in order to encourage these eating machines. This is both very effective and quite stunning to look at.

Certain distinct qualities of a plant have a proven benefit to others, such as fixing nitrogen in the soil. Clover in grass will fix nitrogen, offering the excess nitrogen produced to the surrounding grass which improves the yield. By the same token,

others are less suited as partners. It is never wise, for example, to plant two vegetables side by side that attract the same pests, as this effectively doubles the chances of attack. It is advisable to practise crop rotation or use companion planting in between them.

BENEFICIAL COMBINATIONS

There is little scientific evidence of these associations working, but if you talk to any experienced gardener, they will certainly provide plenty of anecdotal evidence. Tomatoes, for instance, like to be grown near basil and parsley plants. This is, of course, useful for cooks as well as gardeners. Separating rows of cabbages, broccoli or other brassicas with rows of onions has always been a popular combination, possibly due to the onion's strong scent confusing cabbage pests. Tomato plants also grow well next to cabbages and seem to deter caterpillars.

Other beneficial combinations include leeks near carrots as they repel carrot flies, while Swiss chard thrives near carrots and beetroot (beets). Never plant carrot and dill close by each other. This makes the carrots woodier and stronger-flavoured, and the dill milder and with weaker stems.

DECORATIVE COMPANION PLANTS

Certain flowers and flowering herbs offer potential benefits for a variety of vegetables. French marigolds (*Tagetes patula*) are cited as a wonder flower by many allotment gardeners and the bright flowers make a colourful companion crop. They deter many pests, and seem to spur growth in roses. They are also said to reduce the number of soil nematodes, while attracting hoverflies and their larvae, which eat aphids. French marigolds are frequently planted with English marigolds (*Calendula officinalis*).

Right: *Companion plants such as the English marigold (*Calendula officinalis*) can provide welcome splashes of colour in the vegetable patch. In addition to this, the pollen of these flowers will attract beneficial hoverflies and parasitic wasps, both of which can help control large numbers of common pests.*

CROPS AND THEIR COMPANION PLANTS

While it is not an exact science, any practitioner of companion planting will tell you that individual crops have their 'preferred companions'.

Experience is the best guide, but the list below outlines some plant combinations that work well in most situations.

Apples Chives, foxgloves, wallflowers, nasturtiums, garlic, onions
Apricots Basil, tansy, wormwood
Asparagus Tomatoes, parsley, basil
Beans Carrots, cucumbers, cabbages, lettuce, peas, parsley, cauliflowers, spinach, summer savory
Beans (broad/fava) Potatoes, sweetcorn (corn)
Beans (dwarf) Beetroot (beets), potatoes
Beetroot (beets) Onions, kohl rabi, lettuce, cabbages, dwarf beans
Brussels sprouts Nasturtiums
Cabbages Beans, beetroot, celery, mint, thyme, sage, onions, rosemary, dill, potatoes, chamomile, oregano, hyssop, wormwood, nasturtiums, tansy, coriander (cilantro)
Carrots Peas, radishes, lettuce, chives, sage, onions, leeks
Cauliflowers Celery, beans, tansy, nasturtiums

Celery Tomatoes, dill, beans, leeks, cabbage, cauliflowers
Chives Parsley, apples, carrots, tomatoes
Courgette (zucchini) Nasturtiums
Cucumbers Potatoes (early crop only), beans, celery, lettuce, sweetcorn (corn), Savoy cabbages, sunflowers, nasturtiums
Kohl rabi Beetroot, onions
Garlic Roses, apples, peaches
Grapevines Geraniums, mulberries, hyssop, basil, tansy
Leeks Carrots, celery
Lettuce Carrots, onions, strawberries, beetroot, cabbages, radishes, tagetes
Onions Carrots, beetroot, lettuce, chamomile, kohl rabi, courgettes
Parsnips Peas, potatoes, peppers, beans, radishes, garlic
Peaches Tansy, garlic, basil, wormwood

Peas Potatoes, radishes, carrots, turnips
Potatoes Peas, beans, cabbages, sweetcorn, broad beans, green beans, nasturtium, marigolds, foxgloves, horseradish, aubergines (eggplants)
Pumpkin Sweetcorn
Radishes Lettuces, peas, chervil, nasturtiums
Raspberries Tansy
Spinach Strawberries
Squash Sunflowers
Strawberries Borage, lettuce, spinach, sage, pyrethrum
Sunflowers Squash, cucumbers
Sweetcorn (corn) Broad beans, potatoes, melons, tomatoes, cucumbers, squash, tansy
Tomatoes Asparagus, celery, parsley, basil, carrots, chives, marigolds, foxgloves, garlic, sweetcorn
Turnips Peas, nasturtiums

White alyssum (*Lobularia maritima*), by reseeding frequently, helps to break up the soil and adds to its organic content, while chrysanthemums reduce nematodes, making for healthier soil. Mint almost always works with various types of squashes and brassicas to aid plant growth, although it can become invasive. Tansy (*Tanacetum*

Left: *Foxgloves (*Digitalis purpureum*) make excellent companion plants for growing under apple trees.*

vulgare) is said to repel ants, aphids and plant beetles although this, too, can become invasive if not regularly checked.

Chamomile (*Chamaemelum nobile*) is known as the 'plant doctor' by some gardeners because of its alleged ability to encourage other plants to increase their production of essential oil, making plants such as rosemary and lavender taste and smell stronger. Chamomile is easy to grow and looks beautiful anywhere on the allotment, although it should be kept well trimmed to avoid a straggly look. It is also thought that chamomile can help to activate the composting process if it is added to the compost heap.

Lavender (*Lavandula*) is a general insect repellent and makes an excellent small hedge. It is a great addition to the allotment, attracting bees and numerous white and blue butterflies.

Plants that produce berries, such as cotoneaster and the rowan tree (*Sorbus*), will attract birds into the site. Birds, in turn, eat many pests, such as protein-rich

aphids, caterpillars and various flies. Thrushes are the unsung heroes of the allotment because they decrease the snail population quite considerably.

Be prepared to experiment before committing to a companion species. Nasturtiums have been cited as an effective aphid control, although many wonder if they do this by attracting all the aphids to themselves. What works in one area may not always work elsewhere and experimentation is the key to success in this interesting yet uncertain area of gardening.

CROPS AND THEIR ANTAGONISTS

Some plants are highly antagonistic to one another. You should always avoid planting the following combinations.

Asparagus Onions and potatoes
Beans Chives, fennel or garlic
Carrots Dill
Cauliflower Tomatoes
Peas Onions, garlic and shallots
Potato Asparagus, pumpkin and summer squash

HOW TO GROW VEGETABLES

There are three basic growing techniques that you can use to make the most of your space. These are known as intercropping, catch cropping and successional sowing. By adopting the latter two practices, you will extend the cropping season instead of harvesting all at once. You will also make good use of the available space, therefore increasing yields. All that is needed is careful planning to work out which crops to sow and when.

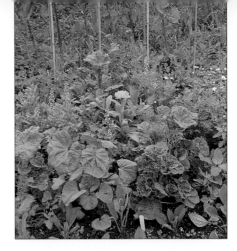

Above: *Catch cropping in close blocks makes the most of available space and allows more crops to be raised in a season.*

INTERCROPPING

This vegetable-growing technique increases productivity and also helps to keep the numbers of weeds down. It refers to the practice of planting a fast-growing crop, such as carrots, radishes and lettuce, between main crops that are slower growing. These include vegetables such as cabbages, peas and potatoes.

Intercropping involves harvesting the quicker-growing crop first before the slower-growing one achieves total foliage cover of the soil or shades out the area. A good example of intercropping is to grow a crop of spring onions (scallions) or lettuce between tomatoes. Similarly, spinach or radishes can easily be planted out early between sweetcorn (corn) or, alternatively, radishes can be planted between cabbages.

Intercropping can also be used to increase productivity. It ensures that no space is left unused and makes the most efficient use of light, nutrients and moisture. It will also reduce the amount of weeds in the vegetable patch by maintaining a continuous plant canopy over the soil.

One slight variation on the theme is to combine the benefits of a green manure with a crop. This can be useful in the case of winter crops because the green manure doubles up as a cover crop, protecting the soil from erosion and leaching as well as stabilizing soil temperatures. If a leguminous green manure is planted in late summer or early autumn in a bed along with leafy crops such as Brussels sprouts, it can provide nitrogen throughout the remaining growing season. It will also provide a boost for early

crops that will be planted out after the green manure crop has been dug into the soil. While intercropping requires careful planning, it can increase the productivity of even a relatively small vegetable plot.

CATCH CROPPING

This technique is when fast-maturing vegetables, such as radishes and lettuce, are grown in an area of ground that has just been cropped and has a vacancy until the next crop is either sown or planted. The sowing of the catch crops can be done in between the main ones or after harvesting at the end of the season if there is time. It is important to know how long a crop takes to mature when planning catch cropping so that you do not sow anything that takes too long to mature in between the main crops.

Left: *Successional sowing of crops in rows allows the same space in the vegetable plot on the allotment to be kept productive throughout the growing season.*

ADVANTAGES OF INTERCROPPING AND CATCH CROPPING

Making the most of the limited space in your allotment is not only productive, but it also has positive environmental advantages, such as the following.

- Suppresses weed growth in the allotment site.
- Increases the productivity of the vegetable patch.
- Planting green manures enriches the soil with nitrogen.
- Helps to protect against the erosion of the soil.
- Helps prevent leaching.

FAST-GROWING CROPS FOR INTERCROPPING AND CATCH CROPPING
Use all the available space in your allotment by sowing vigorous-growing crops in between rows of the main crops. The list below shows the time it will take for some fast-growing crops to mature.

Carrots	9 to 20 weeks
Endives	7 to 13 weeks
Lettuce	4 to 14 weeks
Radishes	4 to 8 weeks
Rocket (arugula)	3 to 5 weeks
Salad leaves	4 to 14 weeks
Spinach	5 to 10 weeks
Spring onions (scallions)	8 to 10 weeks

SUCCESSIONAL SOWING

This is the practice of sowing the seeds of fast-maturing vegetables at regular intervals several times during the growing season. This practice will ensure that you have a continuous supply of crops such as lettuces, carrots and spinach throughout the season. Successional sowing is also useful where crops are sown directly outdoors early in the season where they may be prone to frost damage. Early crops such as lettuce and radish can be sown under the cover of, for example, a cloche where they will begin to develop earlier than would otherwise be possible. Subsequent sowings outdoors will mature later, thus extending the growing season for harvesting.

Above: *The close spacing of rows and successional sowing of new rows allows the maximum use of space on your plot.*

Gardeners with half plots can use this method by sowing only half a row at a time. This process is repeated a week or so later, with further sowings as often as you like. This way you will have fresh vegetables for several weeks and will avoid a glut.

CROPS SUITABLE FOR SUCCESSIONAL SOWING
Successional sowing can ensure a continuous supply of fresh vegetables, avoiding harvest gluts.

Beetroot (beets)	Spring to summer
Broccoli	Spring to summer
Cabbages	Spring to summer
Carrots	Spring to summer
Endives	Spring to summer
Kohl rabi	Winter to summer
Lettuce	Winter to summer
Parsnips	Winter to spring
Peas	All year round
Potatoes	Spring
Radishes	Winter to summer
Rocket (arugula)	Spring to autumn
Salad leaves	Spring to autumn
Spinach	Spring to summer
Spring onions (scallions)	Spring to autumn
Swedes (rutabagas)	Spring to summer
Swiss chard	Spring to summer
Turnips	Winter to spring

Above: *Sweetcorn (corn) is a late-maturing crop that can be intercropped with fast-growing, early salad crops. This enables you to make the most of your growing space.*

HOW TO GROW HERBS

Herbs are valued for their culinary, medicinal, decorative and aromatic properties. They come in a diverse range of sizes, shapes and habits, ranging from ground-creeping thyme through to the tall architectural stems of angelica. The choice of herbs is so great that there is always something to offer an allotment-grower who is also interested in cooking aromatic or unusual dishes. Herbs offer a treat for the senses and these fragrant plants are also easy to grow in an allotment.

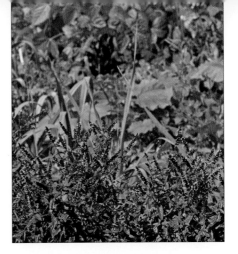

Above: *Herbs are a colourful and useful addition to an allotment and grow quite happily amongst your other crops.*

WHERE TO GROW HERBS

Herbs can be grown in a range of settings, such as custom-designed herb gardens or amongst vegetables, where they can also be used as companion plants. They can also be grown in pots and containers if you want to conserve space, or even in hanging baskets suspended from a shed.

Herbs range from tall showy herbaceous plants such as fennel (*Foeniculum vulgare*) and tansy (*Tanacetum vulgare*) to ground-hugging cushion plants such as thyme (*Thymus vulgaris*). The majority of herbs originate from dry sunny environments and so need sunshine to help them develop their essential oils. It is best to site herbs in an open, sunny spot on the allotment, where they should thrive.

SOIL PREPARATION

Drier sites suit most herbs, and the sunnier and hotter the site the better they will taste. The taste and smell of herbs is usually due to the production of essential oils within the plants. If they are grown in hot conditions, then the concentrations of essential oils will be greater. Growing herbs in very moist rich soils can accelerate their growth, but will result in a milder flavour. They will also look better and flower less than their 'hot-site' counterparts and be easier to harvest.

Herbs are, however, best grown in a soil that is loamy with some added organic matter. The ideal pH is 6.5 to 7.0, which means that herbs can easily be planted among vegetables.

SOWING HERB SEED

Herbs may be sown directly in the soil outdoors, just like vegetables. The preparation of the seedbed and the sowing techniques are exactly the same, and they can easily be interplanted or block planted among other vegetables. Alternatively, herb seeds may be planted under cover, raising them in the same way as early vegetables and then hardening them off before planting out in the allotment. This method is especially useful for more tender, leafy herbs such as basil or coriander (cilantro).

Basil (*Ocimum basilicum*) associates extremely well with outdoor tomatoes. These can be planted out together from an indoor sowing and the crop will be mutually complementary. Indoor sowing can also provide you with herbs that can be cropped earlier in the season than outdoor ones, extending the useful life of your herb patch.

PLANTING HERBS

Herbs can be positioned anywhere in the site as long as it is sunny. They have a range of forms and colours and often make valuable additions to the allotment. Foxgloves (*Digitalis purpureum*), sage (*Salvia officinalis*) and the curry plant (*Helichrysum italicum*) are a few examples of herbs that can be used in annual and herbaceous borders as well as in allotments. Some herbs, such as mint (*Mentha*) and lemon balm (*Melissa officinalis*), can become very invasive if they are not contained in a pot or sunken sink when growing among other plants. Remove the flower-heads from the mint before they have had a chance to seed, as the seed will germinate all over your patch.

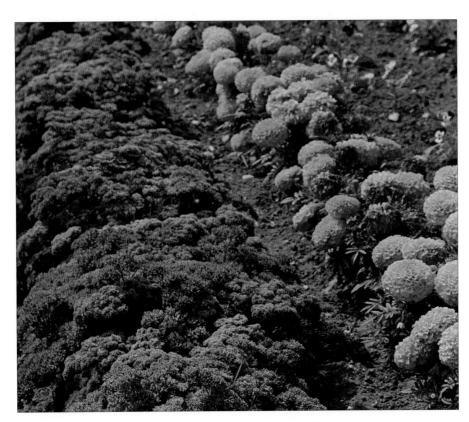

Left: *Herbs that you use a lot of can be grown in rows between other crops in order to make the best use of the space available.*

PLANTING THYME

1 *Thyme plants quickly form a low mound, making them an excellent edge for beds and borders. Start by setting out a row in the position you intend planting them.*

2 *Once set out, remove their pots and dig a hole that is at least one and a half times as wide as the roots. Place them in this, refill the hole and firm the soil around them.*

3 *Once you have finished planting, water the plants in using a watering can with a fine rose attachment. Continue watering regularly in the first year.*

PLANTING HERBS IN CONTAINERS

Herbs make excellent subjects for use in pots and containers and these can be placed around sheds and seating areas on allotments, rather than taking up space in beds. Plants in containers dry out quickly, so water them frequently, especially during hot weather. Always plant them in a free-draining potting compost (soil mix) that will not become waterlogged.

There are numerous cultivars of culinary herbs that can be grown on an allotment, and groups of pot-grown herbs can be extremely decorative as well as supplying you with a range of fresh flavourings. Thyme, rosemary, lavender and sage are all good choices to grow in pots and have many uses in the kitchen.

Herb pots require little maintenance, save for watering and the occasional feed during the growing season. Most are rarely long term and are best restarted yearly or every other year. Herbs that are permanently in pots, such as bay trees, will need repotting every year. Spreading subjects such as thyme can be lifted and both top-pruned and root-pruned prior to repotting.

Mint and other spreading herbaceous subjects may need dividing and repotting from time to time. This is done by splitting the crown of the plant into smaller pieces

and then repotting one of these back into the container with some fresh potting mix. Dividing in this way is best performed annually for very vigorous herbs.

Harvesting on a regular basis is often enough to control the growth of many potted herb arrangements (where a number are planted in one container), but a light trim may also be necessary from time to time.

Potted herbs may also be grown in the greenhouse to ensure a supply both earlier and later in the season. A series of successional sowings will ensure that you have fresh herbs for most of the year.

Below: *Herbs can be grown very successfully in pots and containers, and make an attractive addition to a seating area.*

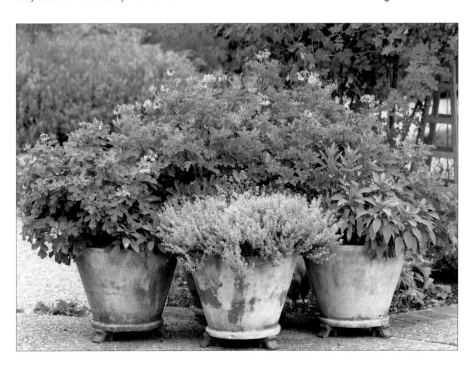

HOW TO GROW FRUIT TREES AND BUSHES

Freshly picked fruit from the allotment tastes absolutely delicious. The warm taste of a juicy sweet raspberry or the crisp flavour of a tree-ripened apple would tempt many a gardener into growing their own fruit produce. The tastes can also be quite different from shop-grown produce where storage, handling, packing, transportation and off-the-tree ripening all take their toll on the quality and taste of the fruit.

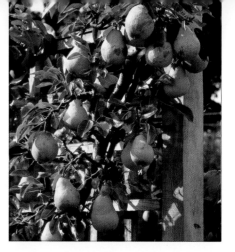

Above: *A sunny place provides an ideal location for growing fruit trees, such as this pear, that need warmth and good sunlight.*

WHERE CAN FRUIT BE GROWN?

Fruit trees and bushes can be grown wherever there is space on the allotment. Strawberries can be used in hanging baskets or tubs, dwarf apple trees can be planted in containers and a number of fruits, such as cherries, white and red currants and figs, can all be grown against walls. Fruits not only provide produce for the kitchen table but many of them have ornamental qualities and can blend well with other plants in the allotment.

CHOOSING A SITE

The best site for fruit, both indoors and out, is a sunny one. Sunlight is essential, not just for the ripening of the fruit itself but also for flower bud formation and flowering. In addition, fruit trees and bushes often appreciate a sheltered spot where even exotic fruit can be raised. Within the allotment a sheltered sunny wall can provide the ideal place to grow peaches, apricots or figs. If cold winters are a problem, then provide winter protection in the form of a portable frame or, alternatively, grow the plants in a greenhouse. It is worth noting that providing your plants with the ideal conditions for healthy growth will reap

its rewards in the end. Not only will you harvest heavier yields, but, more importantly, your plants will be less prone to pest and disease attacks, which is an obvious advantage when growing organically.

SELECTING THE RIGHT PLANTS

Variety selection should not be based purely on hardiness but on personal preference. You may also wish to consider how easy the fruit tree or bush is to grow, fruit size, taste and the time of harvest. Selecting more than one variety can result in having fresh fruit over a longer period as a result of a succession of ripening.

Some fruit trees combine the best qualities of two plants. Grafting utilizes the qualities of the variety as top growth (scion) and other desirable qualities from a rootstock that may be absent from the variety. The scion is the fruiting variety that is budded or grafted on to the rootstock, which is selected for certain characteristics such as dwarfing, nematode insect resistance, soil type, cold hardiness and disease resistance.

The most commonly grown rootstocks for amateur gardeners are the apple semi-dwarfs and dwarfs. Grapes are also grafted on to clonal rootstocks, although they are often supplied on their own roots. Figs, olives and various types of berry are also usually supplied as plants on their own roots.

Dwarf apple trees are very useful in small sites and are eminently suited to container-growing. They produce fruit of the same size, colour and quality as larger standard trees and require the same pruning, nutritional and care regimes as a standard-size tree.

Left: *Most fruit bushes will benefit from a generous application of well-rotted manure or compost in the early part of the year.*

Dwarf trees fruit much sooner after planting and bear less fruit per tree. When harvesting the fruit, you can reach all parts of the tree from the ground without using a ladder and the trees are easier to train and prune on an annual basis. Grafting the desired variety on to special clonal rootstocks 'dwarfs' apples. The most popular dwarfing rootstocks for apple were developed in England and are designated as either EM or M (for East Malling) or MM (for Malling Merton). Dwarfed trees must be pruned annually or size control may be lost. In addition, loss of fruit by frost or pests will also increase growth so necessitating summer pruning.

PLANTING FRUIT TREES AND BUSHES

As with any other type of tree, good ground preparation and careful handling are essential steps to successfully establishing your fruit trees and bushes. The cheapest option when buying fruit trees is to purchase bare-rooted plants. The disadvantage is that they are only available during the dormant season. The most important factor in handling bare-rooted plants is not to let the roots dry out. When you buy trees always check the condition of the roots and packing material. Heel in plants by covering the roots with moist soil in a cool environment outdoors if they are not to be planted immediately.

Dig a hole slightly wider and deeper than the spread and length of the root system, making sure the sides of the hole are not 'glazed' over as this will result in a root girdling. After trimming diseased, dead, broken or extra long roots, place the tree in the hole and spread out the roots. For larger trees, place the stake in the hole and drive it in (remembering to first remove the tree and cover the roots). Place the tree back into

PLANTING A FRUIT TREE

1 *Dig a hole in the ground that is at least half as large again as the roots of the fruit tree. Loosen the sides and the base of the planting hole with a garden fork.*

2 *Remove the pot and check the roots for girdling roots. Tease these out by hand or with a garden fork. Cut out any damaged roots with secateurs (pruners).*

3 *Use a straightedge to make sure that the plant is at the right depth in the hole. Fill around the roots with soil, firm it down and water well.*

4 *Hammer in a stake at an angle of about 60° in order to avoid the roots and place a tie on the tree. Saw off the end of the stake. Nail the tie to the stake to secure it.*

5 *The tree should remain staked for approximately one year. As the diameter of the tree stem increases, loosen the tree tie as required.*

the hole and return the soil, firming in layers of about 30cm (12in) as you go. This avoids large air spaces being left around the roots and ensures that it is set firmly. Trees should be planted at the same depth as they were grown in the nursery. Make sure the bud union (for trees on rootstocks) is about 5–7cm (2–2¾in) above the soil line. Do not place fertilizer in the planting hole as this can be added later. Mulch the newly planted tree with well-rotted manure or compost to suppress weeds.

Container-grown nursery stock can be transplanted at any time of the year. Site preparation is the same as for bare-rooted stock. Make sure that you check the roots as they can become distorted or root bound if they are grown in containers for a long time. Teasing roots out can help avoid root girdling, but the best way to do this is to use field-grown (bare-rooted) stock.

PRUNING NEWLY PLANTED STOCK

Fruit trees must be pruned when they are planted for a number of reasons. If planting bare-rooted stock, the top of the tree must be pruned to counter-balance the loss of the root system which would have been severed in the nursery during lifting. Pruning also forces the growth of laterals from which the future framework of the fruit tree will be selected. Branches that are desirably located can be retained as part of the framework whereas undesirable branches are removed.

FRUIT TREE POLLINATION

Pollination is the transfer of pollen from the male part of the flower to the female part of the flower (the stigma) to allow fruit to set and seeds to develop. Seeds cause the fruit to develop properly. If both the pollen and stigma are from the same flower or from another flower from the same variety, the process is called self-pollination. Fruit trees that set fruit as the result of self-pollination are called self-fruitful, whereas those relying on pollen from a different variety are called self-unfruitful. The latter needs two varieties near to each other for fruit set to occur. This is called cross-pollination.

Apples Apples generally need two varieties for good fruit set. This can be another apple variety or a crab apple that blooms with the edible crop.
Apricots Self-fruitful
Berries (all types) Self-fruitful
Cherries Sweet cherry is self-unfruitful and needs two varieties for good crop set. Sour cherry varieties are self-fruitful.
European plums Self-fruitful
Figs Self-fruitful
Japanese plums Self-unfruitful as a rule, with the exception of Santa Rosa which will set fruit fairly well without cross-pollination.
Nectarines Self-fruitful
Peaches Self-fruitful with the exception of 'J.H. Hale', which has to be pollinated by another variety.
Pears These always need two varieties to ensure good fruit set.

HOW TO GROW FLOWERS

Cut flowers are a wonderful way to brighten up your home but can be costly if you buy them. For this reason, a cut-flower patch on your allotment is the perfect way to ensure that you have a regular supply of flowers that have not been transported across the world. Even a small patch should be able to accommodate a few plants and most are easy to grow. Where space is limited, they can be slotted in among rows of vegetables or raised as catch crops following an earlier harvest.

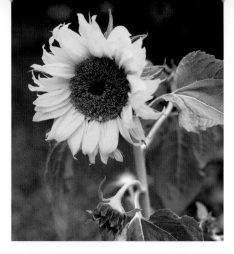

Above: *Sunflowers are easy to grow, and their large, showy blooms make excellent cut flowers, or can be left for wildlife.*

WHERE TO GROW FLOWERS

Generally, the majority of cut flowers prefer a sunny spot on well-drained, fertile soil. Ideally this should be sheltered from strong winds that could blow them over or damage the blooms themselves. Annuals, biennials and some bulbs that are short term are well suited for growing in rows and can be rotated yearly as part of your ongoing rotation regime or grown as catch crops and inter-planting. However, shrubs, perennials and some of the bulbs will need a permanent bed, where they can remain for a longer period.

SOWING

Annual flowers can either be sown directly into the soil in the case of most hardy types, or in seed trays in spring for more tender (half-hardy) types. Biennials, on the other hand, need sowing between late spring

Above: *Flowers make a very colourful addition to the allotment: they can be grown in rows or dotted between other plants.*

and mid-summer, and will flower the next year. Most shrubby species tend to be slow from seed and it is best to plant pot grown specimens or take cuttings under glass to speed up the process.

PLANTING

As a rule of thumb, bulbs and corms are usually planted in a hole that is two to three times deeper than their width, although this can vary according to the species concerned, so check the packet. Pot-grown plants are planted directly into the ground, ensuring there are no air gaps around the root-ball (roots) and that the compost (soil mix) surface is around 2cm (1in) below the soil level. On light, well-drained land, shrubs and perennial plants are best planted in early winter to allow them to establish quickly in spring before drier conditions arrive.

AFTERCARE

Most annuals and biennials simply need to be kept well watered, especially during periods of drought. Early in the year, they can be fed plenty of nitrogen to encourage strong, vigorous growth, but as soon as

PLANTS FOR CUT FLOWERS

HARDY ANNUALS
Helianthus annuus (Sunflower)
Lathyrus odoratus (Sweet pea)
Nigella damascena (Love in a mist)

HALF HARDY ANNUALS
Nicotiana (Tobacco plant)
Zinnia spp.
Cosmos spp.

BIENNIALS
Erysimum cherii (Wallflower)
Dianthus barbatus (Sweet William)
Papaver nudicaule (Iceland poppy)

HERBACEOUS PERENNIALS
Chrysanthemum spp.
Phlox paniculata (Perennial phlox)
Echinacea purpurea (Cone flower)

HARDY BULBS AND CORMS
Narcissus spp. (Daffodils)
Tulipa spp. (Tulips)
Allium spp. (Ornamental onions)

TENDER BULBS, CORMS AND TUBERS
Gladiolus spp. (Gladioli)
Freesia spp.
Dahlia spp.

WINTER AND SPRING SHRUBS
Viburnum x *bodnantense*
Forsythia spp.
Lonicera fragrantissima (Winter honeysuckle)

SUMMER SHRUBS
Rosa spp. (Rose)
Spiraea thunbergii (Baby's breath)
Philadelphus coronarius (Mock orange)

Above: *Gladioli make superb cut flowers, and their upright habit means they are ideal for planting between other plants.*

Above: *Chrysanthemums are herbaceous perennials that inject a welcome splash of colour into any allotment plot.*

Above: *If you want to grow flowers for showing, they often need protection, like these dahlias growing under shade nets.*

flower buds appear switch to a high-potassium fertilizer, such as a liquid tomato food, to promote flowering. After flowering, remove annuals and biennials, and cut back any remaining stems on herbaceous perennials. Tender perennials will need to be lifted or covered with a thick layer of mulch in the autumn to protect them from winter cold.

CUTTING FLOWERS

Regularly picking the flowers you grow on the allotment not only ensures a constant supply but also encourages more blooms and prevents them from setting seed. The amount you can harvest will vary, however,

and, in the case of shrubs, you would be wise to pick more lightly to avoid stressing the plant. Remember that picking is, after all, a form of pruning, and heavy pruning may cause woody plants to produce a flush of leafy growth with few flowers the following season.

Before you start, make sure your secateurs (hand pruners) or scissors are sharp and clean. Ideally, the best time to cut flowers is during cool weather, with early morning proving ideal as the flowers and stems are arguably at their freshest and filled with water. If this is not possible, then evenings can be almost as good. Once cut, flowers can easily become stressed through lack of water, so the best way to preserve them until you get them home is to place their stems into a bucket of water as soon as they are cut. Make cuts

Above: *Sweet peas can be raised from seed and yield a profusion of large, bright, fragrant blooms over a long period.*

in the stems at a 45° angle, as this will ensure the stem has a bigger cut surface area for water absorption.

When choosing which stems you are going to cut, make sure that flowers such as gladioli, which have more than one bud per stem, have at least one or two buds starting to open. Plants with just one flower per stem, such as sunflowers, should be cut when the flower has almost fully opened. Once the flowers have been cut they will last longer if they are conditioned. This involves putting the stem bases in a clean bucket of cool water, cutting the immersed bases once again, and placing this in a cool, dark place for 12 to 24 hours.

HOW TO GROW IN A GREENHOUSE

By providing an environment where plants are protected from the elements, in controlled levels of light, shade, temperature and moisture, allotment-growers can either extend the growing season of their favourite crops or even grow plants that otherwise simply would not survive. This warm, protective atmosphere enables you to propagate plants more easily and shelter tender plants from frosts.

Above: *Warm season crops such as tomatoes can be sown and will crop earlier in a greenhouse than those grown outdoors.*

WHY GROW IN A GREENHOUSE?

A greenhouse, if used to its full potential, is one of the most valuable additions there is on an allotment, offering the opportunity to grow a much wider range of plants; often making these available much earlier or later in the year. Although cloches and cold frames offer similar benefits at a fraction of the cost, neither gives the same amount of dedicated growing space, and it is this space that ultimately proves important, not least when it gives you the chance to work in warm shelter during the cold gloom of winter. Indeed, the prospect of working in the greenhouse can be a positive enticement on to the plot during the winter months. The fact that you can get inside is also useful as crops are protected the whole time you are working on them, unlike cloches or frames, which remain open all the time you work in them.

WHAT GREENHOUSE IS BEST?

Despite the array of designs available, the simplest constructions are usually more than adequate for an allotment. It is more important that you choose one that is the right size for your plot and your own needs. There is little point in erecting a huge greenhouse if it is only ever half full of crops. Having said that, choosing one that is too cramped might limit its usefulness. For most allotments, a greenhouse that is 2.5 x 5m (8 x 16ft) will provide enough space, and if you really need more space you can always get another greenhouse later.

HOW DOES A GREENHOUSE HELP PLANTS GROW?

Almost all plants like to grow in reasonably warm conditions with most growing best between about 16–24°C (60–76°F). While winter light levels may still be sufficient to help power growth, the low temperatures at that time of the year can severely limit this.

The greenhouse simply raises the temperature by trapping daylight, which heats the air and elevates the temperature to one within several degrees above that on the outside. Of course, these temperatures fall during darkness, but this can be offset by heating the interior. Temperature fluctuations are not all bad news though, and a fall of about 4–6°C (39–43°F) at night is actually preferable for most crops.

TEMPERATURE

Controlling temperature is one of the key aspects of successful greenhouse-growing and you will only be able to do this if you know how it varies throughout the day. Although you can't be in the greenhouse all the time you can take an average temperature reading inside using a special maximum and minimum thermometer. This shows two readings; one is the highest temperature achieved in the last 24 hours, the other represents the lowest. Comparing this to a maximum and minimum thermometer outside the greenhouse can help you see how the interior differs from the prevailing climate and assess if the temperature is fluctuating to extremes.

You should note, however, that more than just the outside temperature influences temperature in a glasshouse, as light levels and ventilation also play a part. Limiting the amount of light during the day by shading will cool the house, as will opening the vents and letting the hot air escape. Heating or insulating the house, on the other hand, and keeping vents shut will maintain temperatures if they fall outside.

Right: *A well-lit, warm greenhouse bench is an ideal place to raise seeds, safe from the ravages of often unpredictable climatic conditions.*

Far right: *A thermometer is vital for enabling you to accurately assess the greenhouse temperature and act accordingly.*

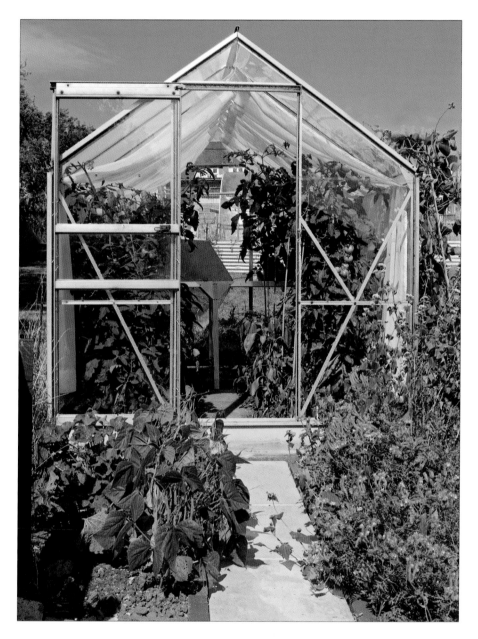

Above: *Even a relatively modest-sized greenhouse can enable you to grow an extended range of crops through the season.*

If night-time temperatures begin to dip, a simple hotbox or burner type heater is usually enough to keep out any night-time chill. These also work by heating the air directly and are used where there is no need to provide heat on a regular basis. During the winter, it is both cheaper and more efficient to insulate a greenhouse by providing additional layers within the structure to trap air. Bubble wrap is a popular method as it is easy to position and allows the transmission of light. In addition to this, careful siting of the greenhouse can help to reduce the chilling or potentially damaging effects of high winds.

LIGHT

Balanced growth requires good glasshouse design and proper planning for the light requirements of the crop. As a general rule, ridged greenhouses should always be orientated with the ridge running east to west to make the best of the available light.

Although natural winter light intensity is often insufficient for certain crops, summer light levels, especially when combined with elevated temperatures, can cause problems. Shading controls temperature and light, and is usually put in place in order to reduce summer temperatures (if excessive) or to protect young plants from intense sunlight.

Right: *Fill watering cans in advance and allow them to warm up, so as to ensure that your plants are not showered in cold water.*

HUMIDITY

Most plants naturally require a humid environment in order to grow healthily and plants grouped together often establish their own small microclimate where the humidity is higher in the immediate vicinity of the plants than elsewhere. Warm air naturally holds much more moisture than cooler air so it is important to increase humidity during the hotter months when it is harder to keep the temperature in protected structures down. Increasing the humidity helps to slow water loss from leaves and may help to prevent wilting or scorch.

Humidity is easily raised by damping down (spraying a hose on hard surfaces, paths or under benches) on hot, dry days. If there are only certain plants, such as young seedlings, that require elevated humidity, then these are best covered with a thin layer of clear plastic.

AIR CIRCULATION

All plants need a constant supply of clean, fresh air around them in order to grow healthily. Outdoors, normal wind movements would supply this, but in a greenhouse you'll need to make provision for it. Ventilators help control excess temperature and air flow. Roof vents should normally occupy the equivalent of 15 per cent of the floor space in order to be fully effective. Side ventilators are also occasionally seen in some greenhouses. If you are away during daylight hours in summer, the time when windows need to be opened on hot days, automatic openers can be used. In winter, windows should be left open as much as possible.

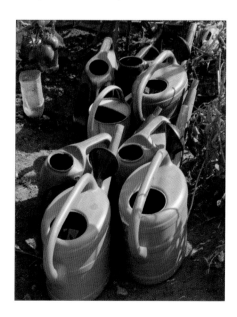

METHODS OF GROWING

Think carefully about how you plan to use your greenhouse and what plants you would like to grow there. Remember also that the true art of greenhouse gardening lies in using every available bit of space. This will involve planning the layout of the growing areas in the greenhouse and making a cropping plan to ensure that you not only use all of the available space, but every 'time space' within the growing calendar.

In open ground Many greenhouse plants will grow well in open soil borders. The soil can be prepared in a similar way to borders outside. Taller crops such as tomatoes are particularly well suited to growing in open borders in the greenhouse, but remember to rotate crops sited in soil to prevent pest or disease build-up.

Above: *Greenhouses are especially prone to disease spread, and any dead or diseased plant material needs to be removed promptly.*

In pots on staging Staging is essentially a shelf or shelves on which plants in pots are arranged, which enables you to work at a comfortable height. It is particularly useful for raising seedlings and propagating plants. The area beneath the staging, which is somewhat shaded, can be used for overwintering dormant plants, as a useful out-of-the-way storage area or to house a water tank.

In grow-bags Grow-bags offer an alternative to open beds where space is limited or no open beds exist. These can be purchased or you can easily make your own by filling large plastic compost bags (about an 80 litre [17.5 gallon] size is ideal) with a mixture of garden compost and a little grit. Each bag will support four tomato plants and an even greater number of smaller plants. They can also be used to raise garden peas or beans.

Climbers and trained plants The growing space available in a greenhouse is not restricted to the floor or staging-height, as the walls and roof can also be used. Ridged houses can be used to raise climbing crops, such as cucumbers or melons, and other climbers such as peas or beans can also be raised under glass during the cooler months.

GREENHOUSE HYGIENE

Practising good hygiene is extremely important for maintaining the health of plants in a greenhouse. Dead leaves and

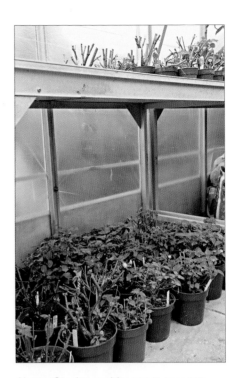

Above: *Staging enables you to use your greenhouse space efficiently, and allows you to work at a comfortable height.*

debris left lying about can harbour pests and diseases, as can badly affected plants if they are not removed promptly.

Once a year, clean all surfaces, including glass and glazing bars, thoroughly with a sponge and hot soapy water. This will pay dividends during the growing season by reducing the number of annually recurring pests and diseases.

WHITENING-OUT GLASS

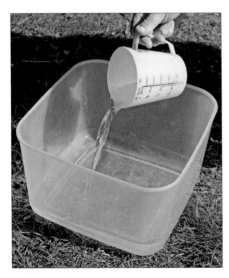

1 *Make up water soluble greenhouse shading by measuring the correct amount of water into a container.*

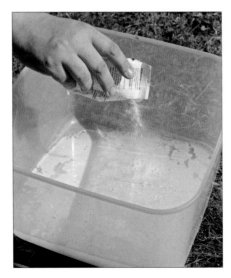

2 *Empty the measured contents of the sachet into the water and mix well with a stick to combine thoroughly.*

3 *Paint it on, paying particular attention to surfaces facing the sun. It is waterproof but can be removed when dry with a duster.*

THE GREENHOUSE YEAR

The information shown here is a sample of how a greenhouse can be used to be productive all year round. The essential point is that you should plan what you want to grow, when you want to grow it and of course how much you want to grow. Once you have decided on these factors, it should be a relatively simple matter to make your greenhouse a productive and enjoyable space on your allotment.

MID-WINTER

Sow carrots, onions and lettuces in open borders and interplant with radishes.

Sow early cabbages and cauliflowers in pots

Bring strawberries in from frames.

Wash glass panes and keep conditions on the dry side.

Watch for winter pests and fungal diseases, and regularly remove dead or dying material.

Provide heat as necessary and ventilate during the day.

LATE WINTER

Make further sowings of winter salad crops.

Sow broad (fava) beans.

Pot on early vegetable seedlings.

Keep an eye on ventilation.

Watch for pests and diseases.

Keep conditions on the dry side unless warm.

Pick over plants to remove dead or dying material regularly.

Provide heat as necessary and ventilate during the day when mild conditions allow.

EARLY SPRING

Sow Brussels sprouts seeds in cool houses or frames.

Sow indoor tomato seed.

Prick out seedlings as they develop first sets of true leaves.

Damp down on hot days and ventilate.

Continue to watch for pests and diseases.

Begin to feed plants as growth increases.

Dig, manure and topdress borders ready for planting if not already productive.

MID-SPRING

Sow outdoor tomatoes, celery and celeriac and pot on indoor tomatoes. Sow melons and cucumbers in individual pots.

Harden off early vegetable plants under cloches.

Remove side shoots of early tomatoes; begin feeding as first flower trusses appear.

Damp down at least twice daily when hot and ventilate.

Continue to watch for pests and diseases.

Dig borders and manure if not already done.

LATE SPRING

Plant indoor tomatoes into prepared borders or large pots of loam-based compost (soil mix).

Continue potting on developing cuttings and seedlings.

Pay particular attention to watering as days lengthen.

Provide shade over sensitive crops with shade or glass paint and ventilate well.

Feed plants regularly.

Watch for pests and diseases and control where appropriate.

EARLY SUMMER

Pick tomatoes regularly as they ripen.

Pinch out and tie in melons and cucumbers as they reach their intended size.

Continue potting on cuttings and seedlings of all plants.

Water regularly, twice daily in hot weather and damp down two or three times daily.

Feed plants regularly.

Watch for pests and diseases and control where appropriate.

MID-SUMMER

Continue potting on cuttings and seedlings of all plants.

Hand pollinate melons and cucumbers.

Mist tomatoes overhead and open vents to help flower set.

Feed tomatoes to encourage development of more trusses.

Water and feed plants regularly; damp down two or three times daily.

Watch for pests and diseases and control where appropriate.

LATE SUMMER

Sow seeds of greenhouse winter leaf crops. Continue potting on cuttings and seedlings of all plants.

Remove lower leaves of tomatoes as fruit ripens. Support ripening melons and remove leaves shading fruit.

Harvest cucumbers as they reach the required size.

Water and feed plants regularly; damp down two or three times daily.

Watch for pests and diseases and control where appropriate.

EARLY AUTUMN

Cut melons as they ripen. Clear tomatoes as they finish.

Prepare borders for winter leaf crops.

Gradually decrease watering and damping down, remove shading and provide gentle heat on cold nights.

Continue potting on cuttings and seedlings of all plants.

Gradually cease feeding plants as growth slows and watch for pests and diseases and control where appropriate.

MID-AUTUMN

Plant winter leaf crops, or sow a green manure.

Gradually decrease watering as days shorten and reduce damping down to avoid the risk of fungal infestation.

Pot on any remaining cuttings and seedlings.

Watch for pests and diseases and control where appropriate

Pick over plants to remove dead or dying material regularly. Provide gentle heat on cold nights.

LATE AUTUMN

Keep winter leaf and salad crops clear of weeds.

Lift crowns of rhubarb for forcing.

Keep conditions on the dry side.

Watch for winter pests and diseases as low light levels stress plants. Pick over plants to remove dead or dying material regularly.

Provide heat as necessary and ventilate on mild days. Beware of gales when ventilating.

EARLY SPRING

Keep winter leaf and salad crops clear of weeds.

Sow seed of early onion varieties.

Lift rhubarb and herbs for early forcing and picking.

Keep conditions on the dry side. Watch for winter pests and diseases as low light levels stress plants. Remove dead or dying material regularly.

Provide heat as necessary and ventilate on mild days. Beware of gales when ventilating.

BASIC TECHNIQUES

Growing crops on an allotment, far from being complex or difficult, is largely the application of commonsense horticultural techniques. The practices described here are at the core of successful allotment-growing and while they can take time to master, they are all essentially straightforward. Knowing that you have been responsible for the produce on your plot is not only very satisfying, but also well within the grasp of even novice growers. The following pages are intended to act as an essential how-to guide to this process; from producing new plants, caring for them while they grow and ultimately harvesting and storing them.

Left: *A flourishing plot is the end result of careful planning and preparation as well as regular maintenance.*

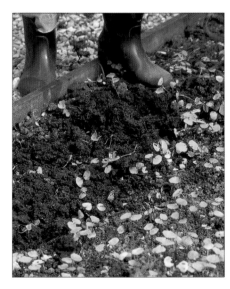

Above: *A well-prepared, weed-free plot is the ideal starting point for successful plant growth and development.*

Above: *Both weeds and crop residues can be recycled in the allotment by composting, and then returned to the soil.*

Above: *Growing fruit such as apples on an allotment is satisfying, but it is important that it is stored properly once harvested.*

WAYS TO GROW DIFFERENT CROPS

When it comes to raising crops on an allotment, there is no one 'correct' way of doing it and there are numerous methods of organizing the layout. Neatly arranged rows of crops are a traditional method, although blocks, raised beds and no-dig systems have become increasingly popular. Each of these has its relative advantages and while some growers favour just one system, others opt for a more eclectic mix.

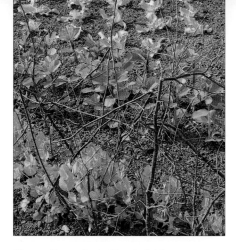

Above: *Peas planted in straight rows are relatively easy to harvest, so this is a very popular arrangement on allotments.*

PLANTING IN ROWS

This is the most traditionally practised and popular form of vegetable-growing. It is an effective method because the spacing of the plants allows the crop to grow without excessive competition. In addition, it is relatively easy to add supports and protection such as cloches to the crops. However, this type of planting does have the disadvantage of needing relatively high maintenance. Due to the large amounts of bare earth left between the rows, the conditions are ideal for weed growth. Rows are spaced according to the optimum growth of the plants and so rows of pumpkins need to be much wider than those for carrots. Setting out rows in this way allows free movement of air along the rows. This results in fewer disease problems which can occur with more closely grown methods such as block plantings.

The rows are quite easily maintained by regular hoeing but can be wasteful of space, particularly in smaller plots. They will produce sizeable vegetables, but this is offset by the actual yield per unit area being smaller than more intensive systems.

BLOCK PLANTING

With this method plants are grown in squares or rectangles rather than in straight rows. Blocks of plants are grown next to each other, for example in dimensions such as five plants by five plants. The numbers of plants grown can be larger or smaller than this. Block plantings use space efficiently, producing many more plants in an area than if grown in rows.

Well-tended soil can support planting that forms a close network of foliage over the soil. The soil will retain moisture extremely well underneath the canopy. It also stops weed seeds from germinating, resulting in a less weedy environment than

other growing methods. However, a close canopy of leaves can have disavantages, such as poor air flow and high humidity, which are ideal for attracting diseases such as botrytis. During dry spells watering is essential for the health of the crops. Double check all watering that has been done because water easily runs off the dense cover of the leaves and never reaches much of the root system.

Blocks can be planted and managed at ground level or in slightly raised beds. They suit modestly sized vegetables, such as root and salad crops, which are usually grown in rows. You may have to be inventive with crop protection for early-sown crops, as cloches and low polythene tunnels do not cover the area well. The blocks are edged with permanent paths for easy access to the centre from any side so you need never walk on freshly cultivated soil. As a result, the soil does not get compacted and the closely grouped plants make maintenance and cultivation easier.

Seeding a block involves sowing the furrows thinly along close rows. For example, instead of the usual 30–40cm

(12–16in) distance between carrot rows, this can be reduced to 20–25cm (8–10in). Further space savings can result from growing as much as you can vertically, rather than sprawled over the ground. Wire fencing, netting or poles and tepees take up less space than blocks of climbing vegetables. This will also keep the climbing plants dry and free of disease.

FLAT BEDS

As the name suggests, flat beds are constructed at the natural ground level of your allotment. They are the traditional way of cultivating ground for growing vegetables and are most suitable for plots that have good soil. Flat beds will naturally raise the level of the soil, especially where organic matter is added on a regular basis as part of the cultivation regime, but the bed remains effectively at ground level. This form of gardening is relatively labour-intensive because all of the bed is cultivated, with large areas then being used as paths between the vegetables. With raised beds, there are no paths and only the growing areas are dug.

Left: *Planting crops closely in blocks is an efficient use of your space. In addition to this, the practice also helps to suppress weeds and conserves moisture in the soil. This will ensure that the plant is less stressed and growth will be quicker, with less pest and disease damage.*

Above: *Beans trained up poles or a trellis use only a limited amount of space, and help maximize the efficient use of ground.*

RAISED AND EDGED BEDS

These can be freestanding beds or beds with wooden or brick walls constructed several inches above the normal ground level. Raised bed gardens not only look good but they can also help solve many problems associated with soils that are difficult to manage. Problems with soil are often aggravated in urban and suburban settings, where topsoil and vegetation may have been removed or the surface level changed during building work.

Raised beds improve the environment for plants by lifting their roots above poor soil. The growing medium can be amended by the incorporation of manure and/or garden compost. Soil in these beds warms up earlier in the spring, allowing the seed sown to germinate quicker than if it is grown in flat beds. Beds should be located where they will receive full sun and some protection from prevailing winds. Do not site the beds in frost pockets or where air circulation is poor.

Drainage is especially important when growing vegetables. Build the beds so that the crops will not become waterlogged. If the bed contains clay soil, incorporate sand, grit or organic matter to improve drainage. It is a good idea to construct the bed so that it slopes about 2cm (¾in) per metre (yard) of horizontal distance away from any structures, or away from the centre of the bed.

NO-DIG BEDS

As the term suggests, no digging is involved in this method, which is an effective way to retain good soil structure within a vegetable plot. Weeding is kept to a minimum and because the soil is not disturbed it will be alive with worms and other organisms. The bed is made on top of the ground and can be built over existing beds, lawns and even hard or rocky ground. Situate the bed in a sunny area that receives morning sun and has good drainage. It can be any size or shape, depending on your space. Start with a small bed – about 2 x 1.5m (6½ x 5ft) – but with a view to expanding in time.

When preparing the site it is not necessary to pull up the existing site if the soil conditions are good, but if the ground is very poor, compacted, or the drainage is bad, initial digging may be necessary.

Above: *Containers are an ideal way to grow a variety of crops where space is limited. These pots contain courgettes.*

The outside wall of a no-dig bed is formed using logs, old planks, tiles, bricks or stones. Line the bed with a layer of plain wet newspaper, at least 6mm (¼in) thick. This layer should cover the enclosed area completely and overlap slightly, so as to kill off any weeds and stop new ones growing. Spread out a thin layer of hay or straw, ensuring that there are no gaps. Place a layer of good fertilizer, such as chicken manure, 20mm (¾in) thick, on top. Cover with a 20cm (8in) thick layer of loose bedding straw. Follow this with a 2cm (¾in) layer of good organic fertilizer and complete the bed with a top layer of garden compost, about 10cm (4in) thick. Make sure the bed is watered in well. Once it is settled you can plant out seedlings, but not seeds. Sowing seeds can begin when the bed has matured and the soil has become fine and crumbly.

No-dig beds that have been recently created are best for growing crops such as potatoes, lettuce, brassicas and cucurbits, whereas root crops grow better when the bed is mature. No-dig beds are best suited to planting vegetables in small blocks of different varieties rather than in long rows.

Left: *Raised beds provide the ideal solution where the soil on a plot is poor, and have the added benefit of warming up more quickly to allow seed to germinate sooner.*

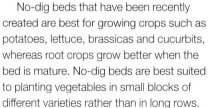

SOWING IN THE OPEN

There can be nothing more satisfying than sowing seeds and waiting in anticipation for them to germinate. Watching the seedlings grow in your plot, making it come alive with leaves, flowers and insects is a fantastic experience. One of the drawbacks of sowing out in the open is that you are at the mercy of the weather, but you can manipulate your allotment environment by using cloches, small plastic bottles and polythene tunnels to increase your chances of success.

Above: *A dibber is a very helpful tool to use when you are transplanting seeds, seedlings or small bulbs outside.*

SITE REQUIREMENTS

If you are a novice allotment-grower, be assured that sowing seed is easier than you may think. In order to germinate successfully, seeds simply need water, air, a suitable temperature and a place into which they can root in order to support the top growth that will follow. For this reason, good soil preparation is the key to success. Most garden soils are able to supply all the necessary elements and only slight modifications are usually necessary. However, it is important that the ground is prepared in a way that will enable the seed to germinate evenly and grow in a uniform environment. The proper prior preparation of a seedbed can provide the seed with the environment that it needs and has the added bonus of making the task of seed sowing easier.

Preparing a seedbed is simple. Following cultivation, the ground is levelled using a rake, held at a shallow angle, to break down any large clods. The art of levelling is to keep the rake angle shallow and move the high spots over into the low spots with even strokes. Hold the rake firmly at the rear and let the shaft run smoothly through the front hand. All stones and large objects, including organic matter such as twigs or previous crop debris, should be removed by combing them out with the teeth of the rake, while holding the tool in a near vertical position. The soil is then firmed with light treading. A light shuffle across the bed is best. Once firmed, lightly rake the soil again at a shallow angle to produce a light 'fluffy' surface that runs freely through the teeth of the rake. This is the perfect environment for sowing and growing seeds.

SEED REQUIREMENTS

The conditions that seeds require to germinate are easy and straightforward to create. A well-aerated moist soil environment is almost all that the seed needs. Most seeds will germinate quite successfully once the temperature gets above 7°C (45°F). Seeds carry their own food supply that provides them with everything they need for those first crucial days following germination. Once the plant begins to establish and grow, it needs soil-borne nutrients. This means that the soil in which it is growing needs to be of the right fertility for the plant. Poorer soils can benefit from the addition of a base dressing with fish, blood and bone prior to sowing to give the boost that the developing plant needs, although loamier soils need only be properly dug and prepared to support germination.

SOWING SEEDS OUTDOORS

1 *Carefully clear the plot of any previous crop residues or weeds, ensuring that all roots or other plant matter is removed.*

2 *Use a rake to remove any clods or stones. Continue raking until the surface is crumbly and runs easily through the rake's tines.*

3 *Once the soil is fine and crumbly it will need lightly firming to make sure that it has no air pockets, using the flat face of the rake.*

Some seeds can benefit from being soaked for a short period in tepid water just before planting to help them take on the water they need for germination. This is especially true of beetroot (beets), but other large seeds also benefit from this treatment.

SOWING IN ROWS

Seed is usually sown in rows. Using a tightly drawn garden line as a guide, draw the corner of a swan-necked (English) hoe along the line to create a shallow drill of about 1–2cm (⅜–¾in) depth, depending upon the seed's individual requirements. Dry ground can be watered after the drill is made. Sow the seed thinly and mix fine seed with silver sand to make it easier to distribute evenly. Mark the end of each row with a label before moving on to the next.

STATION SOWING

Seeds of larger growing plants, particularly those with seed that is large enough to handle, benefit from station sowing. This involves sowing two or three seeds at intervals that will be the eventual crop spacing. If all three germinate, then the two weaker ones are removed or transplanted to gaps where none has germinated.

WIDE ROWS

Certain seeds, particularly peas and beans, benefit from being planted in wide rows. Two rows are effectively station sown at

once, one on each side of a drill that is 15cm (6in) across. The drill is made with the flat of the hoe and after sowing the soil is carefully raked back. Make sure that you do not disturb the seeds from their stations.

BROADCASTING (BLOCKS)

Broadcasting is an ancient method of seed sowing that was used to sow large areas of crops. It involves a 'broadcasting' action that separates the seed to an even spacing. The easiest way to do this in small vegetable plots is to split the seed into two halves, mixing small seed with fine sand. Scatter the seed carefully, letting it run from your hand in even arcs as you move your arm from side to side. Sow each half of the

Left: Station sowing is ideal for larger seeds or seedlings that resent disturbance. Use a marked stick to set the spacing of the seed.

seed at a 90-degree angle to the other, thereby assuring an even distribution. Gently rake the seed in once sown and lightly water if needed.

PROTECTING SEEDLINGS

Seedbeds, with their fine 'fluffed' earth, act as magnets to birds and animals. Some may take the seed from the ground, but, in truth, most will find it more attractive as a dust bath or litter tray. Once the seedlings emerge, however, some birds find them irresistible. They must be kept out with some form of barrier. One of the easiest methods is to form a low tunnel of chicken wire, supporting this on hoops. For larger areas, a series of stakes in the ground can be covered with netting to keep birds at bay. Sticks with thread or string stretched between them are also effective, but less easily removed for you to tend the crop.

LABELLING

When you sow a row or area of seeds, label it straightaway. Re-usable plastic labels are the best option. Each label should have the name and variety of the plant sown. You may also wish to record the sowing date and if the seed was pre-treated.

4 *Stretch a taut string between two pegs to act as a guide, and use one corner of a swan-necked hoe to form a straight shallow drill.*

5 *Pre-water the drill with a fine rose and leave for a few minutes to ensure that later watering does not dislodge seeds.*

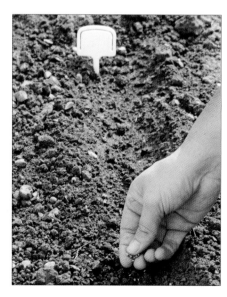

6 *Place a label stating the date and crop name at the row end before sowing seeds according to instructions. Cover lightly.*

SOWING UNDER GLASS

Sowing seed under glass extends the growing season and enables you to raise tender crops that only survive outside in warmer months. It is also ideal for rapidly establishing plants to use as catch crops and as early companion plants. In short, it offers variety and choice for your cropping regimes. Plants raised under glass can be grown on until they reach a size where they are better able to resist pest attack. They can also be planted out at their final spacing, thereby avoiding thinning or gaps in rows.

Above: *A propagator is a useful piece of equipment for raising your seed in ideal growing conditions.*

HEAT REQUIREMENTS

Most seeds have a preferred temperature range within which they will grow. A heated greenhouse will often provide this, although seeds requiring a constant high temperature may need to be grown in a propagator. Such seeds are mercifully rare among vegetables, although cucumbers, tomatoes and (bell) peppers are good examples of crops that will benefit if they are first started off in a propagator.

CHOICE OF CONTAINER

There is a variety of containers that may be used to sow seed under glass. The most common form is the plastic seed tray which has now largely replaced the wooden seed tray. Although more attractive, wooden trays are difficult to keep clean and may harbour plant diseases. Plastic trays can be made of durable polyurethane or sometimes a more flimsy, thin, moulded plastic which is intended for single use. They are available in a variety of sizes, although small 9cm (3½in) pots may be more suitable when you are raising only a few plants.

Modular seed trays are another option. These are made up of individual cells, and a single seed is sown into each one. Seeds that are sown in these trays have the advantage of not suffering any root disturbance when they are planted out in their eventual position. The same is true of some biodegradable pots, which are formed out of paper and coir. These are better (environmentally speaking) than those made from peat, but any recycled material used for these trays is acceptable in the allotment site.

Inventive recycling can also provide an array of useful sowing containers. Re-using plastic cups, vegetable packing trays and any other throw-away items that might

otherwise end up on a landfill site are all possibilities worth exploring. Old plastic bottles make good individual propagation cowls for small pots and plastic bags can also be used to cover the tops of pots and trays in order to maintain humidity.

PROPAGATORS

These are, in effect, mini-hothouses that help to keep the seed in a warm, moist, stable environment both above and below the soil line. Expensive propagators involve the use of electric soil-warming cables and some have thermostats to control the soil temperature. Many are designed for use in the greenhouse. Alternatively, instead of buying the whole

Above: *Modular trays are ideal for planting large seeds and avoid disturbance to roots when planting out or potting on.*

Left: *Many propagators have ventilators on the top in order to aid the flow of fresh air to the seedlings.*

propagator, you can purchase a heating mat on which the seed trays can stand in order to receive heat at the bottom. This system has the advantage of being mobile and easily moved about from area to area. Another cheaper method is to buy soil-heating cables to bed into sand. The seed trays sit on the bed of heated sand to receive an even supply of bottom heat.

AFTERCARE OF SEEDLINGS

Once seeds begin to germinate they can be moved gradually into a less humid environment. Remove the plastic covers from the trays, or open the propagator vents or lids and, after a few days, remove the lid completely. As soon as the seedlings reach a size at which they can be handled, carefully prick them out into individual pots or larger boxes and trays.

Always handle the seedlings by the leaves, gently lifting each one from beneath, using a dibber (dibble). Never hold them by the stems because this can cause a great

Above: *Individual pots can be used for large seeds. Plant two seeds per pot and remove the weaker seedling.*

SOWING IN TRAYS

1 Fill a seed tray with seed and cuttings compost (soil mix) that has been thoroughly mixed. Fill the tray to overflowing and do not firm in the compost.

2 Using a straight-edged piece of board, level the surface of the seed and cuttings compost by carefully moving the board across the top of the tray.

3 Thoroughly water the seed tray and leave to drain for about 20 minutes before sowing the seed. This will ensure that the surface of the compost is moist prior to sowing.

4 Larger seed can be placed on the surface of the compost, spaced at regular intervals. Regular spacing in this way will help to prevent overcrowding.

5 Once the seed has been sown, use a sieve (strainer) to cover the surface with a fine layer of compost and/or propagation grade vermiculite.

6 Do not cover the seeds of plants that require light for germination. Always check the growing requirements of plants before sowing the seed.

deal of damage to the developing plant. When you prick them out, space them at least 5cm (2in) apart to allow room for subsequent development. Water the transplanted seedlings with a fine upturned rose attached to a watering can that has

Above: *Watering from below by pouring the water into the base of the seed tray will prevent damage to newly emerging seed.*

been filled with water overnight, thus bringing it up to room temperature and not giving the transplants a shock of cold water. Keep the pricked-out seedlings in a greenhouse as a constant temperature will promote healthy growth.

HARDENING OFF

Plants that have been raised and grown in a greenhouse cannot be put straight outside once they are a suitable size because their growth will be too soft to withstand the cold. Instead they must be gradually hardened off and acclimatized to outdoor conditions.

The young plants are hardened off by moving them from the greenhouse and into a cold frame, or putting them out under cloches, low polythene tunnels or horticultural fleece. Open up the cloches and cold frames or remove the fleece during the day and replace them at night for a

Above: *Growing vegetables in pots under glass can extend the growing season and also provide a colourful greenhouse display.*

week or two before planting out the seedlings properly or removing the cloches completely. Remove low polythene tunnels after a couple of weeks depending on the weather conditions. If these are severe, leave them in place for longer.

VEGETATIVE PROPAGATION

Many perennial crops are not well suited to being grown from seed. Using part of a parent plant instead ensures that the offspring (essentially clones) are the same variety as the parent and will produce crops of a known quality, something that cannot be guaranteed with those grown from seed. Vegetative propagation methods include stem tip, hardwood and root cuttings, layering runners, simple division and chip budding.

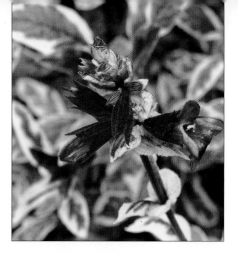

Above: *Herbs such as this tricolor sage are ideal for stem tip cuttings, a very easy way to propagate suitable species.*

PROPAGATING NEW PLANTS

While the majority of annual crops are propagated each year from seed, many perennial types are maintained and increased by a method known as 'vegetative propagation'. This simply involves using all or parts of the stems, roots or leaves to grow new plants. The most obvious example of this is arguably the potato, which is almost always raised from tubers. Despite being called 'seed potatoes', these tubers are actually swollen stem tips that would normally over-winter beneath the ground.

The ease of vegetative propagation varies considerably between crops, and in certain cases (most fruit trees for example) stock is almost invariably propagated using a bud or a twig from a tree that produces exceptionally good fruit. When this bud or twig becomes an adult tree, it has the same qualities as the 'mother' tree and is essentially an identical clone of the 'mother'

plant. This means that you know exactly what you are getting, something that is not always the case when growing from seed, but the genetically identical stock can sometimes be liable to disease, as it lacks what is termed 'hybrid vigour'.

WHICH PLANT PARTS ARE USED?

Plants may be propagated from many plant parts, and in certain species specialized roots, stems and leaves naturally have a tendency to form new plants, thereby making vegetative propagation easy.

Tubers are underground swollen stems or roots that store food, the best known of which is arguably the potato. While potatoes are stem tubers, dahlias and sweet potatoes are root tubers.

Rhizomes are thick, swollen root-like stems that often send out roots and shoots. Jerusalem artichokes are an example of a crop, mostly propagated yearly from swollen rhizomes.

Stolons are similar to rhizomes, but usually grow above ground level, sprouting from an existing stem, whereas runners arise from a crown bud and creep over the ground. Strawberries are propagated from runners.
Bulbs, such onions and garlic, consist of swollen leaves on a short stem. Onions, although sometimes raised from seed, are mostly grown on from small, under-developed bulbs, called sets. Garlic on the other hand is almost always grown from offsets (cloves) taken from a parent bulb.
Stems are used to propagate many trees and shrubs by encouraging a new root system to be formed on a stem, before or after it has been removed from the parent plant. The two commonest methods used are layering and by stem cuttings. The main difficulty with stem cuttings is keeping the stems alive while they form new roots. Some plant stems root better when the wood is soft and actively growing, while others root best from mature wood.

TAKING STEM TIP CUTTINGS

1 *Take cuttings from the tips of the stems and put them in a plastic bag with a little water. The length of the cuttings will vary, depending on the subject, but take about 10cm (4in).*

2 *Trim the cuttings to just below a leaf joint and then remove most of the leaves and side shoots, leaving just two at the top. This will help to prevent stem rot.*

3 *Place up to 12 cuttings in a pot of potting mix that is specially formulated for cuttings or a 50:50 mixture of sharp sand and peat substitute such as coir or leaf mould mix.*

4 *Water well, and cover with the cut-off base of a soft-drinks bottle, a perfect substitute for a propagator. A heated propagator will speed up the rooting process. Place several pots in the same unit.*

TAKING HARDWOOD CUTTINGS

1 *Select healthy, blemish-free pieces of wood about the thickness of a pencil. Cut each of these into sections about 20–25cm (8–10in) long, angling the top cut.*

2 *Stand the cut stems in a jar of water until you are ready to plant them out. Ideally, stand the jar in a cool moist place out of direct sunlight.*

3 *Dig a narrow trench that is deep enough for the cuttings. About 2.5–5cm (1–2in) should emerge above ground. The length of the row will depend on the number of cuttings.*

4 *Loosely fill the trench to about two-thirds full with sharp sand or fine grit. This is essential as it will allow the passage of air around the bases and prevent rotting off. It will also encourage rooting.*

5 *Insert the cuttings about 10–15cm (4–6in) apart, making sure that the angled cut is uppermost. If you place any cuttings in upside down – i.e. with the buds facing downward – rooting will not occur.*

6 *Gently firm the soil, making sure that the cuttings are firm but that the soil surface is not over-compacted. Leave the cuttings for the whole of the growing season before lifting and planting out next winter.*

TAKING ROOT CUTTINGS

1 *Dig up a small section of root from a suitable species with thick fleshy roots. The section must either have a shoot bud or be capable of forming one – in which case the cutting should be taken in the dormant season – if it is to be successful.*

2 *Remove as much of the soil as possible from the root cutting before slicing off the small side roots. Using a sharp knife, remove these as well as dead and damaged portions and any side shoots to leave a section of healthy root.*

3 *Cut the remaining sections of the root into small pieces, approximately 5cm (2in) in length, cutting the bottom end at an angle. Insert the root cutting into propagation potting mix, with the angled end pointing down.*

Cuttings taken from plants that are actively growing are called softwood cuttings. These cuttings are taken from first-year branches that have not yet become woody, with late spring and early summer being the most successful times for this method. Take cuttings 5–10cm (2–4in) long, as larger ones are prone to more rapid water loss. Make cuts slightly below a leaf node (the point where the leaf meets the stem) and remove any leaves on the lower section. Insert them into compost (soil mix), making sure that no leaves are touching each other or the compost. Cover with polythene or place them in a propagator to prevent them from wilting. Remove any cuttings immediately from the tray or pot if they die and pot healthy cuttings up promptly once they recommence growth following rooting. Species suited to this method include vines, figs, peaches, nectarines and plums.

Cuttings taken after the wood is mature are known as hardwood cuttings and these are taken when the plant is dormant. Cuttings can be taken two weeks after leaf fall and before bud burst. Select healthy wood that was produced the previous summer and that is about 'pencil thickness'. Cut it into sections of approximately 15–20cm (6–8in). Several cuttings can be made from the same

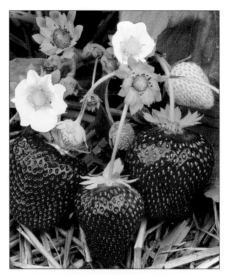

Above: *You can very easily make many more strawberry plants from one adult plant by layering the runners, negating the need to buy more plants the following year.*

Above: *Cherries (*Prunus cerasus*) and apples (*Malus sylvestris *var.* domestica*) are among the species that can be propagated successfully by chip budding.*

branch of some shrubs. The basal cuts are made just below a node, and upper cuts slightly above a bud. The upper cut should be slanted so that a cutting is less likely to be inserted into the compost upside down. Bury cuttings vertically in moist sandy topsoil or sand, leaving 2.5–5cm (1–2in) of cutting above ground, and put them in a cool shady place, taking care not to let

them freeze. In spring, remove the cuttings from storage and plant them at the same depth in pots or open ground in a sheltered position and in dappled shade. Keep them moist until a root system forms and transplant them the following spring while they are still dormant. Species suited to this method include currants, figs, olives and vines.

LAYERING STRAWBERRY RUNNERS

1 *Use a trowel to dig a hole close to a healthy strawberry plant with plenty of runners, making sure that it is large enough to accommodate a small pot.*

2 *Fill the chosen small pot to the brim with seed and cuttings compost (soil mix) and carefully 'sink' this into the hole you made, making sure the rim is just below the soil level.*

3 *The runner will need pegging in place on the surface of the seed and cuttings compost. You can make a peg by cutting a woody branch just below a side shoot to make a small hook.*

4 *Choose a healthy runner, peg it down firmly on the surface of the compost at a leaf-joint and water it in. In a few weeks, it can be detached from the parent, lifted and replanted.*

SIMPLE DIVISION

1 *Water the plant that is to be divided during the previous day. Carefully dig up a clump of the plant using a spade, in this case a Michaelmas daisy (Aster novi-belgii).*

2 *Insert two garden forks back-to-back into the plant and lever apart by pushing the handles together. Keep on dividing until the pieces are of the required size.*

3 *The pieces of the plant can then be replanted in the bed, but dig over the soil first, removing any weeds and adding some well-rotted organic material.*

4 *Alternatively, small pieces of the plant can be potted up individually. After watering, place these in a closed cold frame for a few days before hardening off.*

PROPAGATION METHODS

Layering is where a young branch is bent down to the soil and pegged down. The tip is then bent back upward, forming a 'leg', and the bend is covered with soil. Roots will form at the point where the branch bends as the bend interferes with the flow of sap, thereby encouraging root formation. Sap flow can be further reduced by twisting the stem, or cutting a 'tongue' in the lower side of the bark with a sharp knife. The stem will need earthing-up throughout the summer to encourage stem rooting. Species suited to this method include blackberries, blackcurrant and *Corylus* (hazel).

Division is a method usually practised only on herbaceous plants and it involves cutting or breaking up a crown or clump of suckers into segments. Each segment must have a bud and some roots and these are replanted. The clump is carefully dug up and split apart with two spades or forks, or 'chopped' with a shovel or large knife if the clump is firmly massed. Species suited to this method include rhubarb, globe artichoke and many herbs.

Grafting produces a plant in a relatively short period. In addition to this, however, there are other, very specific applications where it is invaluable. Fruit trees that are self-incompatible (unable to self pollinate) for example, can have a piece of a compatible variety grafted on to them in order to assure fruit. Grafting on to a rootstock might also confer a particular growth habit or give added disease resistance, and is often practised by commercial growers as a consequence.

CHIP BUDDING

1 *Select good bud wood that is free from blemishes and obvious damage, pests or diseases. If you are doing this in the summer, then you must first remove the leaves cleanly using a knife.*

2 *Remove the bud from the step using a clean, very sharp, flat-edged knife. Cut out the bud with a thin shaving of the wood below the bark and leave a 'V' shape at the base.*

3 *Prepare the stock plant by cutting a 'church window' shaped notch from the stem that is the same thickness as the chipped bud and leave a small notch cut into the base.*

4 *With clean hands, place the bud into the notch, fitting the 'V'-shaped base into the notch at the base of the 'window cut'. This should be carried out soon after preparing the bud to prevent it from drying out.*

5 *To ensure a successful union of the bud and the stock, make sure that the bud fits snugly, with the edges of the bud-wood in contact with the edge of the 'window' notch.*

6 *Secure the graft firmly with grafting tape to ensure that the join does not dry out. The graft will usually take in about 4–6 weeks in the summer but winter grafts can take longer.*

CARING FOR NEW PLANTS

Newly propagated plants are at their most vulnerable stage. Even as they begin to establish and grow, young stock remains susceptible to damage for some time to come. The best way to deal with plants, both before and immediately after planting, is to 'toughen them up' over time and this is easily achieved by applying a few simple techniques. Giving young crops a good start in life is a sure-fire way to get a bumper harvest.

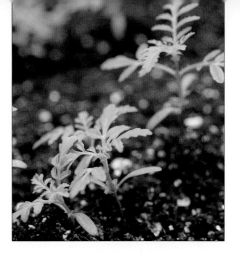

Above: *Growing plants from seed is one of the most satisfying ways of producing new stock for the allotment.*

PLANT SPACINGS

All plants need space to develop and flourish. Plants that are growing too closely compete not only for space, but also for light, water and important nutrients. In addition to this competitive stress, they also become prone to a variety of fungal diseases, as the air is not able to move around them. Thinning the seedlings helps to counteract these problems and will result in larger, stronger and healthier plants.

HOW TO THIN SEEDLINGS

Thinning is essentially two processes in one. Firstly, you are removing all the plants that are excess to requirements and at the same time you are selecting the biggest, healthiest and strongest plants that will be retained to form the crop.

Before starting to thin, dry ground must be watered, preferably the night before you intend to thin. A measuring stick, marked with the appropriate crop distance, can be used to show the approximate position of

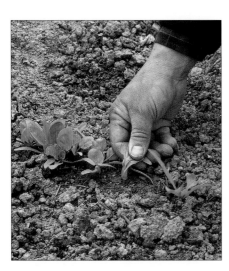

Above: *Rows of seedlings are often too crowded and need to be thinned when the plants are young.*

the individual plants. Remove all the plants in between each of the markers, selecting the healthiest plant at or near the mark on the stick. If there are no plants at the marked point, then you can transplant one of the seedlings that is excess to requirements into this position. When you are removing the excess plants, place a finger on the soil at either side of the seedling that is being kept. This protects it from root disturbance. Once you have finished, water the remaining seedlings with a fine rose on a watering can to re-firm the soil around the plants. The seedlings that have been removed can be put on the compost heap.

Avoid thinning using this method on hot dry days or in windy conditions, as the remaining seedlings in the ground may

Left: *Seedlings grown elsewhere in the allotment can be lifted and replanted in their eventual positions. This method is good for crops that need wide spacing.*

become water-stressed if their roots are disturbed. The alternative, in this case, is to simply snip off the seedlings at ground level with a pair of sharp scissors or secateurs (hand pruners), thereby avoiding root disturbance.

THINNING DISTANCES

The following measurements are the distances that need to be left between thinned seedlings.

Beetroot (beets)	7.5–10cm (3–4in)
Broad (fava) beans	23cm (9in)
Carrots	7.5cm (3in)
Dwarf French beans	
(bush green beans)	20cm (8in)
Florence fennel	25cm (10in)
Kohl rabi	20cm (8in)
Lettuce	23cm (9in)
Parsley	15cm (6in)
Peas	5cm (2in)
Parsnips	15–20cm (6–9in)
Radishes	2.5–5cm (1–2in)
Runner (green)	
beans	25–30cm
	(10–12in)
Salsify	15cm (6in)
Scorzonera	15cm (6in)
Spinach	15cm (6in)
Spring onions	
(scallions)	5cm (2in)
Swedes (rutabaga	
or yellow turnip)	30cm (12in)
Swiss chard	30cm (12in)
Turnips	15–20cm
	(6–8in)

TRANSPLANTING SEEDLINGS

1 *Water your row of seedlings at least an hour before transplanting and preferably the night before if no rain has fallen.*

2 *Using a fork to loosen the soil, gently lift the seedlings. Take care to handle them by their leaves and never touch the stems.*

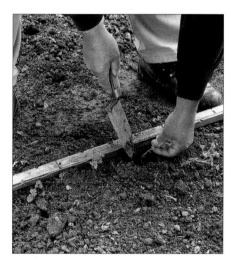

3 *Using a tight line, straight edge or notched planting board, replant the seedlings at the appropriate spacing for that crop.*

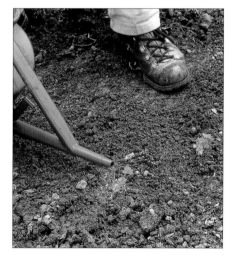

4 *Gently water the seedlings immediately after sowing. Never let roots dry out at any stage during transplanting.*

METHODS FOR TRANSPLANTING

The most common way of transplanting seedlings involves planting container-grown plants into open ground. Early vegetable crops can easily be raised in this way. The other method is to raise seedlings in open ground near to where they are to be planted out. Transplanting outdoor seedlings means that a smaller area of the vegetable plot is needed for sowing and, in consequence, a smaller seedbed is required. Transplanting seedlings is a good way of growing plants such as lettuce that are to be used in catch-cropping beds or where plants are to be planted out in no-dig beds.

The ideal time for transplanting outdoor seedlings is during damp overcast weather because this helps to prevent the seedlings' roots drying out. As is the case when thinning the plants, the seedlings will need watering the evening before. It is best to dig up only a few plants at a time, discarding any that are weak, damaged or appear to be sick. Seedlings can be placed in a plastic bag to maintain humidity around them while they are out of the ground.

A garden line can be set out in the vegetable patch in a similar manner to the way in which it is placed for preparing a seed drill. The position of the plants can then be determined using a measuring stick. Use a dibber (dibble) or thin trowel to plant the seedlings, firming lightly around the base before moving on to the next transplant. Once the row is completed, it is important that you water them in.

For catch cropping or planting among other plants, the surrounding crop may well determine the spacings between the transplants, although the procedure remains exactly the same.

COMMON PLANTING DISTANCES

Always allow the correct spacing between crop plants so that they will grow into healthy specimens.

Asparagus	30–38cm (12–15in)
Aubergines (eggplants)	60cm (24in)
Bell peppers	45–60cm (18–24in)
Broccoli	60cm (24in)
Brussels sprouts	50–75cm (20–30in)
Cabbages	30–50cm (12–20in)
Calabrese (Italian sprouting broccoli)	15–23cm (6–9in)
Cauliflowers	50–75cm (20–30in)
Celeriac	30–38cm (12–15in)
Celery	23–30cm (9–12in)
Courgettes (zucchini)	60cm (24in)
Cucumbers	60cm (24in)
Garlic	15cm (6in)
Globe artichokes	75cm (30in)
Jerusalem artichokes	30cm (12in)
Kale	60cm (24in)
Leeks	15cm (6in)
Marrows (large zucchini)	60cm (24in)
Onion sets	10cm (4in)
Potatoes	30–38cm (12–15in)
Pumpkins	90–180cm (3–6ft)
Rhubarb	75–90cm (30–36in)
Runner (green) beans	25–30cm (10–12in)
Sea kale	30cm (12in)
Shallots	15–18cm (6–7in)
Sweetcorn (corn)	30cm (12in)
Tomatoes	60cm (24in)

Right: *A shade box can protect vulnerable seedlings from strong light and heat while they are being acclimatized.*

AVOIDING TRANSPLANT SHOCK

Even if young plants were hardened off, prior to planting out, they will still suffer a certain amount of stress as a result of their move. The degree to which this affects their growth in the long term will of course vary, and depends upon the steps you take to avoid the problem.

It is worth remembering that no matter how carefully you handle them while planting, some, albeit slight damage, is still likely to occur. Roots, stems and leaves can all be affected, and the plant will need to recover from this while it is also dealing with the challenge of establishing itself in its new home. As a rule of thumb, the younger the plant, the more quickly it will re-acclimatize. Having said this though, very young plants are naturally more susceptible to other stresses, meaning that it may well be better to grow them on a little first.

The fact that the plant experiences a change of location can also cause problems at first, although young plants typically recover from this quite quickly. Plants that have been grown in a sheltered location, for example, initially struggle if they are planted in an open situation, even if this

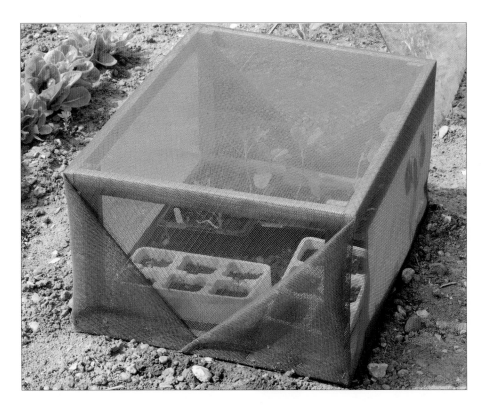

is not particularly windy. Equally, plants grown in an open sunny situation would not benefit from being transplanted into a cool, shady place.

The real trick is to ensure that you gradually acclimatize them to their new setting. Plants not used to an open setting may need a little shelter or light shade for

a few days as they get used to their new home. Remember, also, that even if they come from a similar location to that which they are planted into, they may well have been growing in close proximity to one another, gaining benefit from the humidity this promotes. Once planted or transplanted, however, they will be at their

Below: *Water young plants carefully, as overwatering can be just as harmful to their development as underwatering.*

Below: *Tender seedlings, such as this pumpkin, require very delicate handling when they are planted out or potted on.*

Below: *If pests, such as rabbits, are a particular problem on the site it may be worth installing fencing.*

PLANTING OUT CONTAINER-GROWN PLANTS

1 *Container-grown plants need careful handling to avoid damaging new growth. Pushing them out rather than pulling the stem will minimize harm.*

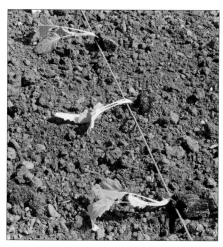

2 *Lay them out in their final spacing or positions prior to planting, using a line to keep them straight if you are planting them out in rows.*

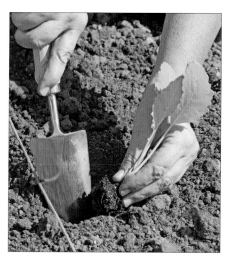

3 *Use a trowel to excavate a hole, planting the root-ball (roots) no more than 1cm (½in) below the soil surface, and gently firm the soil around the plant.*

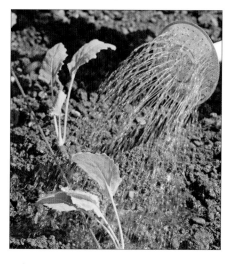

4 *Once the whole row is planted, water the plants using a watering can fitted with a fine rose attachment. Set them back upright and re-firm if needed.*

the height of summer. If you are going to opt for a more permanent protective structure though, it is a good idea to make sure that it can be moved off, as this will allow you access to maintain and harvest the crop easily and ultimately to cultivate the ground in the following spring. A fixed cage structure over a raised bed, for instance, may mean that you have to bend double to work on the area, making reaching some crops and carrying out tasks such as digging and weeding much more difficult.

WATERING AND FEEDING

Even though you will need to water new plants regularly, especially in hot or very windy weather, be careful not to overdo it. Some vegetables, including most root crops and members of the onion family, need only be watered during their establishment and even then do not like to be too wet. A rose attachment is a good investment as it is a gentle way of watering,

Feeding is also not necessary in the early stages, and in many cases can prove detrimental to young, sensitive roots. As a rule of thumb, if you applied a fertilizer before planting, you probably won't need to apply any more for 2–3 weeks after putting plants in the ground, when the plants show visible signs of growth.

Below: *Birds can affect your crop both when plants are young and when it is ready to be harvested, so you need to be vigilant.*

final spacing and this sudden isolation, whilst beneficial in the longer term, can cause a measure of water stress in those first few days. Be prepared to cover them with some fleece if a sudden cold snap threatens and make sure they get enough water while their roots are establishing.

PROTECTING VULNERABLE STOCK

Some newly planted specimens prove a real magnet for the unwanted attention of pests such as birds or rabbits, and it is important to keep these out. Birds often peck out onion sets for example without eating them, and pigeons can easily shred newly transplanted brassicas. Fortunately, these pests can easily be deterred by covering plants temporarily with netting. If birds and rabbits prove a major problem, however, it may be worth making more permanent fences or cages to protect your crops from outside harm.

Frames or hoops, fixed over the bed, can be used to support various protection according to the season; fleece or polythene in early spring and autumn, netting to keep pests out and shade in

COLD FRAMES AND CLOCHES

Individual and multiple plant protectors are useful for covering the transplants or seedlings of warm-weather vegetables or flowers that are set out ahead of the normal planting season. These usually take the form of low plastic tunnels, cloches or individual bell jars. The colder the area in which you live, the greater their usefulness because they effectively extend the length of the normal growing season.

Above: *This is a sturdy brick cold frame with a soil bed for growing winter and early spring vegetables.*

COLD FRAMES

These enable you to sow summer flowers and vegetables some weeks before outdoor planting and may even allow for an extra crop within a season. They are relatively inexpensive, simple structures, providing a favourable environment for growing cool-weather crops in the very early spring, the autumn and even into the winter.

Cold frames have no outside energy requirements, relying on the sun as a source of heat. They collect heat when the sun's rays penetrate the light (the top cover) which is made from plastic, glass or fibreglass. The ideal location for a cold frame is facing the direction of the sun with a slight slope to ensure good drainage and maximum solar absorption. A sheltered spot against a wall or hedge is best. Sink the frame into the ground to provide extra protection, using the earth for insulation. Put a walkway to the front and adequate space behind the frame to help when removing the light.

Designs for cold frames vary. For example, some contain barrels that are painted black and filled with water. These absorb heat during the day and release it at night. Some cold frames are built with a very high back and a steep glass slope. Others are insulated very well and may also include movable insulation. A simple method of providing insulation is to use sacks filled with leaves over the top of the frame and bales of straw or hay stacked against the sides at night in order to protect against freezing.

There is no standard-sized cold frame. The inside depth of the frame should be determined by the height of the plants that you plan to grow. Spring annuals, perennial seedlings or low over-wintering stock may need as little as a 30cm (12in) back board and a 20cm (8in) front board. Potted plants may need a 38cm (15in) front board and a 45cm (18in) back board. A standard glass frame light is usually about 1 x 1.8m (3 x 6ft).

Do not make the structure too wide for weeding and harvesting; a width of 1.2–1.5m (4–5ft) is convenient to reach across.

Cold frames are useful for hardening-off seedlings that were started indoors or in a greenhouse. This hardening-off period is important because seedlings can suffer serious setbacks if they are moved directly from the warmth and protection of the greenhouse to the outdoors. It is also possible to start cool-weather crops in the cold frame and either grow them to maturity or transplant them in the allotment. Cold frames may also be useful for rooting the cuttings of deciduous and evergreen shrubs and trees, and the softwood cuttings of chrysanthemums, geraniums and fuchsias during the warmer months. Ventilation is most critical in late winter, early spring, and early autumn on clear, sunny days when temperatures may rise above 45°C (113°F). The light should be raised partially to prevent the build-up of extreme temperatures inside the frame. Lower or replace the light early each day in order to conserve some heat for the evening.

In summer, extreme heat and intensive sunlight can damage plants. You can avoid this by shading with a lath (a slatted wooden frame) or old bamboo window blinds. Water plants early so that they dry before dark; this helps to reduce disease problems.

CLOCHES

Traditionally a bell-shaped glass cover, a cloche is a movable structure that serves as a mini-greenhouse. Cloches can be used to protect transplanted tender plants from spring frosts. They also help to warm up the soil for crops sown directly in the soil.

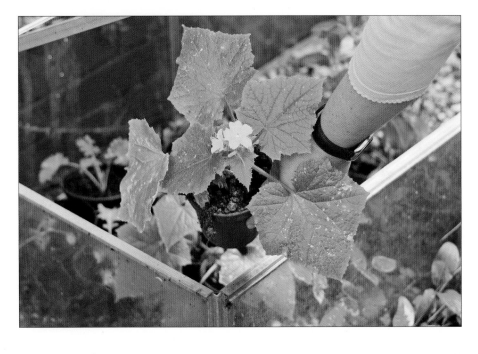

Left: *When the seedlings are fully acclimatized and ready to be planted out, the lights or lids can be left off altogether.*

Above: *A rigid plastic cloche is easy to use. The sections butt up against each other and can be pegged into the soil. End pieces are also available to create a sheltered microclimate.*

Above: *Glass bell jars are simple cloches for covering one plant. They are expensive, but large plastic jars make a good, if not as attractive, alternative.*

The traditional or European cloche is usually built in 60cm (24in) sections that vary in height from 20–60cm (8–24in) and 40–65cm (16–26in) in width. It is made of four panes of glass held together with heavy galvanized wire fittings. It has a handle for ease in carrying and for operating the ventilation system. Several cloches placed end to end make a miniature greenhouse.

Plastic bottles with the bottoms cut out can provide protection for small individual plants. These will last a season or two, but will become brittle over time. Flexible fibreglass sheets held in an inverted 'U'-shape by stiff wire hoops or small wooden stakes can be used to cover rows of plants.

A tunnel-like plant protector can be made with a 1.5m (5ft) strip of plastic or fleece laid over 1.8m (6ft) wire hoops placed 1m (3ft) apart. Elastic tiedowns over the top near each hoop will hold the plastic.

Temporary cloches can also be made by arching black, semi-rigid, plastic piping over the row or bed and sticking it into the ground on each side. Lay clear plastic over the arches. If the beds are enclosed with wood, attach brackets to the inside edges of the boxes or sink short pieces of pipe with a larger inside diameter along the sides to hold the arches. The arches can be used to support fleece or shade cloth to ward off both frost and bright sunlight. When this

cloche is no longer needed, simply remove the plastic sheet and pipe ribs and store them until the following season.

THE BOTTLE RADIATOR

In areas prone to late air frosts, this simple method can protect outdoor crops such as bush tomatoes. Fill a glass or plastic bottle with water and place it next to the plant. The sunlight will warm the water in the bottle, which will in turn release a gentle heat at night. This is sufficient to prevent cold shock to the plant and will ensure good growth and cropping. It can also be used in conjunction with a fleece covering to enhance the warming effect.

Far left: *Upturned, clear plastic bottles with the bottoms cut out are ideal for using as mini-cloches, protecting individual plants. This is also an environmentally friendly technique.*

Left: *Old-fashioned cloches are particularly good for decorative sites. However, they are also very expensive and quite fragile.*

WATERING

In order to cultivate a successful allotment, it is crucial to recognize the water requirements of different plants. It is of vital importance that you know when and how to provide the right amount of water, as well as how to avoid either drought or waterlogging. Conserving the water in the soil as well as storing and recycling this valuable commodity are of key importance in the vegetable, fruit and herb plot, especially in areas where rainfall is seasonal and droughts are common.

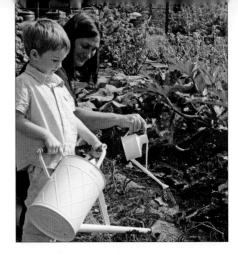

Above: *Seasonal crops often require frequent watering, and this is something that all family members can get involved with.*

PRINCIPLES OF WATER MANAGEMENT

After rainfall or irrigation, the soil pore spaces are filled with water, the air is displaced and the soil saturated. If the rain or irrigation were to continue, then surface pooling or runoff would occur. Water drains from the soil through the pore system and is replaced to some extent by air. After draining, any remaining water may be lost through evaporation or taken up by the plant and lost through its leaves.

All sands and loamy sands tend to have a low available water capacity. Loams and clay have a medium capacity while very fine sandy loam, silt loams, peats and any soil with a high water table have high available water capacity. Clay soils often have a large amount of water within them, but it is held so tightly that plants are not able to obtain it.

Below: *A watering can is ideal for allotment use, and unless you have mains water is often the only practical method available.*

WATER AND THE PLANT

All plants are largely made of water and it is critical that water levels are maintained if the plant is to grow and develop. Soft fleshy subjects, such as courgettes (zucchini), tomatoes and other vegetables, use large quantities of water, particularly during establishment. Plants with large leaves or with extensive branch systems, such as large apple trees, will remove gallons of water from the soil in the course of a hot sunny day.

WATERWISE GARDENING

Since water supplies are limited, we need to do all we can to conserve soil moisture. As the top layer of soil dries out, the dry soil acts as an insulation to further rapid moisture loss. Take advantage of this by avoiding over-cultivation, particularly during

Below: *It is vital to get water directly to the roots of plants; here a pipe is used to channel the water straight into the ground.*

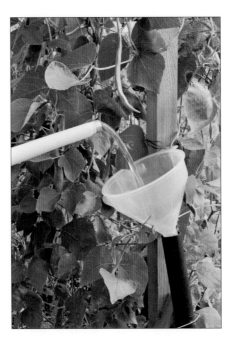

the summer, as this may bring moist soil to the surface to dry out. Always try to maintain a well-structured soil and avoid capping (a hard, partially compacted surface layer) as this can prevent the absorption of rainfall by the soil, leaving puddles that quickly evaporate.

Mulches help to conserve moisture either by holding water or acting as insulation provided that they are deep enough. Keep the soil surface weed-free and provide shelter from drying winds. Maintain drainage, as if this is poor it will lead to limited root growth of the plant and poor soil structure.

STORING AND RECYCLING WATER

Water is a precious resource that is sometimes in short supply. Plants in open ground may acclimatize to the soil conditions, but those growing in pots are more susceptible to drought. Mains water can provide an answer but this can be labour-intensive if only watering cans are allowed on the site.

Storing and recycling household water is a relatively complicated undertaking that is usually best left to specialist contractors. The potential health risks mean that it is not usually wise to store this type of water for any length of time, but it can be used fresh to water non-food plants. You may also find it hard or impossible to transport household water to an allotment site, although you could use large plastic jerry cans if you have a regular supply and can ensure that it will be used fresh.

Rainwater may be a viable alternative and you can collect it on site. The quickest and easiest option is to install water butts to collect water from downspouts from roof drains. This method will rarely provide enough water for your whole plot, but is often plenty to water (or supplement the

MAKING A BOTTLE SEEP TUBE

1 *Plastic bottles can make excellent seep irrigation tubes. Start by making some small holes in the cap and screwing it on tightly.*

2 *Using a knife, sharp pair of scissors or secateurs (pruners), cut the base off the bottle so that it forms an open-ended tube.*

3 *Push or bury the bottle neck firmly into the ground next to the plant and fill the open end with water, re-firming if needed.*

watering of) plants in containers, particularly edible plants such as herbs. Rainwater is naturally acidic and is, therefore, not likely to contain many harmful bacteria. Its acidity also makes it the ideal choice for misting plants under glass on hot days (as it will not mark the leaves with lime) and suits many species sensitive to domestic water additives. Rainwater is also a must for people wishing to grow 'acid-loving' specimens, such as blueberries, in pots.

WATERING PLANTS

In areas where seasonal water shortage is a regular problem, choose drought-tolerant species where possible. Seasonal crops (such as vegetables) tend to suffer the most from drought due to the limited time that they have to develop extensive root systems. If you wish to grow these plants in drier areas, they will need to be watered regularly to survive prolonged dry periods. Perennial fruit and vegetables, on the other hand, may actually become more drought-tolerant if they are watered less. This is because they will have to root deeper to find water. Perennial fruit and vegetables will need to be watered in their first season following planting to ensure their long-term survival.

Remember that applying a good drench on a more occasional basis allows the water to penetrate more deeply and have a better long-term effect because it encourages deeper rooting. Watering little and often can prove detrimental in drier climates by causing

Right: Water butts are both practical and environmentally friendly and ensure that the water is soft and free of added chemicals.

surface roots that may become very drought-prone. After the first growing season following planting, they are better able to cope if not watered at all. Applying a mulch at this time is extremely beneficial.

WATERING METHODS

Plants can be watered in many ways, but all generally fall into two categories: hand watering or automatic systems.

Hand watering The commonest 'tool' used for this method is the watering can. Numerous designs exist but they all rely upon a gradual delivery through a spout. A rose ensures that a fine spray is delivered that will not wash away soil or damage

plants. Hoses can also be used for hand-watering and many nozzles have been designed to deliver a shower of water rather than a jet.

Seep or drip hoses Generally, not many allotments will allow the use of sprinklers, so resourceful allotment-growers often put together a seep or drip hose system, fed from a watering can. These are essentially 'leaky pipes' that gradually release water into the soil over a large area. Bottle seep tubes provide a more localized solution and are a very cheap and easy way of delivering water just where it is needed at the base of a plant.

Standard hoses can also be used on some sites, and these offer the benefit of gradual delivery over a large area and can be operated manually from a mains water supply. A good watering every few days can be extremely beneficial to most plants, especially if recently planted.

WATERING PROBLEMS

These are usually the result of either too much or too little water being applied to the plant. Both over- and under-watering have similar symptoms because both are related to root death. An over-watered plant's root system begins to die off due to a lack of oxygen. The plant becomes short of water and wilts. Other problems can result from the wetting of foliage. Watering in full sunlight can give plants a scorched appearance, so water in the cool part of the day.

FEEDING

In order for plants to grow and sustain their life processes, they require water and air as well as a range of naturally occurring elements. At least 16 different elements are needed by all plants for successful growth and development. Three of these elements – carbon, hydrogen and oxygen – are obtained from the carbon dioxide in the air and from the water and oxygen in the soil. In addition to these, plants also need a selection of other important nutrients, which are described here.

Above: *Foliar sprays are a quick and easy way for the plants to obtain nutrients in a short space of time.*

IMPORTANT PLANT NUTRIENTS

In addition to carbon, hydrogen and oxygen, plants need other important nutrients, which they obtain directly from the soil or compost (soil mix). These nutrients are commonly divided into two groups, depending upon whether they are found in plants in high or low concentrations. When they are found in high concentrations and are needed in large amounts, they are known as macro or major nutrients. There are three of these: nitrogen (N), phosphorus (P) and potassium (K). Every gardener must be fully aware of the functions of the 'essential three'. Nitrogen is basically the shoot and leaf maker and is especially important early in the growing season; phosphorus is used in the formation of roots; and potassium plays a vital role in flower and fruit formation and is also key to hardiness in overwintering plants. Elements that are needed in relatively small amounts are the micro or trace elements, of which there are ten. Among the most important of these are calcium, magnesium and sulphur, although all play a vital role in the growth and development of the plant.

FEEDING PLANTS

Numerous nutrient fertilizers are available. All have their relative advantages, but they should be used only as part of a combined strategy that aims to harness natural nutrient cycles, for example top-dressing the soil with well-rotted organic matter. This is the catalyst to nutrient cycling in the soil as it feeds the vast array of soil organisms that make use of essential plant nutrients. The majority of garden composts do not contain especially large amounts of the major plant nutrients; it is their long-term ability to feed soil life that makes them so valuable.

FURTHER FEEDING

Despite the best intentions, plants can become short of a certain type of nutrient. This is usually avoided by giving the plant a supplement of a 'plant food' that is rich in that particular nutrient. This can be applied as a foliar feed. Foliar feeding involves spraying a fine mist of a low-strength solution of the feed. The exact concentrations vary according to the feed being used, but a rough guide would be to use a quarter strength of that which you would apply as a liquid feed to the soil. The main benefit of foliar feeding is that the nutrient will be taken up quickly. The residue is best washed off after a couple of days. Applying a weak solution of Epsom salts as a foliar or liquid feed is an example of applying such a tonic.

FERTILIZERS

A wide variety of substances can boost nutrient levels. They should be used in addition to composts and manures.

Animal manure Bird manure is an organic source of nitrogen. Use in pellet form, as the fresh substance will burn plant roots.

Bonemeal Promotes strong root growth due to its high phosphate content. When using, always wear latex gloves.

Calcified seaweed This organic fertilizer raises the pH of the soil and adds calcium, like limestone, but also contains magnesium.

Fish, blood and bone A general fertilizer that is normally applied in the spring to promote root and shoot growth.

Ground limestone This raises the pH and supplies calcium where there is a deficiency. It is applied as a powder when it is needed.

Growmore This general-purpose fertilizer is used in spring and summer around the base of shrubs to give them a boost.

Hoof and horn This material gives a slow release of nitrogen where strong growth is needed and is applied in the spring or early summer.

Rock phosphate Used mostly to counter phosphate deficiency and as an alternative to bonemeal.

Seaweed meal Helps to build up humus levels in the soil and is used on a wide range of plants.

Wood ash An excellent source of potassium that can be added directly to the soil or to a compost heap.

Bonemeal

Calcified seaweed

Fish, blood and bone

Hoof and horn

MAKING COMFREY TEA

1 *Cut a large bundle of comfrey leaves from the patch in your allotment. Choose good, green, leafy growth. Remove the leaf and stem, but avoid using the crown.*

2 *Place in a plastic container with holes in the base. Weigh down the leaves. Line a second larger container with a plastic bag and place the first container inside. Tie the bag at the top.*

3 *The thick dark liquid from the decomposing comfrey leaves collects in the bag below. The lower bucket allows this to drip down and stores it until the process is complete.*

4 *Decant the finished liquid into a jam jar for later use. The liquid feed must be diluted before it is applied to plants at a ratio of about 10 parts water to 1 part concentrate.*

LIQUID FEEDS AND TEAS

Compost tea is easy to make. Comfrey is ideal for this, but stinging nettles are also very good. You could also use sheep or goat manure, or finely sifted compost from the heap. Simply fill an old pillowcase or burlap bag with your chosen material (comfrey, nettles, compost or manure) and sink it into a large bucket, dustbin (garbage can) or barrel of water. Cover the container and let it steep for a few days. Remember, the longer you steep, the stronger the tea will be. You may use the final 'brew' as a light liquid feed, and it can also be used as a foliar feeding medium, provided that it is well diluted. Don't throw the plant residue in the bag away as it can be used as a very effective mulch. An alternative method for making the tea is shown above.

Worm colonies in containers also produce a liquid feed that is a tonic for your plants. It should be diluted to a ratio of about 10 parts water to 1 part liquid feed. It is generally high in potassium and phosphorus. Wormeries can be bought on-line.

SYMPTOMS OF DEFICIENCY

Plants exhibit varying symptoms of a nutrient deficiency. General ones are stunted growth, discoloured leaves, including mottling and inter-veinal coloration, and the premature death of leaves or other parts of the plant. Plants may also display twisted or distorted growth as well as poor root growth and development. In many cases, the symptoms are often seen first in the plant's extremities, such as the tips of the shoots, as these are furthest away from the nutrient source. If a plant cannot obtain enough of any nutrient from a soil it will be because there is either little or no nutrient present in the soil, or the nutrient is not 'available' to the plant.

Any element can also be toxic to the plant if it is present in sufficiently high amounts or out of balance with other elements in the growing medium.

OTHER FEEDING METHODS

1 *An alternative method of feeding is to use a good-quality liquid feed. This is most useful for plants that are growing in containers. Add the fertilizer of your choice to one of the waterings, according to the manufacturer's instructions.*

2 *Granular fertilizer can be applied by hand, spreading it over the area covered by the roots below. Follow the manufacturer's instructions. You may wish to protect your hands when applying the fertilizer by wearing a pair of gloves.*

3 *Apply a layer of well-rotted organic material, such as farmyard manure or garden compost, to the surface of the soil around the plant. If the plant is not shallow-rooted, lightly fork the material into the top layer of the soil.*

PLANT NUTRIENTS

The following table highlights the characteristics of the soil nutrients. Symptoms of deficiency may be seen on different parts of the plant at different stages of growth, although it may not always be immediately obvious that a plant is suffering from a nutrient deficiency. Some of the more important symptoms that can be seen on plants are listed below, together with remedies and toxicity causes.

PLANT NUTRIENT	NATURAL ORGANIC SOURCE	PLANTS MOST IN NEED	SOILS MOST IN NEED	SIGNS OF SHORTAGE	HOW TO AVOID SHORTAGE	TOXICITY CAUSE
Major plant nutrients						
Nitrogen (N) The 'leaf maker'	Bird manure, blood and bone, grass clippings	Vegetables grown for their leaves, such as lettuce and spinach	Sandy soils in rainy areas	Stunted growth; small pale green leaves; weak stems	Apply a base dressing before sowing or planting. Top-dress in spring and summer with organic matter.	Excessive use of nitrogen-rich fertilizer
Phosphates (P_2O_5) The 'root maker'	Comfrey, seagrass, horse manure, blood and bone	Young plants, root vegetables, such as carrots, and fruit	Sandy soils	Stunted roots and stems; small leaves with a purplish tinge; low fruit yield	Apply a base dressing of bonemeal. Use fish, blood and bone when top-dressing plants.	Excessive use of fertilizer
Potash (K_2O) The 'flower and fruit maker'	Comfrey, horse manure, seagrass	Fruit, flowers and potatoes	Sandy soils	Leaf edges turn yellow, then brown; low fruit yield; fruit and flowers poorly coloured	Apply a compound organic fertilizer or wood ash as a base dressing or top-dressing.	Excessive use of fertilizer; lack of magnesium
Minor plant nutrients						
Boron (B)	Beetroot (beet) leaves, horse manure, compost, seagrass, untreated sawdust	Root vegetables, top fruit (apples, pears etc.)	Sandy soils	Brown heart (roots); narrow leaves; corky patches on fruit	Top-dress with compost or apply borax in severe cases.	Irrigation water
Calcium (Ca)	Dandelion, lucerne hay, comfrey, horse manure, compost, blood and bone	Fruit, vegetables, flowers	Acid and potash-rich soils	Similar to nitrogen shortage – stunted growth and pale green leaves	Apply lime or use gypsum or calcified seaweed.	High pH causes toxicity for some acid-loving plants
Copper (Cu)	Nettles, yarrow, horse manure, dandelion, chickweed, compost, untreated sawdust	Fruit, vegetables	Sandy soils	Dieback; brown spots on leaves	Top-dress with compost.	Copper-based fungicides
Iron (Fe)	Stinging nettle, compost, dandelion, horse manure, spinach and seaweed	Soft fruit, strawberries and carrots	Chalky soils	Yellowing of younger leaves	Trouble can occur on chalky, peaty, very light and acid soils. Iron shortage in chalky soil is due to lock-up by calcium and hard to avoid.	Rare
Magnesium (Mg)	Grass clippings, seagrass	Tomatoes	Sandy, peaty and potash-rich soils	Yellow or brown patches between veins of older leaves	Apply a mulch of compost or Epsom salts if deficiency is severe.	None
Manganese (Mn)	Chickweed, compost, untreated sawdust	Many crops, especially peas	Chalky soils	Yellowing between the veins of older leaves	Shortage in chalky soils is due to lock-up by calcium (see iron). Acidification for some plants.	None
Molybdenum (Mo)	Cornstalks, compost, grass clippings	Brassicas, such as cabbage	Acid soils	Narrow leaves	Apply lime and top-dress with compost.	None
Sodium (Na)	Seaweed	Root vegetables, fruit	Sandy soils	Very rare except in a few seaside-loving plants	Not usually warranted.	Land reclaimed from sea
Sulphur (S)	Cabbage leaves	All plants	Soils in rural areas	Stunted growth and pale green leaves	A light dusting of flowers of sulphur during the year.	Industrial sites and acid rain
Zinc (Zn)	Horse manure, corn stalks, garden compost, untreated sawdust	Fruit, vegetables	Sandy soils	Dieback	Top-dress with compost.	Leaching from containers

Above: *If you are using a bought fertilizer, always read the label and only apply the recommended dose, to avoid overfeeding.*

Above: *Excessive fertilizer use results in nutrients leaching into watercourses, causing problems such as algal bloom.*

PROBLEMS CAUSED BY OVERFEEDING

While we tend to associate nutrient-related problems with a shortage, applying excessive fertilizer also brings a host of problems, both for your plants and ultimately for the wider environment. Overfeeding plants is, at its most basic level, wasteful. Plants can only take up a certain amount of nutrients, and the majority of any excess is usually lost through leaching (being washed away by water). Leaching of nutrients does not destroy them, however, and while lost to your own plants, the soil water that seeps away from your plot ultimately must go somewhere. This is usually to groundwater (aquifers) or slow-flowing underground rivers, and from these sources it can enter drinking water supplies, surface-flowing rivers or ultimately the sea, causing problems such as eutrophication, which can lead to a reduction in oxygen levels in that water. Although your own contribution to this would of course be very small indeed, it does no good when it is leached away, and is ultimately a form of pollution – one that is easily avoided.

Before leaching of excess nutrient happens however, high concentrations of fertilizer in the soil can cause considerable damage to the roots of your crops. In essence, a high concentration of plant food in the soil starts to reverse the process that roots use to remove water and dissolved nutrient from the soil. The effect is akin to burning the roots and the knock-on effects will be seen through changed growth patterns and an overall loss of condition to the plant.

Leaves and new shoots on your plants are often the first things to show visible signs of overfeeding, and the symptoms are often very similar to drought stress – due to the loss of healthy root – but in young plants can easily be mistaken for lack of nutrients. Indeed, young plants are especially sensitive to overfeeding, particularly in the time following transplanting or planting out.

A simple rule of thumb for spotting the symptoms are: leaves that curl under from the outside margins or hook downward at the tips (as the plant tries to retain moisture), gradually becoming darker green and brittle or glossy, are the commonest sign of overfeeding; discoloration, spotting or mottling of older leaves, accompanied by reduced leaf and shoot size of new growth, on the other hand, are all common signs of underfeeding.

Even if plants are not directly harmed by overfeeding, imbalances to their nutrition can still cause unwanted growth patterns, so it is important to try and get it right. Excessive nitrogen applied to fruiting crops may encourage large amounts of foliage while inhibiting the production of flowers and ultimately fruit. If nitrogen is applied late in the year, plants make excessive 'soft' growth that is less hardy and root crops overfed with nitrogen may become tough, fibrous or poor-tasting.

MAKING LIQUID MANURE

1 *Fill a permeable bag or sack with some fresh animal manure using 1 litre (1½ pints) manure for every 10 litres (2 gallons) of water you intend using.*

2 *Tie the top of the bag with string and submerge the bag in a dustbin (garbage can) filled with water. Leave for 1 month in warm weather or 3 months if cooler.*

3 *Once the manure has soaked sufficiently, dilute with water in a 2:1 ratio, wearing gloves. Avoid using it directly on crops that will be harvested soon.*

STAKING AND SUPPORT

Staking the plants on your allotment not only makes the area look tidier, but it also allows crops to grow and bloom without toppling over, breaking, or smothering smaller plants nearby. It will also save you a considerable amount of space. What is more, staking improves air circulation, meaning that your plants will be less likely to suffer from common fungal diseases. Staking must be done early on in the growing season, preferably when the plant is young, if you want the full benefit from it.

Above: *Young, straight branches, such as these hazel rods, make an excellent method of support that you can even grow yourself.*

WHICH PLANTS NEED STAKING?

The decision to stake a plant depends largely upon what it is. Low-growing sturdy crops often need no support, whereas taller heavy cropping types, such as tomatoes, usually require robust supports in order to help them carry a full load of fruit. Equally, cut flower species, such as dahlias, can also benefit from a strong stake in order to support heavy flower heads from toppling and breaking the stems, particularly during windy spells or heavy showers. Many fruit trees require staking, either when young or if they are grown as cordons. Soft fruit bushes, especially cane fruits, also benefit considerably from support.

Staking your crops generally results in cleaner produce that is less susceptible to damage, allows more air and sunlight to reach the plants, and makes cultivation and harvesting easier. In addition, it is a more efficient use of space and this, combined with the other advantages, can ultimately mean that you get higher yields from your available space.

Having said this, this 'intensified' approach to your plot can mean that more frequent watering is needed and that extra time is spent preparing the plot and tying in the growing plants. Many allotment-growers believe that this is time well spent, so it is worth trying.

STAKING MATERIALS

There is a wide range of materials that can be used to stake your plants and each of these has their relative merits and drawbacks. Ideally, the best materials are those you have to hand, but if you have to purchase materials then you should think carefully about what you want them to do before spending too much money.

Natural materials such as timber, bamboo, branch-wood or twigs are freely obtainable and, provided that you are careful about their origin, tend to be a renewable resource. The fact that they are natural in origin does mean that they tend to rot and need replacing, sometimes on a yearly basis.

Right: *An excellent way of recycling old materials is to use scrapped scaffold poles and clips to make a robust frame for climbing plants. Nets and wires can be fixed on to the frame to support runner (green) beans, sweet peas and gourds.*

Far right: *Bamboo is traditionally used for staking and support. Bamboo canes are strong, light and durable. If cleaned at the end of the growing season and stored in a dry area, the canes can be used for a few years.*

Above: *Wooden trellises are a lightweight, durable and cheap way to divide the plot, providing an ideal place to support climbers.*

Left: *Although a shed takes up space, using it to support a climber such as this vine makes it a productive area once more.*

Wires may be attached to a wall or fence to provide support for climbing plants in a similar way to a trellis. Wires can also be stretched horizontally between posts or stakes to provide support for plants such as cane fruits, or as a crisscross framework for climbers.

Sticks and twigs are used either as protection for seedlings or support for low-growing plants. Twiggy sticks are often called pea sticks by gardeners, due to their suitability for supporting shorter varieties of peas and beans.

TYING MATERIALS

The way that you attach the plant to a support is arguably just as important as the support itself. Ideally, ties must be flexible and slightly loose to allow the plant room to grow without tearing, ripping or scarring the plant stem. Natural materials such as raffia or twine do of course have the advantage of being biodegradable and if combined with natural supports mean that the whole system is derived from renewable sources.

Synthetic materials are mostly made of coated wire, Velcro, plastic or rubber and there are a numerous 'systems' available. Although some of these can be reused, the majority cannot, and they must be disposed of and not composted.

There is a range of synthetic materials, including plastics, uPVC, carbon fibre poles, and galvanized or plastic-coated metal. A huge number of brands and designs are available, almost all of which have two things in common: they are durable and, as a consequence of their manufacture, quite costly. Arguably, however, their longevity offsets these initial costs.

STAKING METHODS

Stakes are an ideal way to support individual plants, particularly those with one central stem, such as young trees.

Cages and frames are particularly good for bushier specimens that need all-round support and have the added bonus of cutting out the need for tying. Having said this, the design of some types can make pruning or pinching out side-shoots difficult, resulting in crowded growth inside the cage itself.

Trellises are essentially a lattice-work panel traditionally made of timber, although synthetic substitutes are increasingly common. There are many designs available, some of which can be fixed on to a wall to provide support for climbers, while others can be used as free-standing supports.

BASIC PRUNING

The task of pruning can seem a daunting prospect to some gardeners, but there is, in fact, no great mystery surrounding pruning and a few basic rules are all you need to get started in most cases. At its simplest level, pruning should be regarded as a way of introducing some order to your allotment, giving your plants space to grow and look their best, while also controlling them within a set area. The following section provides some basic advice to enable you to prune with confidence.

Above: *Cuts should be made like this one, just above a bud or a pair of buds, but not so close that you risk damaging the buds.*

WHY IS PRUNING NECESSARY?

Pruning is usually carried out to control the growth of stronger subjects that may otherwise damage those of a weaker habit growing alongside; it also ensures plants do not outgrow their allocated space and cause an obstruction. Pruning is also used especially on fruit trees and bushes to train a plant to a specific shape or form; to maintain or improve flowering; and to improve the shape or 'balance' of an individual shrub or tree. Finally, it is used to remove dead, damaged, diseased or pest-infected growth. This last type of pruning is referred to as hygienic pruning and helps maintain plant health and vigour.

Constant pruning, however, is not always necessary for the good cultivation of plants. Once a plant has become established and the initial framework has been formed, pruning is often reduced to a minimum. The major exceptions to this include plants that are pruned annually in order to improve flowering, fruiting or quality of foliage. Apples, peaches and other fruit trees and bushes are regularly pruned to increase the yield of fruit.

SUCCESSFUL PRUNING

There are arguably two hallmarks of good pruning: a well-planned, careful and methodical approach to the work undertaken; and a good knowledge of the requirements of the plants that are to be pruned. The real results may not always be apparent for months and, in the case of trees, for years.

With secateurs (hand pruners), always try to place the thin blade on the trunk/ branch side of the cut. This will result in a short stub and will also prevent a layer of damaged cambium tissue being left immediately under the line of the cut, which could lead to disease entering the wound.

Cuts should always be made immediately above a bud or a pair of buds and should be done as cleanly as possible. Use well-maintained secateurs that are regularly sharpened. Make sure that you do not position your blade too close to the bud or the tissue connecting the bud to the main plant body could be damaged and this would affect fruiting. As a guide you should cut 1–3mm ($\frac{1}{16}$–$\frac{1}{8}$in) above a bud to ensure it is not damaged during cutting.

Be careful when using a saw close to a trunk or stem to remove heavier thicker branches. The weight of the branch can sometimes cause splitting and tearing to the main stem wood or bark. Injuries such as these often increase the likelihood of disease affecting the plant.

A simple rule of thumb when deciding what to cut is to remember the 'D's. These are: dead, dying, diseased, displaced or deformed branches. All of these must be

Above: *Long-handled pruners are essentially secateurs on long handles, and will cut through thicker wood and more inacessible shoots compared to secateurs.*

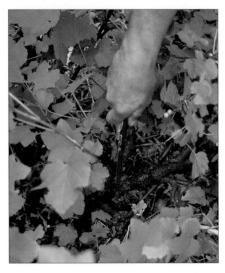

Above: *It is important that you always cut out and remove any dead or diseased wood. For thicker material, you may need to use either secateurs or a saw.*

Above: *Most soft and bush fruit needs to be pruned back once it has been planted. Remove any weak growth completely, then cut back the longer shoots by half.*

PRUNING AUTUMN RASPBERRIES

1 *Autumn raspberries are pruned differently from summer ones. As with all raspberries, during the winter they consist of a mixture of fruited and new canes.*

2 *Regardless of what sort of raspberries they are, the canes should all be cut right down to the ground using secateurs (pruners) and completely removed.*

3 *Once the canes have been cut back, new growth quickly appears. Once the canes are tall enough, they should be tied in to supporting wires.*

removed as the first stage of any pruning work. Then add to this list the 'C's: criss-crossing branches and crowded growth, taking care (arguably the most important 'C'!) all the time to ensure that you avoid removing too much growth. Finally, once you have cleared this material, it is possible to see what further work needs to be done.

Many species have very specific pruning requirements, based largely upon their growth habits, its effect upon cropping and ultimately their tolerance of the treatment. Reading up on the specific requirements of the bush or tree in hand is essential,

therefore, if you are going to get the best results, and well worth the time that it takes. Make a few notes in a notebook to help remind you what these are before you start and always be prepared to take a little time when pruning. Acting too hastily can easily spoil the job. Finally, remember that pruning is best viewed intermittently from a distance. You can only cut a branch once, and if you cut the wrong one, you cannot effectively rejoin it. Always check that you know the full extent of a branch and what effect its removal will have, therefore, prior to making the cut.

Above: *Cutting back new growth on a pear or apple tree at just the right time will reduce its vigour and promote the formation of fruiting spurs.*

Above: *It is often necessary to thin out some of the foliage on a fig bush in order to expose the developing fruit to sufficient sunlight to ripen well.*

PRUNING EQUIPMENT

There is a range of tools that can be used for pruning. It is advisable to use the correct tool for a specific task because it will make the process both easier and more efficient.

Pruning knife Using a pruning knife requires both skill and a sharp blade. A blunt knife can easily damage the plant. Cut away from you and keep hands clear of the direction of the cut.

Secateurs (hand pruners) When small branches are to be removed, it is easiest to use secateurs and remove the branch in one go. Secateurs are the commonest type of pruning tool and are best used on twiggy material up to about the width of a pencil.

Loppers Use these on branches up to 2.5cm (1in) thick. Loppers are useful in situations where secateurs may not easily reach, such as in dense tangled shrubs. Loppers should not be used for very thick branches or they may easily be damaged.

Extension loppers Ideal for cutting out-of-reach branches up to 2.5cm (1in) thick. They are a useful tool but they can be tiring to use and require some practice.

Ratchet and snap cut shears These have three times the power of conventional shears. Used for branches up to 4cm (1½in) in diameter.

Narrow curved Grecian saw Use on branches up to 5cm (2in) in diameter where the branches are very crowded. It cuts on a pulling cut, making its use above shoulder height very easy.

Extension saw This is similar to the Grecian pruning saw, but has an extended handle. It is very useful where larger branches need removing from smaller fruiting trees.

Bow saw Used for cutting larger branches. Available in various sizes. It cuts with a pushing cut, making its use above shoulder height tiring.

HARVESTING AND STORING VEGETABLES

There are few hard and fast rules for harvesting your crops, but you need to plan how you intend to do this. When you go out into your allotment, it is tempting to pick only the good vegetables and leave the rest. You should, however, always pick and compost poor or rotten ones as well as harvesting the best of the crop. Diseased or damaged crops can begin to rot and could infect or damage the remaining harvest.

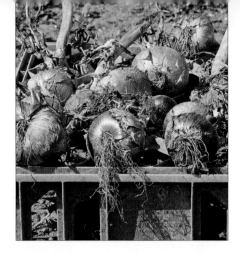

Above: *Onions are an easy crop to store and last for several months provided that you dry and ripen them thoroughly first.*

PLANNING A SUCCESSFUL HARVEST

The key to a successful harvest lies not just in its execution, but in careful advanced planning. If you staggered the sowing or planting of crops, you should ensure that vegetables mature and ripen over a longer period, and this of course has the advantage that you don't need to deal with it all at once. It is also important that you have set plans in motion as to how you intend to store the inevitable excess. Crops stored incorrectly often deteriorate very quickly and can become unusable. Storing fresh produce may also need plenty of space: space that is cool, dry and free from unwelcome visitors such as mice or other pests.

You need to think about storage from the outset then, and have your plans in place ahead of the start of the harvest season for the crops in question. After all, once the harvest begins in earnest, you will find that you have very little time, between gathering the 'fruits' of your labours, preparing it for storage and getting the plot cleared and ready for a new crop.

TIMING YOUR HARVEST

The timing of a harvest will of course vary according to the crop in question. Winter and spring crops such as some brassicas and root crops, can be harvested intermittently throughout the cool season. Other crops only grow in warmer seasons, meaning that the availability of produce is markedly seasonal. In addition to this, some crops are only fit for consumption once they have passed a particular growth stage or fully ripened. For others though, the

Above: *Harvested marrows and pumpkins can be stored in trays that should be kept in a cool, dark place.*

decision as to when they are ready to be picked fresh from the plot is simply a matter of taste. Some people prefer to pick young less developed beans for instance, whereas others prefer their beans more 'mature.' Salad leaves can be taken as baby leaves, as can squashes and courgettes (zucchini); picking what you need at the time that you need it, meaning that you gather a little and often rather than waiting for a heavy harvest later.

WHY STORE CROPS?

Whilst it is always preferable to have fresh rather than stored vegetables, this is only really feasible for most crops during their growing season. As the yearly harvest inevitably peaks during late summer times of glut ensue, and there is only so much that can be traded between you and your neighbours. The problem with a large and sudden amount of fresh produce, however, is that it rarely stays that. If left, it quickly goes past its best and in the worst case scenario, rots or otherwise spoils. In addition, harvest times are often followed by shortages. As the summer glut subsides, the autumn pickings gradually become

CLAMP-STORING POTATOES

1 *Clear a patch of ground approximately 1m² (1 sq yd), and dig a trench, 10cm (4in) deep, filling it with clean, dry straw.*

2 *Pile the potatoes into a pyramid shape on top of the straw, the base of which should be no more than 50cm (18in) across.*

3 *Cover the potato pile with a further layer of straw, piling this to around 15cm (6 in) thick over the whole of the pile.*

4 *Dig a trench to improve drainage, and pile 15cm (6in) of soil over the clamp, leaving a straw-filled hole in the middle.*

LIFTING POTATOES

1 *Unless you need new-potatoes, wait until the top growth withers as they continue to grow under the ground until then.*

2 *Use a fork to lift the potatoes, shaking free any soil that is attached to them; leave them to dry on the surface for a couple of hours.*

3 *Once they have dried, brush off any remaining soil and carefully inspect them; avoid storing damaged or blemished ones.*

more meagre and the range of winter produce, whilst each may be individually satisfying, is rather limited to a few of the hardiest crops. Ironically the time between early to late spring often marks what is known as the 'hungry gap', a period between the last of the winter crops and start of the early crops where fresh produce can be scarce. Storing produce helps alleviate this, and means that you get the best all-year-round value possible from your plot.

HOW TO STORE VEGETABLES

When it comes to storing crops, there are several options. Root vegetables and some brassicas can be left in the ground in all but the coldest winters, lifting them as and when they are needed. Some, such as parsnips, actually develop a better taste after they have been subjected to frost and cabbages become all the sweeter in the cooler months. In very cold areas, or if heavy frost threatens, root crops can be lifted and stored in a cool dark place. Brush away as much soil as possible (do not wash them) before laying them on around 1cm (½in) of sand or a layer of newspaper in the bottom of a wooden box, making sure they don't touch each other. Cover the crop with a mixture of sand and a sterile organic substance such as coir, untreated sawdust, fine leaf-mould, fine bark or sterilized soil before adding another layer of roots. Repeat this layering until the box is full to the top and all are covered. Repeat with another box if necessary. Place in a frost-free environment such as a shed or cellar.

Other vegetables can be stored on shelves or in boxes, ensuring that they do not touch each other. Onions and garlic may be kept in open sacks or in strings. Cabbages can be kept in nets, hung in a cool dark place until needed for up to 2–3 months. Other brassicas, such as sprouts, are best kept outside, harvesting them as needed.

FREEZING AND PRESERVING

Vegetables usually need some preparation prior to being frozen to make the process more successful. This is usually done by blanching them for a couple of minutes in order to destroy enzymes that would otherwise cause the vegetables to deteriorate quickly. Blanching also helps to keep the colour, texture and flavour and to retain vitamin C content. The vegetables are mostly prepared as you would normally before being plunged into the boiling water for about 2–3 minutes. They are then removed, drained immediately and plunged into a bowl of iced water to cool them as quickly as possible. Once cooled, they are drained once again, patted-dry on kitchen paper, packed and frozen in single-portion bags. The other option is to cook the vegetables as part of a recipe, then freeze them.

Lastly, a good way to preserve fresh vegetables is to pickle them or make other forms of preserve such as chutneys. As with so many things, the way you choose to store your produce will largely be a matter of taste. The best option is often to try as many methods as you can to maintain the maximum variety through the winter.

HARVESTING AND STORING HERBS

Many commonly used culinary herbs such as basil, coriander (cilantro), chives and parsley can be grown successfully outdoors during the summer months. If you are not able to spare growing room on allotment vegetable beds, they are easily grown in pots and can be sited around sheds or seating areas. Herbs are very easily harvested and most of the storage techniques are simple and straightforward.

Above: *Aromatic herbs such as rosemary (*Rosmarinus officinalis*) can be used to flavour bottles of vinegar or olive oil.*

HOW TO HARVEST HERBS

Various parts of herbs, including the leaves, flowers, fruits and seeds, are gathered at different times, depending upon the plant and the part that provides the desirable properties. Annual leafy herbs such as basil (*Ocimum basilicum*) and parsley (*Petroselinum crispum*) should be carefully picked, never taking more than about 10 per cent of the growth in a single picking.

The same is true of perennials such as sage (*Salvia officinalis*), thyme (*Thymus vulgaris*) and rosemary (*Rosmarinus officinalis*) because severe pruning or over-stripping of the leaves will weaken the plant. It is important that you do not remove more than one-third of the growth at any one time. If you harvest carefully, you will get a more vigorous leaf growth that will result in healthier plants.

As a general rule, pick herbs just before the plant is about to flower, which is when they have the strongest flavour. Pick the leaves when they are fresh and at their sweetest, selecting blemish-free, upper leaves. Collect the leaves in early morning or late evening, provided they are dry, rather than in bright afternoon sun when the plant's sap is rising. This is when the aroma of herbs is at its strongest and is easily lost if picked during this time of day. Flowers such as borage (*Borago officinalis*) and lavender (*Lavandula angustifolia*), however, are best picked just before they reach full bloom and once they begin to open in the heat of the day.

Rhizomes, such as ginger and turmeric, are collected in autumn, just as the leaves begin to change colour and the maximum amount of nutrition has been stored. Use a fork to gently free the roots from the soil and always avoid 'hand-pulling' them. Choose only the best ones and use a vegetable brush to gently loosen any dirt. If you do need to wash them, do so quickly in cold water and avoid soaking them, as this can result in lost flavour.

Harvesting seeds tends to vary from plant to plant. Some seeds, like those of borage, simply fall to the ground as soon as they are ripe. Thyme seeds are very small and hard to see. Parsley and coriander seeds shake off very easily, and frequently the plants will have sown next year's crop for you before you realize they have gone to seed. One method of harvesting any seed that is difficult to collect is to tie a small paper bag over the flower head when the seeds start to form, ensuring that you can collect the seed without losing any. It would be advisable to use this method for collecting from plants with small seed as they can drop off when ripe or sometimes spring from the plant.

Above: *The best time to harvest herbs is usually just before they flower. This is when they have their strongest flavour.*

Above: *Herbs can be dried for later use by hanging them in bunches in a dry place out of direct sunlight.*

DRYING HERBS AND FLOWERS

Store herbs in a cool, dry place with minimum exposure to air and sunlight. One of the most popular methods of preserving them for use during the winter months is drying. This method can actually improve the flavour of some herbs, particularly the leaves of bay trees (*Laurus nobilis*). Herbs may be dried in bundles secured with a rubber band or string and hung upside down from a rack in a dry location such as an airing cupboard or shed.

When drying the herbs, the temperature of the area should not exceed 30°C (86°F) because the plants' essential oils will evaporate at or above this temperature. Do not dry your herbs in the kitchen where they will be spoiled by the humidity caused by cooking.

Fresh herbs can also be placed in brown paper bags. Remember to label the bags because it will be hard to distinguish between the herbs once they have dried. Store in a dry, dark, cool place until the herbs inside are dry, shaking the bags occasionally so that the plants dry evenly. Remove any stems and store the dried herbs in airtight jars. Keep the jars away from light to protect the colour and flavour of the herbs. Roots are best chopped into small pieces and dried in an oven. In general, you can expect those that you have grown and dried yourself to last at least two years.

STORING HERBS

Herbs can also be preserved in other ways, so that you can use them in cooking throughout the year.

Herb salts In a cool oven, spread a layer of ground salt on a sheet of baking parchment. Sprinkle the chopped fresh herbs on top of the salt and bake for 10–20 minutes. When the herbs are dry, let them cool and place in a jar. Chives, oregano, thyme, lemon balm, lemon thyme, parsley, rosemary and basil can all be treated this way.

Puréeing This method involves mixing approximately 60ml (4tbsp) of olive oil with 2 litres (8 cups) fresh basil leaves which have been washed and dried. These are blended in a processor until puréed before being transferred to a jar. Stir each time you use it and top with a thin layer of oil afterwards. The purée should keep for up to one year in a refrigerator.

Above: *After herbs have been hung up to dry, separate the seeds from the dry flower heads before storing in tightly sealed jars.*

Freezing herbs Herbs such as dill, fennel, basil and parsley freeze well. The herbs should be cleaned and put into separate, labelled freezer bags. Alternatively, chop the leaves and freeze them with a little water in ice-cube trays. Chop the herbs finely, filling each cube, half with herbs and half with water, before freezing. Transfer the frozen cubes to plastic bags and label. Frozen herbs are best used within six months.

HERBAL INFUSIONS

You can also make a hot infusion of leafy herbs by placing the herb and any fine-quality olive oil in a glass bowl. This is then placed over a pan of gently simmering water and heated gently for about three hours, ensuring that the water in the pan does not dry out. The strained oil, once it has cooled, should be stored in airtight bottles or jars.

A cool infusion of flowery herbs involves using fresh herbs such as chamomile which are ground with a pestle and mortar and packed into a large jar and covered with oil. The sealed jar is then left in a warm, sunny place for two to three weeks and shaken occasionally. It is then strained and placed into airtight jars or bottles where it can be stored for up to a year.

A simple way of creating aromatic olive oil is to simply add a large sprig of your chosen herbs – rosemary and mint are good choices – to a bottle of olive oil. Store the bottle in a cool dark place for about ten days before using.

You can also make you own herbal vinegars by adding fresh herbs such as tarragon or rosemary or cloves of garlic, slices of ginger, chillies or peppercorns and all-spice powder to white vinegar. Crush about a quarter litre volume (1 cup) of loosely packed fresh herbs for each litre of vinegar. If you are using dried herbs, use half the amount of herb stated above. It is important that you use only commercially prepared vinegars, as home-made vinegar may not have a low enough pH to prevent bacterial growth. Place the vinegar in a pot on the stove and heat, but do not boil. Place the herbs in a clean, sterilized jar and slightly crush them. Pour the vinegar over the herbs and cover the jar tightly. Let the herb-vinegar mixture steep in a dark place at room temperature, shaking the jar every couple of days. After a week, strain the vinegar and place in bottles and store for up to six weeks.

DRYING AND FREEZING HERBS

1 *Pick seed just as it is ripening. Place the seeds on a tray or in a paper or muslin (cheesecloth) bag. Leave in a cool, dark place for a few days until the seed is dry.*

2 *Herb seeds that have been dried can be stored in old glass jars with an airtight lid. Store the jars in a cool, dry, dark place and label them for future reference.*

3 *Herbs can be frozen in ice-cube trays. Fill the trays with water after you have added the herbs to make ready-to-use cubes. Herbs can also be packed into freezer bags.*

HARVESTING AND STORING FRUIT

When harvesting your fruits, you will find that there is only so much you can eat fresh or give away. There is always surplus fruit left over and you are faced with the question of what to do with it. Leaving some on the plant to help feed the wildlife at your allotment is a good idea, but storing the rest of the excess fruit using a variety of methods will ensure that you can eat your home-grown produce over a longer period of time.

Above: *Damaged fruits are no good for storing but if left on the plant they will feed a whole host of visiting wildlife.*

HOW TO HARVEST FRUIT

The key to successfully storing fruit begins well before harvesting commences. Your first objective should be to grow fruit that is as healthy as possible because it will be the best for storage. Harvesting immature crops or attempting to save those that are in poor condition – due perhaps to a lack of water or nutrients or to pest and disease damage – can lead to many storage losses.

There are several ways that fruit can be stored and the condition of the picked crop will usually be the deciding factor as to which of these you should use. Top fruit such as apples and pears can often be stored fresh through most of the winter, whereas stone fruits and berries, such as peaches, strawberries and raspberries, must be quickly consumed, turned into a preserve or frozen.

Careful handling, both during and following harvesting, is essential because, from the moment they are harvested (and in many cases well before), crops have no means of repairing any physical damage

that they may suffer. Even firm, strong-looking fruit such as apples can easily be bruised, although the damage may well not show up immediately.

As well as good handling, a careful selection of the fruits during harvesting is essential for successful storage. You should inspect the picked fruits and select only those of the best quality for fresh storage. Reject any that have a broken skin or show any sign of pest or disease damage. Do not throw them on the compost heap yet, however, because damaged fruit may well be useful for making preserves such as jellies and jams, or for freezing.

It is also a good idea to leave a small percentage of mature fruit on the plants when you are harvesting to help feed the surrounding bird and insect population.

STORING FRUIT

In general, the storage area for fruit must be frost-free, safe from pests, rainproof and ideally kept at a constant temperature. The long-term storage of any fruit calls for

---

STORING FRUIT

To store surplus fruit and avoid the risk of rotting, make sure that you use the appropriate method.

Apples, pears and quinces Store in a cool place for up to 12 months, depending on the variety.
All other fruit Eat immediately or freeze. Alternatively, preserve fruit by bottling or making into jam. Fruit can be kept for up to 12 months, depending on the method of preservation that has been used.

Below left: *Pick soft fruits such as strawberries, raspberries and gooseberries carefully to avoid bruising the fruit.*

Below: *Pears can last for up to 12 months, depending upon the variety. Lay them in a recycled box, ensuring that the fruits do not touch and air can circulate around the fruit.*

Above: *Fruit trays, recycled from supermarkets, make ideal storage boxes for surplus fruit. The trays should be kept over winter in a cool, dry place such as a garage or shed.*

Above: *Soft fruit is best placed in small individual containers as it is picked to prevent it being squashed and spoiling. Store in a refrigerator or other cool place.*

cool conditions with adequate ventilation. If you have space, consider having a separate refrigerator for fruit storage, or choose an area with a low temperature that does not go below freezing. A shed or garage can be ideal, in many cases, but even these spaces may need extra insulation if winter weather conditions become especially severe. Some houses have a basement, cellar or unheated room that may be ideally suited for the task. Attics, however, are not recommended for fruit storage because of their wide temperature fluctuations and variable humidity.

It is worthwhile trying out a variety of different storage methods. This can be done by splitting the crop up and then trying out different locations in your home. You will soon find which are the best places to store fruit, and what areas are best for storing a particular kind of fruit.

Ensure that you check the stored fruit regularly, at least weekly, removing any that show signs of decay. Remember the old adage that 'one bad apple spoils the whole barrel'? This can be true for your crop too unless you prevent rots from spreading. The unblemished parts can often still be used for eating or cooking. If lots of fruits begin to rot simultaneously, it could be that the storage conditions are not suitable, the crop has reached its maximum 'shelf-life' or the fruit was not of sufficiently good quality to start with.

FREEZING AND PRESERVING

Storing fruit in the freezer is an excellent way of storing all the surplus crop that has been produced in your plot. Unfortunately, fruit tends to lose its firmness once it has been frozen, although the taste will remain more or less the same. Raspberries, for example, are best used for making pies or flans after they have been frozen and will be of very poor quality if they are eaten raw. Most fruits can be frozen after they have been stewed or puréed; this is true of fruits such as apples and plums.

Fruits such as strawberries and blackcurrants that do not easily submit to long-term storage are excellent candidates for jam-(jelly-) making. This is surprisingly simple to do and there are many recipes available in cookbooks and on the Internet.

Above: *Bottling fruit in alcohol is an ideal way to preserve soft fruits such as peaches, nectarines and apricots.*

Above: *One of the simplest ways of preserving fruit is to freeze it, although once frozen, most fruits are only good for cooking.*

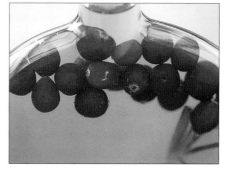

Above: *Adding a favourite fruit such as these cranberries to good wine vinegar can produce interesting flavours.*

PLANT HEALTH

The main concern for allotment-growers is that their plants will be attacked by pests and diseases. There is an array of techniques to control these undesirables, although the successful gardener must first learn to recognize signs of distress. However, you are unlikely to experience more than a handful of the problems described, all of which are relatively easy to solve. Pests, for example, are eaten by creatures known as beneficials and so the ecology of the allotment, once stabilized, will be enough to keep most problems at bay. There is always a technique to control more persistent problems and so ensure the health of your plants.

Left: Companion plants such as these French marigolds can provide welcome colour in the allotment vegetable plot.

Above: *Ladybirds provide a natural form of pest control in allotments because when their eggs hatch, the larvae eat aphids.*

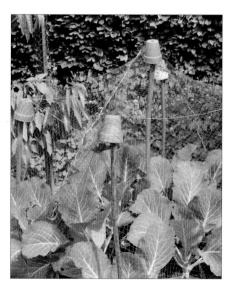

Above: *Netting crops, such as brassicas, can help protect them from attack by flying pests, which cannot permeate the nets.*

Above: *Different types of netting provide a barrier between vegetables, such as carrots, and specific pests, such as carrot fly.*

WHY PLANTS GET SICK

Plants are prone to numerous ailments, some of which can pose a serious threat to their survival. Pests and diseases are only one of the potential pitfalls that you will meet during a normal growing season though. A basic knowledge of the other main factors that can affect plant health are all you will need to help your allotment to flourish. While the sight of your plants suffering can be alarming, there are, in general, only a few potential health threats that you are likely to encounter.

Above: *Temporary netting is a very good way of protecting vulnerable crops from pests and diseases and preventing potential problems.*

FROST

This can cause serious problems and is actually more critical than average minimum temperatures. Most harmful are unexpected frosts that can cause severe damage even to hardy subjects, especially when they may have produced 'soft' new growth.

While warm air rises, cold air will settle and collect in hollows and depressions. Cold air is laden with water vapour and is therefore heavier. Any valley or low-lying area is, therefore, a potential frost pocket. Cold air will accumulate in a depression and then back up the sloping sides as the build-up increases. Any barrier, such as a hedge or a wall, will obstruct the passage of the cold air and a frost pocket will form. Any plants growing in the vicinity will be exposed to the frost and may be damaged by it.

When the soil is frozen, water is no longer available to the plant and shallow-rooted plants are not able to access any water to replace that which they are losing through transpiration. The plant will dehydrate and the foliage will brown and shrivel. Ground frosts may also cause the soil to 'heave' and plants will be lifted out of the ground.

Alternate freezing and thawing is often more damaging to the plant than the initial frost itself, especially for tender or half-hardy subjects. A particularly severe frost can split the bark on woody subjects and may also distort leaves.

The damage caused by frost is directly related to its duration. A temperature of -4°C (25°F) for one hour may cause little or no damage, while the same temperature for four hours may be disastrous.

WATERLOGGING AND DROUGHT

The build-up of water in the soil, particularly where this occurs over a prolonged period of time, can be highly detrimental to the health of your plants. This is of greatest concern with plants that are not adapted to such waterlogged conditions. As a result, the roots of the plants will suffer and probably die from asphyxiation.

Water shortage or drought only tends to occur during the summer months when temperatures and light intensity are at their peak. The most obvious sign of the effects of water shortage on a plant is when it wilts and loses its turgidity. Water shortage also causes plant functions to slow down dramatically and prolonged drought can result in permanent cell damage.

WIND

The effects of wind damage to plants, especially woody trees and shrubs, are sometimes only too obvious. Not only can they knock over and break plants, but wind-rock can cause a plant to move about so that it becomes loose in the soil or it can create a hole around the point at which the plant enters the soil. This fills with stagnant water and the plant can rot. A dry or hot wind can remove moisture from leaves, making them wilt. Cold winds create wind-burn, which shrivels leaves.

It is not all bad news, however, as wind can be tamed to some extent by creating windbreaks. The best defence is a hedge, which filters the wind without creating turbulence, but this may not be a viable option on an allotment plot. Plastic netting that is designed to be used as a windbreak is a more practical solution on many sites. While it is not pretty to look at, it is very functional. Make sure the poles supporting it are anchored securely because the netting will act as a sail and exert enormous pressure on the supports. A double row of netting or hedges set a few yards apart is the very best option if possible, as this will reduce any turbulence to an absolute minimum and give greatest protection.

Left: *Frost and snow can have a negative impact on crops such as these leeks, especially if they alternately freeze and thaw.*

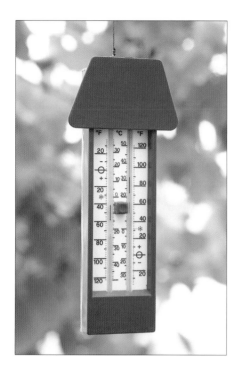

Above: *A maximum/minimum thermometer is ideal for keeping track of the temperature in the greenhouse and outdoors.*

Above: *If a frost pocket is caused by a thick hedge, cut a hole in the base so that air can pass through and continue moving.*

LIGHT IMBALANCES

A plant's growth is always directed towards the available light. Plants growing in shade often become drawn and etiolated. Conversely, strong sunlight damages plants by scorching the foliage. To prevent such problems it is best to select plants that will grow well in the prevailing site conditions.

NUTRIENT IMBALANCES

Plants exhibit varying symptoms that point to a nutrient imbalance depending, in general, upon the severity of the problem. Symptoms of deficiency may include stunted growth, discoloured leaves (including mottling and interveinal coloration), the premature death of leaves and parts of the plant, twisted and distorted growth and poor root growth and development.

The symptoms are usually noticed first on the shoot tips, although problems may appear on any part of the plant and in different stages of growth. Determining a cause may involve an analysis of the soil.

Any nutrient can be toxic to the plant if it is present in sufficiently high amounts or is out of balance with other elements in the growing medium.

Right: *It is important to provide plants such as these raspberries with the correct light and temperature conditions so that they flourish.*

POLLUTION

Specific symptoms of pollution may include leaves turning brown at the tips and margins, leaf discoloration or premature leaf fall. Growth may also be stunted. Soil pollutant damage can be very severe and rapid in its effects on a plant and its growth. Common problems that you may encounter include extreme soil acidity or alkalinity, chemical toxicity, salt toxicity or pesticide residues. Of these, only soil acidity is relatively easy to cure. If serious pollution is suspected, then this requires specialist help. Such situations, however, are thankfully rare.

PESTS AND DISEASES

It is important to bear in mind that a certain level of pest and disease invasion is normal even on healthy crops. However, it is also true to say that healthy vigorous plants are more resistant to serious attack than plants that are growing under stress. The best form of pest and disease control is obviously prevention. You will need to be able to find and recognize a range of pests and diseases in order to prevent outbreaks of them in your allotment and, if necessary, take prompt action. This is examined in greater detail later in this chapter.

Below: *This healthy row of carrots on an allotment is a tribute to good plant care and the result of much hard work.*

PREVENTING PROBLEMS

Effective allotment gardening is about working with nature to create an environment in which plants can grow and be productive and withstand attack from pests and diseases. If plants become infested, they may fail to give a good display and crop yields can suffer. Prevention is better than cure, and a keen eye and regular checks will help you to anticipate and prevent the worst of any potential problems.

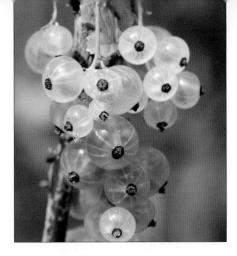

Above: *A healthy crop, such as these ripe white currants, is more likely if you position the plants in an appropriate site.*

GOOD CULTURAL PRACTICE AND HYGIENE

Many pests and diseases can survive without a susceptible host even under the most unfavourable conditions. Myriad plant diseases survive from one growing season to the next on plant debris, in the soil, on seeds or on alternate hosts (some pests and diseases affect different plant species at different times of the year e.g. peach-potato aphid). This means it is vital to remove and properly dispose of any infected plant materials. It is also important for the allotment-holder to be aware of the diseases that can threaten an individual crop and recognize the conditions in which these potential threats to plant health can thrive.

GROW DISEASE-RESISTANT CULTIVARS

Plant varieties and cultivars were mostly chosen for other reasons than their disease-resistant qualities. Often they become so commonly grown that their diseases become widespread. Many plants have disease-resistant strains or cultivars, but this does not necessarily guarantee that they will be immune to a disease. However, they will be better able to resist the worst of its ravages.

AVOID PLANT STRESS

A plant that is stressed – by drought or an unfavourable temperature, for example – will be predisposed to pest or disease attack. Plants that are not subjected to higher levels of stress than they can cope with will remain healthy and better able to deal with potential attackers.

Stressed plants often show signs of physical disorders (e.g. being tall, drawn and pale due to lack of light). These can be due to the weather, the plant being wrongly sited, nutrient imbalance or the presence of a toxic substance in the air or soil. Physically stressed plants may become sicker than if a pest- or disease-causing organism actually had invaded them. Stress can kill a plant if the problem is not quickly remedied.

RIGHT PLANT, RIGHT PLACE

Plants all have their preferred locations and the occurrence or lack of a particular environmental factor or factors will ultimately determine whether a plant will prosper in the position in which it has been planted. Ferns, for example, need a cool moist site. Placing one in a hot sunny site will lead to its death as it struggles to keep its moisture. Plants that become stressed will neither grow as well, nor be as disease-resistant, as they would otherwise. Choosing an appropriate site in the first place will at least help to ensure the initial health of your plants and will render them more able to resist other potential threats to their health.

RECOGNIZING THE PROBLEM

Allotment-holders who understand pest life-cycles and behaviour are better able to determine when control will be most effective. Insects living in your plot are all part of nature's complex ecosystems and food chains. Less than one per cent of species that you are likely to encounter are considered pests. Since few insects are actually harmful, gardeners must learn which are pests, which are beneficials, and which ones will have no effect on the allotment whatsoever.

Despite the fact that they are not always popular, insects play an important role in our sites. Beneficial insects, such as bees, are necessary in the allotment to pollinate fruit and some vegetable crops. Others,

Far left: *The regular washing down of the glass panes in a greenhouse can reduce the build-up of disease-causing organisms.*

Left: *Regular deadheading of old or damaged blooms will help to reduce the spread of some fungal diseases.*

Above: *Using mesh to prevent the adult carrot fly reaching a carrot crop is an excellent preventative measure.*

Above: *Sturdy wire mesh can help keep out unwanted visitors, such as rabbits and rodents, while allowing light, air and water in.*

Above: *Fine netting is useful for protecting crops from smaller, often flying pests, such as cabbage whites.*

such as springtails, also help to break down dead plant tissue, while wasps and ground beetles capture and eat other pest insects and are called predators. Wasps and midges have larvae that attack pests by living inside their bodies and are called parasitoids. Allotment-holders must learn to cherish this 'willing army' of helpers in their plots.

PEST AND DISEASE CYCLES

Often gardeners believe that their plants have been attacked overnight. This may be true in the case of damping-off disease or with larger pests such as rabbits. More often, however, much has occurred before the symptoms are actually visible.

The pathogen (the pest- or disease-causing organism) must be introduced (inoculated) to the host plant. Most pathogens either move by themselves (as with most pests) or must be carried to the host plant (as with the vast majority of diseases). Rain, wind, insects, birds and people usually spread plant diseases.

Splashing rain carries spores of apple scab fungus from infected apple leaves to uninfected leaves. Wind blows fungal spores from plant to plant, while aphids and whiteflies transmit many common plant diseases. Believe it or not, smokers can transmit tobacco mosaic virus from a cigarette to tomato plants.

Once the pathogen has been transferred to the host plant, it begins to multiply, change or grow into a form that can then enter the host. In many fungal diseases, the pathogen arrives on the plant as a spore, which must germinate before it can begin to grow and invade the plant. Once

the fungal spore germinates, it sends out thread-like tubes called hyphae. These penetrate the plant through wounds or natural pores in the outer skin of leaves, stems and roots.

The roots of plants that have been damaged during transplanting are a common entry point for root-rotting fungi. A single aphid that lands on a plant can give birth to a clone every 12 hours and can eventually form a small thriving colony within a few days, leaving the allotment-holder with the impression that it suddenly appeared out of nowhere.

Once established, pests or diseases can grow, spread or increase in number very rapidly and begin damaging plant tissue. As they consume nutrients or plant tissue, evidence of the damage to the plant begins to appear. Symptoms may be seen on any plant parts and include mottling, dwarfing, distortion, discoloration, wilting, shrivelling or holes and notching in the margins of leaves. The first signs of pest infestation may not appear, however, until well after the parent insect has laid its eggs on the plant and disappeared.

Seeds or cuttings from infected plants will also transmit disease. Certified organic seed guarantees that at the time of sale the seeds are free of all diseases. Always try to obtain disease-free stock as this should ensure that the plant is not infected and will not introduce disease into your plot. This is particularly important with crops such as raspberries and other small fruits.

Pest insects and mites may carry diseases that infect plants. Many gardeners use the term 'pest management' rather than pest control or pest eradication. It is

impossible to eradicate pests from your allotment completely. The best option is to try to keep pest numbers low in order to minimize the damage that they can cause in your plot.

ADOPT AN INTEGRATED STRATEGY

Allotment-holders should learn how to use a range of pest management techniques, such as introducing beneficial predators into their plots (often referred to as biological controls), making sites less attractive to harmful pests, and encouraging conditions in the plot that favour beneficial predators of all types (cultural controls).

Below: *Companion planting is an environmentally friendly way of deterring pests, and also looks good in your allotment.*

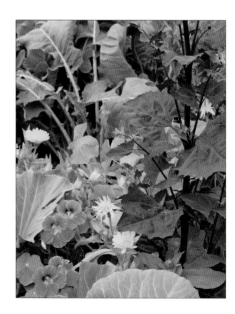

TREATING PROBLEMS

It is essential that you act quickly to safeguard crops as soon as they start to show signs of stress. Knowing what is causing the problem is an important first step, although choosing the most effective treatment is vital if you intend to limit the damage and prevent further losses. A range of strategies is available to the allotment-holder and each of these has its own advantages and disadvantages, meaning that the best approach usually involves a combination of treatments.

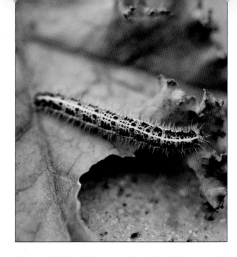

Above: *Caterpillars can do a lot of damage in a short amount of time , so it is important to be vigilant and keep an eye on your crops.*

CHEMICAL PESTICIDES

The word 'pesticide' is a broad term, covering a range of products that are used only to control pests and disease-causing agents such as fungi, as well as weed killers, repellents and other chemical agents. Although people usually think of pesticides as purely synthetic (man-made) chemicals, they actually include a huge range of products, some of which are considered to be entirely 'natural' (despite their existence being the result of human endeavour). Examples of these include pyrethrins (a chemical extracted from *Chrysanthemum cinerariaefolium* and *C. coccineum*), plant oils (such as neem, garlic and citronella) or inorganic compounds such as sulphur or copper salts. Yet more are merely slightly altered versions of otherwise 'natural' chemicals.

RISKS OF USING PESTICIDES

While many allotment-holders are quite happy to use pesticides that are of a natural origin, the use of any synthetic chemical as a pesticide is often something they would rather avoid. At first, this would seem to be rather unsurprising, given that concerns over food safety often act as a prime motivation for growing your own food. Although the use of synthetic pesticides does indeed have to be considered with great caution, both for environmental reasons and your own personal health, the simple fact of the matter is that many synthetic products are actually less toxic than their 'natural' (organic) counterparts. It is also worth remembering that just because a poison is derived from a 'natural' source, does not mean that it somehow becomes 'healthier' or less dangerous than synthesized versions.

Left: *Slug gel and other pesticides will protect young plants, but you should be aware that they may have an impact further up the food chain.*

Right: *Hand-removal of pests such as snails is more environmentally friendly than using pesticides. Relocate them to a wild area.*

Before you decide to use any pesticide then, natural or synthetic, you should weigh up the true dangers of using them. Any pesticide is a form of poison or at the very least an irritant. Even if they are specifically targeted, they represent some degree of hazard, albeit slight in many cases. Put simply, hazard is the potential of a substance to cause harm to people. This cannot be

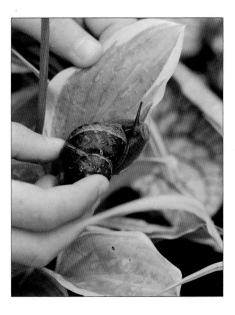

SPRAYERS

Before choosing a garden sprayer, you should consider the use it will get. There are many different types of sprayer on the market, with plenty of shapes and sizes to choose from. Dimensions vary from small hand-held misters to large-capacity backpack or trailer types, so finding a model to suit your needs shouldn't be hard.

Sprayers have many uses beyond simply applying synthetic pesticides. They can be used for applying foliar feeds, misting plants to aid fruit set, and even for applying micro-biological control agents.

Ideally, then, you will need at least two sprayers: one for herbicide and one for pesticide, and if you intend to apply biological agents, then this will need a third separate one. This is because residues from any pesticide can be very difficult to remove completely from inside a sprayer tank and, if used to spray crops afterward, could potentially harm them.

Make sure you label each sprayer according to its use.

changed and a hazardous substance should always be treated with caution. Risk, on the other hand, is the likelihood of a person being harmed by exposure to a hazardous substance. The more hazardous a substance therefore, the greater the risk involved with its use, particularly if it is misused or used in an unsafe manner. Remember also that neither hazard nor risk is the same thing as toxicity. The toxicity of a chemical, whether high or low, cannot be changed by the person applying it.

Having said this, synthetic pesticides do pose significant problems, other than those directly associated with their relative hazard or toxicity. Chief among these are the fact that many pests and diseases have built up tolerances to them, rendering their use ineffective in many cases. In addition to this, the increasing legislative burden upon the manufacturers of pesticides has made their creation and supply less economic and many have been withdrawn from the market as a result.

BIOLOGICAL CONTROL

A living organism that is used to control another specifically targeted pest or disease is called a biological control. This chosen organism might be a predator, parasite or disease and, in effect, it is a way of manipulating nature. In essence it is almost like a 'living pesticide' and, like its namesake, it is not without its problems.

Using a biological control involves careful planning, often taking a good deal of time, patience and sometimes considerable personal research if it is to be effective. The results are not as dramatic or quick as those produced by pesticides, meaning that they are sometimes ineffective in controlling sudden outbreaks. They are also less effective in outdoor settings than the controlled setting of a greenhouse and, in some cases, biological agents (harlequin ladybirds, for example) are inclined to become invasive, even out-competing the native species in areas where they are intentionally or even accidentally released.

PHYSICAL CONTROL

The term 'physical control' often simply means removing the problem entirely or preventing it from reaching the crop in the first place. It is therefore essentially a cultural control and mostly refers to mechanical or hand controls. It often proves most useful in respect of weed control, although cultivation, pruning, burning, and simple removal by hand all have their place in pest control as well. Some insects, for example, may also be destroyed by cultivation, as this can destroy their eggs, overwintering larvae or adults.

Below: *Insecticidal soaps affect only those pests with which they come in contact, meaning they can be targeted at specific areas.*

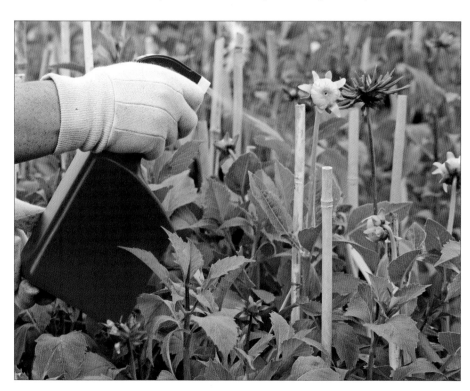

PESTICIDE SAFETY
Essentially pesticides work in one of three ways:
- Those that kill on **contact**.
- Those that work their way inside the plant – either to kill a weed or provide an internal protection against pests or diseases – called **systemic** or **translocated** pesticides.
- Those that leave a long-lasting barrier on the leaves or in the soil – known as **residual** or **protectant** pesticides.

The mode of action is no guarantee of safety, although protectant and residual types tend to be the least preferable due to their longevity in the environment.

If you do choose to use a pesticide, the following steps should be considered:
- Is there a safer alternative?
- Work out how much pesticide you will need; buying the right amount prevents your having to store leftover product.
- Read the manufacturer's instructions very carefully and make sure you understand how to mix and use the product safely and effectively.
- Ensure you know what safety clothing you will need, and be sure to use it.
- Make sure you know what type of application equipment is needed for the job, and use it properly and accurately.
- Mix just enough of the product to complete the job.
- Once you have finished, clean, store, and maintain the application equipment according to the manufacturer's instructions, ensuring that all chemicals are stored safely and locked away where children and animals can't access them.

Reducing stress factors, such as drought or cold exposure, can also make your crops more resistant to attack from pests or diseases, and practices such as crop rotation or soil sterilization as well as the use of traps and barriers are also essentially physical controls. While physical control does have an important place then, it is essentially preventative, relying upon considered plant selection and correct cultural care in order to avoid problems, and is only rarely a treatment in its own right.

PLANT PESTS

Pests can be described as those creatures that harm your plants and, if left unchecked, they can quickly cause a great deal of damage. There is a huge army of these pests, but most allotment-holders are unlikely to encounter the vast majority of them. A basic knowledge of the commonest types that occur in allotment sites is all that you should need to be familiar with in order to protect your plants and guarantee their health and successful growth.

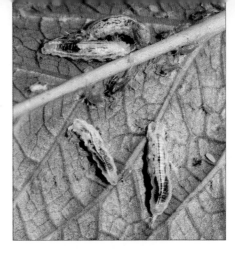

Above: *Pests may well be present before symptoms appear. Close examination may reveal them before the plants start to suffer.*

HOW CAN YOU TELL IF A PEST IS A PROBLEM OR NOT?

Deciding whether a pest is a problem or not is very much a matter of opinion. Commercial growers assess the importance of a pest in terms of their financial losses. Allotment gardeners, however, tend to grow fewer plants or crops and mainly grow these for the pleasure of eating home-grown produce. The final decision as to the importance of a pest will rely upon the circumstances and experience of individual gardeners. All gardeners must be willing to accept a certain number of pests in their plot as these form part of the intricate food webs that result in natural control. If there are no pests, then the animals that eat them will disappear and open the door to future, potentially serious, pest outbreaks.

RECOGNIZING PESTS

It is important that you are able to accurately identify a pest that has been attacking your plants so that you can take the appropriate action. Just because an insect is seen walking on an affected plant does not mean that it is the one causing the damage. The only real way to control pests involves getting to know them.

Many pests produce characteristic symptoms that make it possible to diagnose the cause with relative certainty. Some have a wide range of host plants, and symptoms may not always be as conspicuous on all affected plants. Close examination – perhaps with a hand lens – may be necessary for the final diagnosis. With careful observation and experience, it is possible to keep one step ahead of the pests in your site.

CONTROL OPTIONS

It is important to control pests before they become a problem. A single black bean aphid (*Aphis fabae*) that lands on a broad (fava) bean at the start of the summer could theoretically give rise to 2,000,000,000,000,000 aphids by the start of the autumn. This would be about a million tons of aphids. Quantities such as those cannot occur as the food supply would run out and a host of predators would move in before this can happen, but it does go to show that early control is essential as, in just a few days, a small number of pests can cause considerable damage to your plants, and this may have irreparable consequences for your harvest.

Effective allotment-holders must employ a full range of control measures to ensure their plants survive this seasonal invasion, including cultural practices (crop rotation, good hygiene and encouraging biodiversity in the surrounding area), physical controls (hand picking, traps, repellents and barriers) and biological control (using other animals that naturally eat pests). These are covered more extensively later in this section but for now it is important to stress that pests can only really be controlled in a responsible and sustained manner by an integrated strategy that uses a variety of techniques.

CAN PESTS BE TOLERATED?

It is worth pointing out that we tend to be unduly concerned with pests damaging our plants. Supermarkets have conditioned us to expect blemish-free produce. We need to judge the overall health of a plant rather than react when we see a pest. If there were no pests in the allotment, then there would be no predators. Step back and look at the whole picture and remember that everything, even pests, has its place in nature. They all add to the interest and diversity that is the most unique quality of a green space.

Above: *Birds can be serious pests in the allotment. Here, large bites have been taken out of a brassica.*

Above: *Rabbits can devastate a plot overnight, leaving nothing but chewed-off stumps as a result of their visit.*

Above: *Although fascinating to watch, squirrels are closely related to rats, and are a pest on the allotment.*

COMMON PESTS

There is a seemingly endless array of creatures that are waiting to devour and attack your allotment plants. The most common pests are almost worldwide in their distribution, but they can be controlled relatively easily.

It can be discouraging to see how many potential pests may attack your plot, but it is important to bear in mind that you will only encounter a handful of these in your allotment-holding career.

PEST		PLANTS AT RISK	TREATMENT
Ants and termites		Ants are not really pests, but they 'farm' aphids for sticky sugar. Termites can attack some woody species.	Few effective treatments, but baits based on borax are useful. Use a herbal spray of essential oil (citronella and lavender) or lukewarm water as a repellent.
Aphids		Most cultivated plants growing in the open, under glass or indoors.	Encourage beneficial insects to feed on them. Insecticidal soap can also be useful, particularly if the aphids are being 'farmed' by ants.
Birds		Some birds will attack fruit and brassicas as well as brightly coloured flowers, including blossom.	Bird scarers may be employed as a deterrent and netting will also provide cover for individual crops and plants.
Cabbage root fly		The small maggots grow and develop on and within the roots of the developing cabbage plant.	Place a collar around newly planted seedlings, sinking it into the ground to prevent the newly hatched maggots from reaching the plant roots.
Carrot fly		These root-feeding maggots feed on carrots.	Try companion planting and avoid large monocultures of carrots. Erect plastic or fleece barriers, about 45–50cm (18–20in) high and 2–3m (6½–10ft) apart.
Caterpillars		Many different species of plant, especially those in the cabbage family.	Birds and other predators will reduce populations. Biological control, using a bacterial agent, and pesticides such as derris. Hand-pick off individual plants.
Chafers		Raspberries, strawberries, potatoes, lettuce and young trees.	Keep the ground weed-free and well cultivated in order to reduce the number of bugs. Roll lawns in late spring.
Deer		Browse on many plants. Male deer rub their antlers against trees, causing damage to the bark.	Notoriously difficult to control, often best kept out by fencing. Repellents are available, based upon formulae such as bear or even lion droppings.
Fruit flies		Troublesome on softer fruits in warm conditions, especially tomatoes.	Cover the fruit with a small piece of rag. Paper bags are also good to use, but can be difficult to get around a truss of tomatoes.
Gall mites and wasps		These pests affect a wide range of trees and shrubs.	Generally not problematic or life-threatening. They are a good indicator of healthy biodiversity in an allotment.
Leaf hoppers		There are many different types, affecting a wide range of plant species.	Difficult to control. Remove dead leaves to reduce overwintering eggs and nymphs. Encourage predators such as lacewings.
Leaf miners		There are many hundreds of species that all have their preferred host species.	Hand-picking of severely affected leaves. Biological controls exist but the problem is rarely serious enough to warrant their artificial introduction.
Leather-jackets		They feed on roots just below the soil surface.	Can be difficult to control. Damp sacking over the soil can lure them up to the surface where they can be hand-picked or left for birds to eat.

PEST		PLANTS AT RISK	TREATMENT
Mealy bugs		Suck the sap of many species and produce a sticky honeydew that supports the growth of sooty moulds.	Biological controls are available. Cultural control is more difficult and involves drenching plants with a soap solution and then rinsing.
Mites		A common pest of many plants, especially those growing in hot dry conditions.	Biological controls are available. For a cultural control, improve humidity around the plant or spray foliage with a soap solution and then rinse.
Moles		Damage roots by lifting small newly planted trees.	Best controlled by trapping or using repellents. Sonic repellent devices are rarely effective. Removing one mole can simply 'open the door' to another.
Nematodes (eelworms)		A few species cause disease-like symptoms. A problem when the same plants are grown in the same place.	Regular crop rotations can help to reduce damage. If numbers build up or plants become badly affected, avoid growing the affected species.
Rabbits and hares, squirrels, voles and mice		Rabbits gnaw shoots. Mice and voles eat small bulbs and corms in winter. They all ring-bark young trees.	They may be trapped or a variety of repellents are available. Tree and shrub shelters are useful against voles and mice, as is fencing for rabbits and hares.
Sawflies		Developing larvae eat plant tissue. Fruit sawflies are notorious. Slugworm sawfly attack ornamentals.	Control slugworm by applying insecticidal soap. Control fruit sawfly larvae with derris. Both these treatments reduce numbers of beneficial insect predators.
Scale insects		Several species, some of which have specific host plants.	A cultural control consists of swabbing woody stems with a strong organic soap solution or pruning and removing affected parts.
Sciarid fly (fungus gnat)		Tiny flies that feed on soil fungus. The larvae attack the roots of young plants in water-logged compost.	Control by preventing the potting mix becoming too wet, although biological controls of nematodes are also available.
Slugs and snails		Common pests of a wide variety of plants. Snails, in particular, cause damage and defoliation of plants.	Often difficult to control although they can be caught in traps containing beer. A variety of barriers and deterrents are also available.
Thrips		Small insects suck the sap of soft foliage and attack flowers. Rarely a problem outside in cooler climates.	Remove seriously damaged foliage. Several natural predators (usually mites) are available for use against thrips.
Weevils		Larvae attack roots, stems or flowers and fruit of a range of plants. Adults feed on affected plants.	Wet acidic composts favour ground-living types such as vine weevil. Biological control possible with parasitic nematodes if temperatures sufficiently high.
Whiteflies		A greenhouse pest in cooler climates that may occur outside in warmer areas.	Biological controls are available but the best option can be to avoid growing susceptible species.
Woodlice (pill bugs)		Usually a pest indoors of crops such as cucumbers. May chew through young seedlings.	Often more an indication of poor hygiene than a problem in itself. A sign that you must clean up the greenhouse.

PLANT DISEASES

The early detection of plant disease can help to halt the widespread infestation of your crop. Try to establish a routine of regularly checking your plants and crops. Look closely for any tell-tale signs, using a hand lens if necessary. Remember that the first or most obvious symptom may not always be the only one or even the most important. Always check to see if there are other symptoms to ensure that you get the full picture before making your final diagnosis.

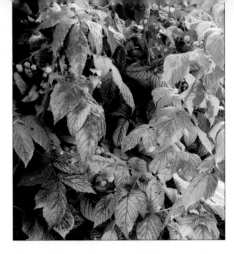

Above: *This raspberry is exhibiting symptoms of damage caused by a virus. Having identified the cause, appropriate action can be taken.*

RECOGNIZING PLANT DISEASES

Vigilance is the key to success in controlling plant disease. Carefully inspect leaves, stems, roots, flowers and fruits for any sign of disease. You may even find it useful to cut open a branch or stem to look for problems such as discoloration of the tissue, which may explain leaf or stem wilting and sudden wilting of a section of or a whole plant.

Stand back and look at the overall picture. Consider the whole environment. This will include the weather, soil, the stage of development of the plant (and any pathogens present), cultural practices and the condition of other plants in the area. All of this information can help to indicate what may be wrong with the plant. Remember that a plant growing in the wrong location may be stressed.

Try to determine when the symptoms became apparent. The onset of a problem may be due to a cultural practice, the seasonal appearance of a disease or insect, or a weather-related event. Remember that long-term stress is slow to appear, taking a year or more at times.

It is important to establish whether the problem is spreading, as this may indicate that it is a disease. Check whether plants of other species have been affected, as diseases are usually (but not always) species-specific. Problems caused by environmental factors do not spread, although the symptoms may become more severe.

You must know what the plant should look like in order to be able to recognize any abnormalities. Reading up a little on 'the species that you are growing in your allotment can help you to make a more accurate diagnosis of the problem.

Remember that there is usually no single cause of a disease infestation. The primary cause may be associated with cultural or environmental conditions. And just as there is probably no single cause, there is usually no single symptom.

When you are attempting to diagnose the cause of plant illness, always inspect symptoms that appear on parts that are still alive (or at least partially alive). Dead plants are often invaded by secondary infestations of decomposer fungi, which may hide the original problem. If possible, make an examination of the entire plant, including roots, although this may not be possible for large specimens such as trees.

CONTROL OPTIONS

Ultimately, where a serious disease is suspected, it may be advisable to avoid growing susceptible species altogether, or, in the case of fruit and vegetables, to rotate the crop as part of a regular cycle. Make notes that provide details on disease occurrence (the type of disease and when it appeared), the plants affected, the weather and environmental conditions in your allotment each year. By doing this you can better anticipate what problems are likely to occur in your plot during the growing season.

Finally, remember that even the best gardeners lose plants to disease. This is only serious when large numbers of plants are affected. A diverse allotment site will contain other highlights, and diseases will claim only a fraction of the planting.

Above: *Inspecting plants regularly will help you spot damage and begin the process of assessing what may have caused it.*

Above: *Bacterial problems, such as the leaf spot on this pelargonium, are often most active in moist and warm conditions.*

Above: *Disease-causing organisms can enter a plant each time it is cut or pruned, or when branches break off in strong winds.*

COMMON DISEASES

There are all kinds of diseases that can affect your plants. Most of these are mercifully rare, but every site will suffer from its share of diseases during the growing season. Most of these conditions are relatively easy to deal with, but a correct diagnosis is essential. As always, it is preferable to try to prevent these diseases taking hold and spreading in the first place rather than treating them when they occur.

DISEASE		PLANTS AT RISK AND THE SYMPTOMS	TREATMENT
Apple common scab		A bacterial disease that causes the formation of large (albeit harmless) scabs on the surface of the apples. Commonly encountered in damp weather and on trees with crowded branches.	Rake up and dispose of affected leaves. Prune out cracked or scabby shoots to remove places for the fungus to overwinter.
Bacterial canker		Many different tree fruits. Reduces vigour and the rate of growth of the affected plant. Leaves turn yellow, wither and die. Branches become girdled and die back. A sticky secretion will ooze from cracks or welts in the bark.	Difficult to control once a plant is infected. Cut out and destroy infected material. Confine the problem to one specimen by cleaning pruning tools between cuts and before moving on to another specimen of the same type.
Clubroot		This fungus attacks all plants in the brassica family, including cabbages, radishes and cauliflowers. The spores can live in the soil for up to 20 years. Plants wilt during the day and grow weakly.	Remove and destroy infected plants. Practise crop rotation, lime acidic soils and avoid planting out in waterlogged soils.
Coral spot		A common fungus affecting many woody plant species, including fruit trees and bushes and figs. Appears as pink or bright red, raised pustules on wood that is showing signs of dieback.	Prune out infected tissue and destroy it. Regular 'hygienic pruning' can help to prevent it taking hold in the first place.
Fireblight		Attacks plants of the Rosaceae family, notably apples, pears, plums and cherries. Flowers and leaves turn brown, wither and die. The affected plant dies back rapidly from the branch tip.	Remove and destroy all affected material, cutting back to at least 50cm (20in) below the point of infection. Best to remove diseased plants, replacing them with a non-susceptible fruit tree or shrub.
Fungal canker		Affects many fruit trees. The bark tissue shrinks, cracks and begins to peel and flake away around the affected tissue in concentric rings. The infected area swells up and new growth ceases.	Prune out the affected material, about 15cm (6in) below the point of infection, and burn it. Clean tools with disinfectant between cuts and especially between pruning individual plants.
Honey fungus		A soil-dwelling fungus that parasitizes the roots of woody plants. Leaves tend to discolour and wilt and fail to develop in the spring. Ultimately, this can weaken and kill the plant. Affects tree and bush fruits, rhubarb and strawberries.	Difficult to control. Remove and destroy all infected plants, including the roots.
Mosaic virus		This group of viruses affects a very large number of species, including marrows (large zucchini), pumpkins, cucumbers and aubergines (eggplants), and is characterized by an irregular, angular mottling or streaking of the leaves.	Winged insects that feed on plants, then migrate to another, can rapidly spread the virus. Control the pests themselves where possible. Dig up and destroy infected plants.
Onion neck rot		This is a fungus that will cause onions in storage to rot. The bulbs become soft and transparent.	Regular checks must be made on stored crops, and remove any infected material. As the fungus can be soil-borne, rotate crops next year.
Potato blight		This is a fungal disease that is spread by the wind and rain. The leaves turn brown at the tips and can have white mould underneath. Eventually the leaves wither and collapse. The tubers have dark patches and the inside turns slimy and rots.	Spray with Bordeaux mixture as a preventative measure, especially when it is warm and humid. Remove infected material and purchase disease-free seed potatoes next time.
Potato common scab		This bacterial disease is found in most soils. It is more prolific in hot, dry years. Brown textured patches are found in the potato skins, but are still safe to eat.	It is best to grow varieties resistant to potato scab. Water regularly to prevent attacks.
Powdery mildew		Affects many plant species. The leaves become covered with white powdery patches that may distort growth or even cause leaf drop in severe cases. Thrives in warm, humid or wet conditions.	Remove and destroy infected leaves. Sulphur and Bordeaux mixture can provide protection, but these are easily washed off in wet conditions. Avoid growing susceptible species if conditions favour the spread of the disease.
Rust		A common fungal disease affecting many species. Characterized by rusty coloured patches or spots, known as pustules, on leaves. Tissue around the pustules yellows and dies, and this, in turn, may distort growth or cause leaf drop in severe cases.	Commonly seen on soils rich in nitrogen. It may have a noticeable effect on seasonal crops or those grown for their leaves. Bordeaux mixture can reduce its spread but it is difficult to control completely. Avoid susceptible crops and varieties if the problem is persistent.
Silverleaf		Affects fruiting and ornamental species of *Prunus*, including cherries, plums, peaches, apples and pears. The leaves on some branches gain a silvery sheen, dying back a year or two later. A purple fungal growth appears on the dead tissue.	The affected wood should be pruned out below the point of infection and disposed of in late summer after fruit has set. Badly infected specimens should be removed completely and disposed of, preferably by burning.
Tomato blight		The leaves have brown patches and curl up, eventually drying out and dying. Stems have brown patches and darken with the fruits turning brown and rotting.	Remove and destroy infected parts of the plant. A Bordeaux mixture will provide protection. Avoid growing tomatoes in the same place next year.

PLANT DISORDERS

Many external factors can affect allotment plants. Weather seldom does what we want it to – there is either too little or too much rain or it is too cold or too hot. If you combine these climatic disappointments with other factors that can affect your plants, such as pollution or nutrient deficiencies, you will see why these difficult conditions can produce a number of disease-like symptoms. They can all put severe stress on a crop and so precipitate attack from living organisms.

Above: *Nutrient deficiencies can cause discoloration of the leaves. This plant is short of magnesium.*

RECOGNIZING DISORDERS

Plants can be susceptible to a long list of outside forces. Extremes of weather, nutrient deficiencies and physical damage can take their toll on the health and vigour of a plant. Other environmental factors, such as too much or too little water, or pollutants in the soil, can also encourage disease-like symptoms.

Soil pollution can be caused by nutrient deficiency, misapplied fertilizer (resulting in too much nutrient and, therefore, toxicity) `or buried inert material. Airborne pollution can be more insidious and more difficult to determine or detect.

Weather events such as high winds or frost may go unnoticed if you are not there to witness them. A huge storm will leave evidence in its wake. The effect of a sharp early morning frost, however, or a steady drying wind on a sunny afternoon may not show the damage caused until several days have passed.

Disease can result from a combination of factors, affecting growing conditions and actual disease-causing organisms. Plants may initially be placed under stress, making them vulnerable to attack by living agents. For instance, drought may damage roots, which in turn renders them more liable to infection by fungal diseases.

It is important to determine whether the problem is the result of a pathogen or due to a problem in the environment. Look to see if the occurrence of ill health is random or uniform in terms of its distribution. As a general rule, randomly distributed symptoms on injured plants are usually caused by a living factor, such as diseases or a pest. In addition to this, infestations, particularly those caused by diseases, tend to radiate out from central points. Uniform patterns are generally associated with non-living or non-infectious agents such as poisons, fertilizers, environmental stress or mechanical damage.

Above: *While rain is essential for a plant's growth, excessive water and waterlogging can kill a vulnerable, young plant.*

CONTROL OPTIONS

If the cause of the problem is physical, you will need to find out whether it is due to a recurring environmental factor inherent in the site, such as constant buffeting by strong winds, or whether it is caused by 'one-off' events such as unseasonable frosts or contamination from a careless neighbour's weedkiller spray. Some factors can often be removed, such as polluted soil, and windbreaks can be planted and fleece draped over tender specimens on cold nights. If plants continue to be affected, it could be that the plant is in the wrong place and you may have to try relocating it elsewhere.

Left: *Weather can have a big impact on an allotment, with sudden sharp frosts and high winds being particularly damaging.*

COMMON DISORDERS

Disorders are the result of either an imbalance of essential nutrients or of a range of stresses that are caused by adverse or difficult environmental conditions. Many of the disorders and conditions described here can resemble diseases. This means that is very important for you to diagnose the cause of the distress in the plant before taking any remedial action. A plant disorder will call for a different response to a plant disease.

CONDITION		PROBABLE CAUSE	TREATMENT
Bare patches or areas of poor plant establishment		The patchy establishment of cover crops or turf can be due to soil compaction or underground obstructions. Soil can easily become compacted if it is walked on a lot, particularly when it is wet. Buried obstructions such as rubble can also cause similar growth distortions.	Remove all buried rubble prior to planting or replanting. Relie' compaction by cultivating and replant if required. If treating tui on an allotment, aerate and scarify to relieve compaction and improve drainage.
Blackening of leaf tips		Usually the result of overwatering, particularly with container- grown plants. The waterlogged soil or potting mix forces oxygen out of the soil, thereby suffocating the roots, which suffer a form of drought-stress.	Plants that are waterlogged are best left to dry out. Do not water until the potting mix is dried out, not only on the surface but throughout the pot. Always check to see if plants need watering before doing so.
Etiolation		Sun-loving plants kept in low light conditions quickly become starved and will be significantly weakened. If kept in these conditions for any length of time, the plant will eventually die.	Choose specimens that are appropriate for the light levels in the allotment. If growing in a greenhouse, ensure that correct light levels are achieved. Remove shading and clean glass in winter to increase the levels.
Leaf blackening		Frost damage on buds and leaves in early spring, even to hardy specimens, is usually noticed on new growth that has not yet become acclimatized. It is the sudden shock that often causes the problem, not the actual temperature itself.	Cover slightly tender plants with fleece in the winter. Lightly spray plants with water in the evening to help protect against late frosts. Crops grown in the greenhouse prior to planting out need to be properly hardened off before being planted outside.
Leaf scorch		High winds and bright sunlight, especially on shade-loving species. Some plants can also be damaged by watering in bright sunlight, by providing too little or too much water, or by applying too much fertilizer to the soil. Hail can also cause leaf spotting or holes.	It is best to water first thing in the morning or in the evening to prevent leaf scorch from water that has splashed on to the leaves.
Mechanical or physical damage		High winds, which are especially damaging to deciduous woody plants in full leaf. Tall vegetables can easily break if not adequately staked, as may newly planted fruit trees and shrubs. Animals visiting the allotment, for example foxes, can also flatten or snap plants.	Stake plants firmly and ensure that animals are excluded from areas where plants could be damaged. Stakes used to support newly planted fruit trees should be kept in for at least one year.
Nutrient deficiency		A lack of or too much of a particular nutrient. Nutrients can also become in short supply if other nutrients are present in large amounts. Nitrogen deficiency (shown left) is extremely common. The leaves turn pale green or yellow and the plants become stunted.	Deficiencies are best treated with the application of fertilizer, or choose plants that are adapted to deal with the site conditions. To prevent deficiencies, ensure that the soil is properly prepared before planting and add generous amounts of organic matter if needed.
Poisoned ground		Leaked fuel or lubricants used in construction work can leave the ground contaminated. This is usually more of a problem in allotments near building sites. Underground gas pipes can leak, flooding the ground with gas that is lethal to plant roots. Other chemical spillages could come from machinery such as a strimmers or rotavators.	Remove all affected soil and replace with fresh topsoil. If pipes are leaking, make sure that they are fixed before replacing soil. Fill lawnmowers with fuel over a plastic sheet.
Root girdling		This can cause instability and the collapse of fruit trees and shrubs. Tree and shrub roots become woody following the first year's growth and, if these are constrained in round pots, they tend to grow in spirals.	At the establishment phase, try to use bare-rooted stock whenever possible if using pot-grown trees. Tease out roots from the root-ball immediately prior to planting, even cutting out older woody roots. This will ensure that the root system grows out into the soil instead of spiralling.
Wilting		A normal response in many plants to either a lack of water or high temperatures, and not necessarily a cause for great concern. Squashes habitually wilt on hot summer afternoons, therefore mulching the crop with generous amounts of organic matter aids in reducing stress.	Water if required. A good preventative measure is to mulch, even around vegetables. Use sieved (strained) garden compost or leaf mould as manure can hold too much moisture and this can cause problems with rotting. Choose wind-resistant species, if appropriate. Apply fertilizer at recommended rates. Do not over- or under-water plants.

BENEFICIAL PREDATORS

A thriving population of natural predators and parasites can significantly help to keep pest populations down. The allotment-holder should strive to create and maintain an environment in which these welcome visitors to the allotment or greenhouse can prosper. This usually means avoiding using pesticides, which can wipe out beneficial predators and so upset the natural balance in the allotment or greenhouse.

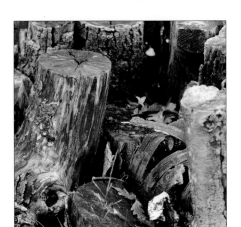

Above: *Biological controls are a successful way to fight pests. The control insects are released, here from a sachet, to attract pests.*

BIOLOGICAL PEST CONTROL

Nearly every species of plant-feeding insect has another insect that is its predator or parasite. Some pests, such as aphids, are eaten by ladybirds (ladybugs), hoverflies and midge larvae, parasitized by wasps and infested by fungal diseases. Large pest populations are a food larder for many 'natural enemies', including carnivorous animals, parasites and diseases.

Biological methods of control use these natural enemies of pest insects to keep their populations under control. It is like having an army of insects and other creatures doing the work for you. Biological controls can be encouraged into the allotment by creating a suitable habitat. Ironically, this means that the pests must be present first. They must also be present in sufficient numbers to support a viable population of the beneficial predator. This can be a complex area and the easiest way is to encourage the conditions that will favour a balanced food web to develop. Purchasing beneficials is only generally recommended for use in greenhouses, although a few (particularly microbes) are suitable for use outdoors.

Above: *Parasitic nematodes can be used in specific cases to attack pests that live in the soil. Here they are watered into the area.*

CREATING SUITABLE HABITATS

The greater the variety of habitats your plot has, the more biodiversity it will support. Ponds (if these are allowed), long grass, log piles, and food plants for animals with varied tastes all encourage a stable ecosystem where pests are kept at relatively low levels.

Many birds and bats eat insects. Bats need a roosting site, so place a purpose-made bat box on the shady side of a tree. Position the box at least 3m (10ft) high with a clear airspace in front. Night-scented flowers encourage the moths that bats feed upon. This is the key. The predators must be able to live in your site or they will go and find a more suitable habitat elsewhere.

The longer you use this approach, the more balance will appear in your allotment. This is simply because the ecosystem begins to stabilize and diversify over time.

BENEFICIAL INSECTS

Predators (those that devour pests directly) and parasitic insects (those whose young hatch inside and devour pests) are often termed 'beneficials'. Predators include lacewings and wasps. Parasitic insects

Above: *Log piles encourage beneficial predators such as beetles to colonize and take shelter in your allotment site.*

(more correctly termed parasitoids) are less well known than predators, but equally effective. They lay their eggs in a pest species. When the eggs hatch, the larvae feed on the pest insect, killing it. The majority of these insects are tiny wasps, although some flies and mites also fall under this category. Learning to recognize beneficial insects is crucial if you want to avoid killing your army of allotment helpers.

BENEFICIAL PREDATORS IN THE ALLOTMENT

There are many beneficial predators that will willingly take up residence in your allotment and help to control populations of pests in a natural way.

- Anthocorid bugs or red kneed capsids
- Bats
- Birds (robin, blue tit and thrush)
- Centipedes
- Earwigs
- Frogs, toads and newts
- Ground beetles
- Harvestmen
- Hedgehogs
- Hoverflies
- Lacewings (adult or larva)
- Ladybirds (ladybugs)
- Mites, e.g. *Phytoseiulus*
- Nematodes, e.g. *Heterorhabditis*
- Parasitic wasps (*Encarsia* or *Aphidoletes*)
- Slow worms
- Spiders on web or wolf spiders
- Tachinid flies
- Wasps (solitary and social)

BIOLOGICAL CONTROLS IN THE GREENHOUSE OR ALLOTMENT

The application of biological controls in the greenhouse or allotment involves using predatory insects or other beneficial animals to control commonly occurring pests. Many pests are only a problem because their natural predators are missing from the allotment. Introducing a biological control usually results in the rapid control of the pest.

PREDATOR SPECIES	PREFERRED TEMPERATURE RANGE	PEST SPECIES THAT THEY CONTROL
Amblyseus cucumeris (predatory mite)	25°C (77°F)	The nymphal forms and adults consume large quantities of immature thrips.
Aphidoletes aphidimyza (predatory midge larva)	21°C (70°F); needs 80%+ humidity	Tiny mosquito-like midge larvae that control substantial populations of more than 60 species of aphids.
Cryptolaemus montrouzieri (predatory beetle)	20–25°C (68–77°F); needs 70%+ humidity	This ladybird is effective in controlling mealybugs on houseplants and in greenhouses.
Encarsia formosa (parasitic wasp)	18–25°C (64–77°F)	Minute, flying parasitic wasps, which lay their eggs inside whitefly scales (the pupa stage) and eat them in two to four weeks
Heterorhabditis megidis (parasitic nematode)	Minimum soil temperature of 14°C (57°F); if temperature drops below 20°C (68°F), they become less effective	Patrol the soil to a depth of about 18cm (7in) and quickly take care of the slow-moving grubs, such as vine weevil grubs and chafers. Very effective in pots and containers. Soil must be moist.
Metaphycus helvolus (parasitic wasp)	20–30°C (68–86°F)	These tiny, black and yellow wasps are effective against several soft-scale species, including brown scale. The females lay their eggs under the body of first- and second-stage scales. The grubs feed on scales and develop into adults within two weeks. Adults also provide control by feeding on non-parasitized scales. *Metaphycus* are most effective in semi-tropical conditions.
Phasmarhabditis hermaphrodita (parasitic nematode)	Minimum soil temperature of 5°C (40°F)	Useful for slug control. Should be applied during the early growing stages of vulnerable plants. Needs moist soil.
Phytoseiulus persimilis (predatory mite)	Use once temperature is regularly above 15°C (60°F). Best at 18–25°C (64–77°F); needs 60%+ humidity	Predator mites, slightly larger than the two-spotted mites (also known as red spider mites) upon which they feed.
Steinernema feltiae (parasitic nematode)	Minimum temperature of 10°C (50°F), although they remain effective when the soil temperature drops below this	Aggressive predators used to control fungus gnats, mushroom flies and leatherjackets. They can be used in flower and vegetable plots and greenhouses.

Above: *Ladybirds are just one of the many beneficial insects that will help to keep the unwanted pests of your allotment in check.*

MICROBES
Bacteria, fungi, viruses, protozoans and parasitic nematodes are microorganisms that attack insects. These microscopic hordes are generally effective against very specific pests and present little risk to humans and the environment. Many experienced gardeners may well be familiar with a popularly known, microbial-based insecticide known as Bt or *Bacillus thuringiensis*. This commonly available product, which is used to kill many different kinds of moth and butterfly larvae, is a bacterium. It produces a toxin that kills specific caterpillars. The larval pest usually dies within four to seven days. There are many strains of Bt, each type controlling specific pests.

Parasitic nematodes are also very effective against certain pests that live in the soil. However, the nematodes require moist conditions in order to survive and their temperature requirements further limit their use to greenhouses in many cases.

Despite their potential, very few fungi, viruses and protozoa are commercially available because these living organisms are difficult to raise, store and apply. The best way to encourage these willing and tiny helpers into your plot is to maintain a healthy soil that is rich and diverse in terms of the life it contains.

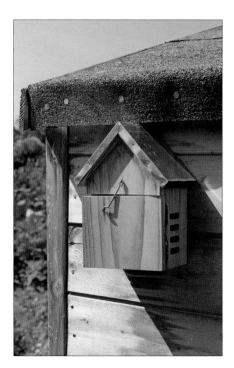

Above: *Providing convenient shelter, such as this lacewing hotel, for beneficial insects can help to increase their numbers.*

OTHER CONTROL METHODS

There are many ways of dealing with the different pests that appear in the allotment. Some of these methods have been tried and tested for generations, others are individual to the gardener and are often the result of a happy accident. As an allotment-holder, it is useful to learn and experimenet with as many different tricks as possible to manage the pests in your plot and to protect your plants.

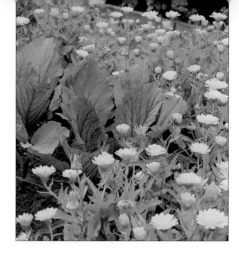

Above: *Companion plants such as these marigolds confuse or deter pests that would otherwise attack plants.*

GOOD GARDENING PRACTICE

The selection and culture of plants can reduce the potential for pests and diseases. Cultural practices are methods the gardener can use to change environmental factors that affect plants and their pest populations. It is essential, therefore, that you know the cultural or growing requirements of each plant. Providing the correct conditions results in a vigorous plant that is less likely to be attacked by pests and diseases and can tolerate some damage.

ASSESSING THE DAMAGE

When problems do arise, you must decide whether a pest is causing enough damage to warrant control. In other words, you will need to assess how far the problem can

Above: *Compact discs are an unusual and amusing way of scaring away marauding birds from your allotment crops.*

be tolerated before action is necessary. Some form of pest damage is inevitable with any crop, but you will need to establish limits. To do this, you will need to take into consideration the amount of damage that can be tolerated, the numbers of an individual pest that can cause significant damage and the plants' stage of development. The health and vigour of the plant can also have a direct bearing on when or if you need to take action. A few holes on a leaf may not require control, but, if most of the leaf has been eaten, the plant may die.

TAKING ACTION

Monitor your plants to determine when action is necessary. A thorough inspection of the plant allows you to identify a problem before major damage occurs. You should also inspect the plant's entire environment for clues to the problem. Observing and keeping records of weather conditions, for example, can help provide clues to growth patterns and problems.

Above: *Slugs and snails are notorious allotment pests that are easily kept at bay using a water trap around vulnerable crops.*

TYPES OF CONTROL

Control options can be arranged by their mode of action and their impact on the environment. These methods of control can be grouped from least to highest impact: cultural and mechanical controls and 'permitted' chemical controls (soaps, oils and botanical insecticides).

Cultural control includes hand removal of larger pests, the use of screens, barriers, and traps, freezing and crushing. These methods generally have little or no negative effect on the environment.

COMPANION PLANTING

This is commonly used to protect plants from pest attack. The theory is that the companion plants – flowers growing next to a food crop, for example – disrupt the searching pattern of the pests looking for host plants. They literally smell these hosts but become confused with the more diverse planting style. Separating rows of cabbages, broccoli or other brassicas with rows of onions has always been a popular combination, possibly because the onion's strong scent confuses cabbage pests. Tomato plants also grow well next to cabbages and seem to deter caterpillars, while growing leeks near carrots repels carrot flies.

SCREENS AND BARRIERS

Any material that is fine enough to keep pests out can be used as a barrier. A variety of screens of different mesh sizes can keep out large insects, birds and rabbits, but they can also prevent pollinating insects from reaching a plant, resulting in lack of fruit. Cardboard and metal collars will prevent cutworms from reaching young transplants. Sticky bands placed on tree trunks trap beetles and soil-hibernating pests. Copper strips are available for slug control. These supposedly react with the slugs' slime to shock them. Sharp particles, such as crushed eggshells, are also used to control slugs.

TRAPS

Certain insect pests can be monitored by using traps. Sticky coloured traps, pheromone traps and pitfall traps can all be used to monitor the occurrence of some pests. Whiteflies and aphids are attracted to bright yellow, and this colour is used for sticky cards upon which they become trapped.

You may want to apply a control and then enclose the plants in netting to keep further infestation from occurring – perhaps putting up netting and then releasing predators.

Right: Garden birds can be dissuaded from attacking your allotment plants if you stretch string and shiny foil over the crops.

Traps usually serve as a monitoring system, warning of the presence or increase in undesirable pest numbers. Traps can also be useful in timing control measures by showing the presence of migrating or emerging adults. The control measure can then be introduced at the best time to control the particular pest. Codling moth traps for use around fruit trees are a good example of this. They are sometimes used to control numbers, but most types are limited in their real effectiveness. Yellow, sticky traps attract whiteflies, aphids, thrips, leafhoppers and other small flying insects.

Traps that use pheromones or attractive scents to tantalize adult insects are best used as a way to check presence and numbers. Pitfall traps can be cups or jars dug into the ground then filled with yeast and water or beer to attract and trap slugs.

WATER

A jet of water from a hose washes aphids, spider mites and other small insects from plant foliage. This must be done frequently as it does not kill insects or eggs and it does not prevent some insects from crawling back on to plants.

INSECTICIDAL SOAPS

These are made from the salts of fatty acids. Fatty acids are components of the fats and oils found in plants and animals.

These soaps should not be confused with ordinary cleaning soaps. Insecticidal soaps kill only what they touch and are effective against soft-bodied pests such as aphids, thrips, crawler stage scales, whiteflies, leafhoppers and mites. Insecticidal soaps may cause burning on some plants, particularly those with hairy leaves. Test insecticidal soap on a single leaf if you are unsure – burning will usually occur within 24 hours.

BOTANICAL INSECTICIDES

Derived from plants, botanical insecticides include pyrethrum, citrus oil extracts and the extract of the neem tree. They act rapidly to stop feeding by insects, although they may not kill the pest for hours or days. There are also disadvantages to the use of botanicals. They must be applied frequently, may be difficult to obtain, and, although generally less toxic than many pesticides, they are still toxic and may harm other beneficial allotment residents.

Above: *Sticky traps are another form of pest control in greenhouses. Here, pheromones attract pests to the trap, where they get stuck. Other traps consist of sheets of plastic covered with a non-drying glue.*

Above: *Sheets of horticultural fleece, which can be stretched over developing young plants, provide an effective physical barrier against some of the smaller types of allotment pests, such as flying insects.*

TRAPS, BARRIERS AND DETERRENTS

The prevention of pest and disease attacks is an essential part of allotment gardening. Plants that are infected by pests or diseases are weaker specimens that are difficult to treat and never quite recover their former vigour. Many allotment pests can be trapped or kept at bay using relatively inexpensive materials and sometimes recycled household items. Put the barriers in place when the plants are young and always ensure that pests are not trapped inside the barrier.

CONTROL METHOD	HOW IT WORKS
Beer traps and deterrents (granules, copper strips and greasebands)	Traps are effective ways of both controlling pests, such as slugs, and finding out which ones you actually have. Deterrents are physical barriers over which the pest cannot or will not pass. There are many types and their effectiveness can vary.
Bird scarers (e.g. scarecrows)	Bird scarers have the drawback of a limited lifespan before the birds learn that they are not a real threat. They can, of course, be changed and most bird scarers are only needed on a seasonal basis.
Bug nets in the greenhouse	Greenhouse vents are problematic in terms of pest control in that they allow both pests in and purchased biological controls out. Bug nets are put in place to avoid this happening.
Fleece on frames	Frames covered in horticultural fleece can be used over outdoor crops to help keep pests out and control the temperature.
Fleece stretched over a crop	Fleece can be used to create a favourable microclimate around young plants. It also acts as a barrier to airborne pests. On the downside, however, it can also keep out airborne predators from pests that overwinter in the soil.
Fruit nets over fruit	Fruit nets are especially useful for summer soft fruit crops that can quickly be devastated by birds.
Individual cloches	Cloches can act as barriers to a wide variety of airborne pests. Any pests that are sealed into this environment may, however, find the perfect environment within which to thrive.
Mesh cages for trees	Mesh cages are usually used to keep rabbits and hares at bay. They are usually simple constructions formed from three or more stakes driven into the ground with chicken wire (or similar) attached to them.
Rabbit fencing	A continuous barrier to prevent rabbits entering areas where plants are growing. The base of the wire should be buried below ground level to prevent the rabbits burrowing a passage beneath it.
String or wire netting stretched over seedlings (e.g. peas)	Aerial barriers can protect against bird attack. They may only be needed for the duration of the crop's life or even less.
Traps (pheromone)	Pheromone traps are used to detect the presence of insects. The pheromones attract members of the opposite sex and the appearance of the target species allows you to begin looking for and controlling the young that cause the damage.
Traps (sticky, coloured traps used in the greenhouse)	Sticky traps can provide a certain degree of control against the flying adults of insect pests. However, they are not as effective as they are sometimes thought to be and are, in fact, of more use for showing whether a particular pest is present or not, thereby allowing appropriate control measures to be put in place.
Tree guards (spiral)	Spiral guards are useful for protecting the bark of newly planted trees from rabbits and hares, especially in winter and early spring. These guards expand as the tree develops, but they are best removed completely after about a year.
Tree shelter	These protect newly planted trees from vertebrate pests and from the worst rigours of the environment by providing a favourable microclimate around them. They naturally degrade under the action of sunlight, but are best removed after two to three years.
Twiggy branches over plants	Arched over young plants, these can be an effective deterrent to pests such as birds and cats. They do not prevent the migration of beneficial predators to the plants.

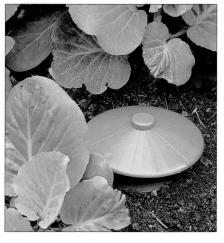

Above: *Slugs and snails can be caught in a trap that is filled with stale beer, or water that has been mixed with yeast.*

Above: *Ring tunnels that are covered in a fine mesh will prevent flying insects from attacking your allotment vegetables.*

Above: *Plastic netting, stretched over the crop and carefully secured, provides an effective barrier against birds.*

Above: *Old plastic bottles make an ideal barrier to protect young plants from pests. These are cheaper than traditional cloches.*

Above: *Chicken wire, stretched over young plants, will prevent garden birds from reaching and eating them.*

ORGANIC PESTICIDES

Although you can use conventional pesticides, it may well be worth considering some naturally occurring substances to protect your plants from pests and diseases. As with standard pesticides, these should only be applied when and where absolutely necessary and not on a regular basis.

ORGANIC PESTICIDE	HOW IT WORKS
Bacillus thuringiensis	These are bacterial spores that produce a toxic protein that is useful against caterpillars but will not cause any harm to beneficials. *Bacillus thuringiensis* works quickly, paralyzing the caterpillar and so preventing any further damage, although it quickly degrades in sunlight and needs frequent re-application throughout the growing season.
Bordeaux mixture	A compound containing copper and sulphur used to control various fungal diseases including apple scab and potato blight. It is harmful to fish and livestock, and frequent use can lead to a build-up of copper in the soil that can be harmful to worms.
Derris	A chemical extracted from the roots of the derris and longocarpus plants. It is useful against a variety of insects including aphids, caterpillars, sawflies and plant-eating beetles. It can prove harmful to beneficials, although it is not a threat to bees.
Insecticidal soap	This is not soap, like the domestic washing soap, but is made from the salts of fatty acids, extracted from plant material. It can be effective against a wide variety of insect pests, although it can damage sensitive plant species.
Plant oils	Their effectiveness varies but most depend upon coming into contact with the pest itself and suffocating it, although some, such as neem tree oil, do appear to have insecticidal properties.
Pyrethrum	This organic pesticide is extracted from the flower-heads of *Chrysanthemum cinerariifolium* and is especially effective in controlling aphids. However, it does not persist for long and can also cause harm to beneficial insects.
Sulphur	An effective fungicide against a variety of plant fungi, including powdery mildew, grey mould and blackspot. Sulphur can also prove harmful to predatory mites and can cause damage to certain sensitive species.

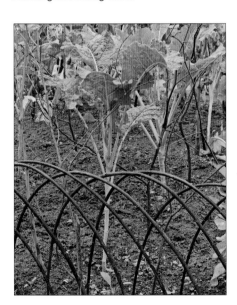

Above: *Twigs and willow can be used to make a barrier to protect plants from rabbits and other unwelcome larger animals.*

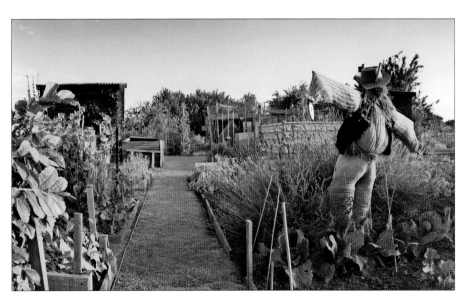

Above: *Scarecrows are an attractive method of deterring birds and occasionally large pests away from your vegetable plot. They should* be moved around the allotment and redressed occasionally so that the birds do not get too accustomed to them.

WEED CONTROL

Even the most successful allotment-holder must fight a constant battle against weeds, which if left unchecked for just a couple of weeks will begin to reassert themselves. Weeds take vital nutrients, compete for light and water and, if not controlled, will overrun, spoil or even kill all but the most vigorous crops. As if this wasn't enough, weeds can also harbour pests or diseases. You needn't be disheartened though as, if they are dealt with early, a short time spent each week is enough to control them.

Above: *From clearing a plot when you first take it on to keeping the site clear when growing crops, weeds are a common problem.*

WHAT MAKES A PLANT A WEED?

A plant that we describe as a weed is one that without help or encouragement establishes itself on your plot, and competes with those that you have planted. They do this by robbing cultivated specimens of nutrients, light and (arguably) most important of all, water. They are able to do this because they are species that have evolved to colonize, compete and become dominant. Most of them are specialists in establishing on disturbed ground – which is often found on a cultivated plot – and usually have rapid growth rates when compared to cultivated specimens. In natural habitats this competitive capability is often held in check by established neighbouring plants, but natural stability is very rare on the average allotment as cropping means that the vegetation is constantly cleared and the soil disturbed by the regular cycle of cultivation.

Below: *Hand-removal of weeds using a small hand fork is fast and effective, so long as you remove all traces of the weed.*

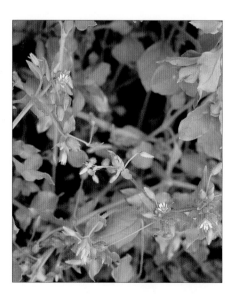

While many common weeds are native plants and owe their competitive edge to this alone, many others are introduced species that have become weeds because they do not have the constraints of the habitats from whence they came. These are often the most serious weeds in an allotment and can become so troublesome that they assume a national importance.

The term weed is a relative one, however, and any plant that is able to propagate itself and spread freely can become a weed. Weeds may also be the remnants of a previous crop, called 'volunteer' weeds. Although many of these can easily be dealt with, some can interfere with the crop rotation as they can act as a host for diseases in the intervening time between cropping cycles. Equally, some 'wild' weeds also host plant diseases that can subsequently spread to cultivated crops. Charlock (*Sinapis arvensis*) and shepherd's

Below: *Annual weeds, such as chickweed, are adept at exploiting opportunities to grow and spread very quickly.*

purse (*Capsella bursa-patoris*) for example, can host clubroot, while eelworm can be harboured by chickweed, fat hen and shepherd's purse. Cucumber mosaic virus, a potentially devastating disease affecting not only cucumbers, but also melons, courgettes (zucchini), marrows (large zucchini) etc., is carried by a range of weeds including chickweed and groundsel (*Senecio vulgaris*).

Most weeds are easily dealt with, although there are always a few that seem to resist all efforts to eradicate them. No weed is completely invincible, however, and the only really successful strategy for weed control is persistence.

WEED TYPES

The weeds that may plague your plot share some attributes with the crops they compete with and, as such, they can be divided into three groups.

Annual weeds are those that germinate, grow, flower and set seed within one growing season. Among these are some species known as ephemerals, which are extremely fast-growing and complete their lifecycle well within a growing season, allowing them to produce several successive generations over a year. This strategy means that they can exploit brief windows of opportunity – during mild winter spells, or between crops – in order to grow and set seed. Many of these are known then as winter annuals, due to their habit of germinating in late summer or autumn, overwintering and setting seed the following summer. A few hardier examples, such as chickweed (*Stellaria media*), can actually germinate under snow cover, meaning they commence their growth at the first sign of spring, often before the surrounding crops appear.

Biennial weeds are actually short-lived perennials that grow from seed during one growing season, overwintering as a rosette of leaves close to the soil surface, before flowering, setting seed and dying the following growing season. This strategy means they are rarer on allotments due to the cropping cycle, although a few such as spear thistle (*Cirsium vulgare*), can occasionally prove problematic.

Perennial weeds live for more than two years and can become established either by seed or by vegetative parts, such as roots or rhizomes being moved around during cultivation, or contained in imported topsoil or compost. Seedling perennials are usually no more difficult to control than any other weed seedlings, although once established, they can be difficult to control and often prove very competitive among vegetable crops. Examples of perennial weeds include blackberry (*Rubus fruticosus*), nettle (*Urtica dioica*), dandelion (*Taraxacum officinalis*) and dock (*Rumex obtusifolius*).

WAYS TO CONTROL WEEDS

Physical control of weeds usually involves hand-weeding, hoeing and forking over and, despite the effort they involve, in most cases it is a perfectly viable strategy if done regularly. It also represents the least environmentally detrimental method of weed control. The real trick is to be able to recognize weeds when they are very young, preferably when they are just seedlings, as it is then that they are most vulnerable and your efforts at weeding can be most effective. In the case of shallow-rooted crops such as brassicas and onions, any control needs to be limited to shallow hoeing as any digging can cause root disturbance to your crops. Perennial weeds may be difficult to control by hand weeding alone, especially those with extensive root systems or which spread by rhizomes in the soil, such as couch grass (*Elymus repens*), bindweed (*Convolvulus arvensis*) and horsetail (*Equisetum arvense*).

Machinery has a limited use on the allotment, although rotavators can be used to destroy seedlings on vacant areas, and strimmers are useful for clearing overgrown areas.

Mulch is a layer of a material that is laid over the surface of a soil or other growing medium, often to suppress growth or prevent germination of weed seed. To be effective, mulches must be laid on a bare surface, as they will not inhibit established weeds. They should also be laid on soil that is warm and moist, in either autumn or spring, depending upon the crop involved.

DIFFERENT TYPES OF WEEDS

Annual meadow grass (*Poa annua*)
A very common annual weed that thrives in just about every situation on an allotment plot. Very variable and adaptable, and able to grow and set seed all year round.

Bindweed (*Convolvulus arvensis*)
Common perennial in well-drained soils that is difficult to control on account of the very deep roots from which the stems arise directly. Seeds prolifically.

Bittercress (*Cardamine hirsuta*)
A diminutive annual plant that often grows in mild periods in the winter. Sheds many seeds and can become invasive if not controlled.

Blackberry (*Rubus fruticosus*)
A highly persistent woody perennial, meaning that hand removal of young seedlings as soon as they are seen will save a lot of hard work later.

Charlock (*Sinapis arvensis*)
An annual plant that occasionally becomes problematic due to its ability to act as a host for clubroot in between normal crop rotations.

Chickweed (*Stellaria media*)
A common annual found on soil that is well cultivated and rich in organic matter. Spreads to make a large mat and seeds prolifically.

Couch grass (*Elymus repens*)
Spreads via perennial underground rhizomes to form thick masses in the soil over time. Can be difficult to eradicate but it will not stand constant cutting.

Dandelion (*Taraxacum officinalis*)
A common yellow-flowering perennial with long, strong tap roots that readily regenerate unless the whole plant is dug up and removed. Seeds prolifically if left in the ground.

Dock (*Rumex obtusifolius*)
A persistent perennial that is difficult to dig out and can regenerate from even a small section of root. Seeds prolifically if not controlled.

Groundsel (*Senecio vulgaris*)
Extremely common annual, often unnoticed beneath crops. It can tolerate very harsh conditions and varies greatly in size depending on site and soil.

Horsetail (*Equisetum arvense*)
Non-flowering perennial spreading via thin black roots to cover large areas. Difficult to dig out as the brittle stems and roots break easily when pulled.

Nettle (*Urtica dioica*)
An extremely common perennial in rich, fertile, frequently cultivated ground. Relatively easy to control but hated because of its stinging ability.

Shepherd's purse (*Capsella bursa-patoris*)
A very short-lived, prolifically seeding annual weed that often completes a whole life cycle in a mild winter period. Can also harbour clubroot.

Spear thistle (*Cirsium vulgare*)
One of a few biennial weeds, which can occasionally become a problem if it establishes between crops. Usually best controlled by cultivation.

Herbicides can give quick results when used correctly and these are split into two groups. 'Contact herbicides' are usually applied as a spray and kill only those parts with which they come into contact. 'Systemic (translocated) herbicides' are also applied as a spray, but are absorbed by the foliage and translocated to all parts of the plant. A few among these are selective, meaning that they target only one group of plants, and thereby leave the crop unharmed.

DO I NEED TO USE HERBICIDES?

This is occasionally a debateable point and, as a rule of thumb, the answer is likely to be no. The majority of herbicides (weed-killers) are toxic compounds that can kill other crops or persist in the environment, so should generally be avoided. The exception to this might be where highly persistent weeds cannot be effectively controlled by hand-weeding or mulches, but try these methods first.

GARDENER'S CALENDAR OF CARE

Understanding the yearly growing cycle is an important part of successful allotment gardening. Plants are acutely sensitive to the changing climate through the year and often require action to be taken within a narrow window of opportunity if the plot is to be fully productive. In order to do this, it is essential that you plan everything on paper in advance, foreseeing potential mistakes or opportunities, avoiding problems and allowing you to budget not only expense but also time. The following pages offer guidance, but over time you should develop your own seasonal planner.

Left: *Mangetouts (snow peas) are ready to harvest when the pods are plump but not fully grown, from late spring until late autumn.*

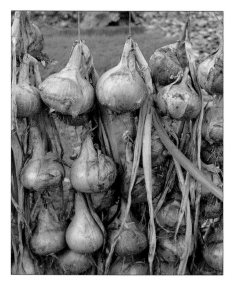

Above: *Late summer onions signal the start of the harvest which, whilst a busy time, represents the fulfilment of your labours.*

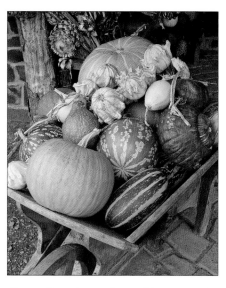

Above: *Squashes and pumpkins are a real sign that autumn has arrived, and mark the impending end of the growing season.*

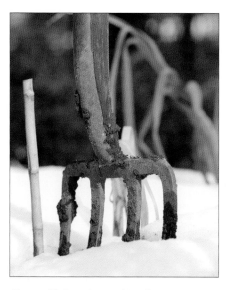

Above: *Allotments need tending even in the depths of winter, when a layer of snow may be covering the ground.*

EARLY SPRING

Marking the traditional start of the gardening season, early spring is the point in the year when the weather starts to warm up, days become longer and the strength of the sun becomes noticeable. Although frosts begin to subside now, winter can be reluctant to give way to spring, and allotment gardeners still need to keep an eye on weather forecasts and be prepared to protect crops at short notice. Many will still require protection for several more weeks.

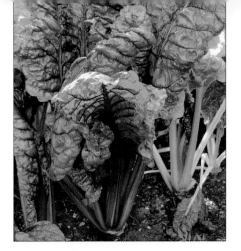

Above: *The beautiful stems of Swiss chard add colour and interest to the winter and spring vegetable patch.*

OVERVIEW

Spring is a magical time for allotment-holders, although the longer days and the strengthening sun can easily lull you into a false sense of security. It is the time when outdoor seed sowing really starts, although these first spring-like days are notoriously erratic. If the allotment is in a frost-prone area, delay sowing and planting outdoors, or warm the ground up well with cloches, fleece or black plastic for a couple of weeks before sowing, rather than risking damage to vulnerable seedlings.

Winter rains often have the dual effect of compacting the soil surface while depleting nutrient reserves in the soil. An easy way to give over-wintering crops a boost is to apply a general-purpose, compound fertilizer. Gently fork this into the surface of the soil, being careful not to damage any roots around established crops. Take particular care around plants such as asparagus, whose crowns are still lying dormant below the surface.

VEGETABLES

SOWING OUTDOORS NOW:
- Broad (fava) beans
- Brussels sprouts
- Calabrese (early)
- Cauliflowers (early)
- Leeks
- Parsnips
- Peas
- Radishes
- Summer cabbages

SOWING UNDER COVER NOW:
On a heated bench or propagator:
- Aubergines (eggplants)
- Celeriac
- Courgettes (zucchini)
- Cucumbers
- Self-blanching celery
- Sweet (bell) peppers
- Tomatoes (early indoor)

Above: *Sow early tomato seeds indoors.*

Under cloches:
- Beetroot (beets)
- Broad beans
- Brussels sprouts
- Carrots (early)
- Lettuces
- Parsnips
- Peas (early)
- Radishes
- Salad leaves
- Spinach
- Spring onions (scallions)
- Turnips

In module trays:
- Lettuces, sown at two-weekly intervals

PLANTING OUTDOORS NOW:
- Asparagus
- Broad beans
- Garlic
- Horseradish
- Jerusalem, globe and Chinese artichokes
- Leeks
- Onions (sets and autumn-sown)
- Potatoes (early, once chitted)
- Sea kale
- Shallots

PLANTING UNDER COVER NOW:
- Cauliflowers
- Peas (second early)

HARVESTING NOW:
- Beetroot
- Brussels sprouts
- Cabbages (Savoy and winter)
- Calabrese
- Cauliflowers (winter- and spring-heading)
- Chicory and endives
- Chinese and Jerusalem artichokes
- Kale and sea kale
- Leeks
- Lettuces (winter-protected)
- Parsnips
- Radishes
- Salsify and scorzonera
- Spinach (winter)
- Spring greens
- Spring onions
- Sprouting broccoli
- Swiss chard

GENERAL:
- Remove any remaining covers from forced rhubarb.
- Apply a nitrogen-rich fertilizer to spring cabbage at 30g (1oz) per lm (1yard) row.
- Clean and weed existing asparagus beds before growth commences.

LAST CHANCE TO:
- Sow celeriac, early peas and onions.
- Plant garlic, onions (sets), shallots and asparagus.

FRUIT
PLANTING NOW:
- Drought-prone fruit trees and bushes that need watering in their first season
- Outdoor vines, such as grapes
- Strawberry runners

PRUNE:
- Blackcurrants to within 5cm (2in) of the ground.
- Complete the pruning of cobnuts and filberts.
- Cut out older wood from acid cherries on established trees.
- Newly planted redcurrant and gooseberry bushes hard, by about half their length.

HARVESTING NOW:
- Rhubarb

GENERAL:
- Apply nitrogen-rich fertilizer to blackcurrants and give a second application of nitrogen to fruit trees if growing in grass.
- Apply a potassium-rich fertilizer to cane fruits.
- Check for wind damage, especially following high winds.
- Inspect stakes and ties of newly planted trees.
- Remove any weeds from around the bases of young trees, bushes and cane fruit, then mulch the area.
- Untie and retrain canes of blackberries and related fruits, which have been bundled together against winter damage, and train on wires before bud burst.

LAST CHANCE TO:
- Plant rhubarb, fruit trees and bushes.

Above: *Train blackberries on wires.*

HERBS
SOWING OUTDOORS NOW:
- Chervil
- Coriander (cilantro)
- Parsley

SOWING INDOORS NOW:
- Basil
- Curled parsley
- Marjoram

HARVESTING NOW:
- Parsley

GENERAL:
- Divide overcrowded perennial herbs, such as chives.

Above: *Divide chives, as necessary.*

PLANT HEALTH
Pests and diseases:
▷ Look out for signs of all pests from now on. Aphids are usually the first to appear.
▷ Pinch out the top of broad (fava) beans when in flower to reduce attack from black fly.
▷ Slugs can strip young plants of new growth, doing irreparable damage. These become more active now as the temperatures rises, so keep an eye out for them.
▷ Peaches and nectarines can be sprayed to protect against peach leaf curl. Apply sticky bands to apple trees.

Soil and climate:
▷ Hoe frequently for weed control and soil aeration.
▷ Complete all digging and manuring, adding fertilizer in final soil preparations.
▷ Apply a good general fertilizer to all open ground.
▷ Use nets for frost protection on early blooms and young fruitlets on fruit trees, on still cold nights.

Above: *The hazy, weak sunshine of early spring heralds the arrival of a new season.*

MID-SPRING

Mid-spring brings the real promise of the main growing season to come. Lengthening days combined with steadily increasing temperatures and light levels mean that crops start to grow in earnest as the summer approaches. The effect of the longer daylight hours is extremely important for us too, meaning that we now have the opportunity to get out into our precious patches in the evenings for an hour or two while it is still light. Just as well as it is all go on the allotment from now on!

Above: *The first young stems of asparagus are a very welcome sight; make the most of them as the season is short.*

OVERVIEW

While the risk of a hard frost is generally slight by mid-spring, plants can still be damaged by wide fluctuations in temperature and will either need to be grown under protection or their sowing and planting delayed. Despite this, this is the time where sowing vegetable seed really gets under way.

Mid-spring also marks the start of the pretty blossom period, which reaches a crescendo toward the start of late spring. The buzzing of bees eagerly pollinating these blooms is a welcome sight, but remember that with it come some less welcome guests: the insects and other pests that can ruin a crop if left unchecked.

To survive the coming season, your plants will need a good start. It is most important, then, that they are given proper care and attention now, ensuring they have enough food and being vigilant about pests and diseases. This will mean that they begin their lives in the best possible condition and you will reap the rewards later.

VEGETABLES

SOWING OUTDOORS NOW:
- Asparagus peas
- Beetroot (beet)
- Brussels sprouts
- Cabbages
- Calabrese
- Carrots (early and maincrop)
- Cauliflowers
- Kale
- Kohlrabi
- Leeks
- Lettuces
- Onions (bulb and spring),
- Oriental greens (seedling crops and bolt-resistant types)
- Parsnips (in situ)
- Peas
- Red chicory (Belgian endive)
- Salsify
- Scorzonera
- Spinach
- Sprouting broccoli
- Swiss chard
- Turnips (early)

SOWING UNDER COVER NOW:
- Aubergines (eggplants)
- Capsicums (sweet and chilli)
- Courgettes (zucchini)
- Cucumbers (indoor)
- Dwarf French (green) beans
- Marrows (large zucchini)

Above: *Sow courgette seeds indoors.*

- Pumpkins
- Runner (green) beans
- Self-blanching celery and celeriac
- Squashes
- Sweetcorn (corn)
- Tomatoes (outdoor)

UNDER CLOCHES:
- Lettuces
- Mixed salad leaves
- Spring onions (scallions)

PLANTING OUTDOORS NOW:
- Potatoes (second early)

HARVEST NOW:
- Asparagus (early)
- Cauliflowers (spring-heading)
- Celeriac
- Chicory (Belgian endive)

- Endives
- Jerusalem artichokes
- Leeks
- Oriental greens (seedling crops)
- Radishes (summer and winter)
- Salad plants
- Salsify
- Scorzonera
- Sea kale
- Spinach (winter)
- Spring cabbages
- Spring onions
- Sprouting broccoli
- Swiss chard

GENERAL:
- Start hardening off seedlings of brassicas, leeks and onions from prior sowings in the greenhouse in a cold frame.
- Transplant cabbages, cauliflowers, leeks or broad (fava) beans sown earlier to their final positions.
- Plant up a new asparagus bed.

LAST CHANCE TO:
- Sow spring varieties of broad bean, Brussels sprouts, cabbage (summer/autumn), cauliflower and celery (under cover).
- Force chicory or sea kale.
- Plant maincrop potatoes, Chinese artichoke, globe artichoke and sea kale.

Above: *Harvest forced rhubarb.*

FRUIT
SOWING UNDERCOVER NOW:
• Melons

PLANTING OUTDOORS NOW:
• Raspberries
• Strawberries

PRUNE:
• Figs (before the buds break)
• Gooseberries
• Newly planted raspberry canes to encourage good root establishment and strong new shoots
• Red and white currants if left unpruned through the winter, to reduce bird damage
• Young pyramid plums

HARVESTING NOW:
• Rhubarb (forced)

GENERAL:
• Apply nitrogen (light dressing) to established strawberry plants if growth is poor and apply a foliar feed at least every two weeks.
• Hand-pollinate wall-trained peach and nectarine flowers and mist spray at midday to help setting in dry weather.
• Ventilate plants under cloches and add straw mulch as flowering commences.
• Water all newly planted trees, bushes and canes if necessary.

LAST CHANCE TO:
• Plant blackberry plants.

HERBS
SOWING OUTDOORS NOW:
• Borage
• Coriander (cilantro)
• Dill
• Feverfew
• Marjoram
• Pot marigold

SOWING INDOORS NOW:
• Basil
• Parsley

PLANTING OUTDOORS NOW:
• Bay
• Mint
• Oregano
• Parsley
• Rosemary
• Sage
• Tarragon (all types)
• Thyme

HARVESTING NOW:
• Bay
• Parsley
• Russian tarragon
• Sage

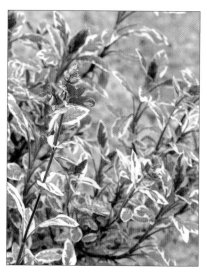

Above: *Pick sage (tricolour sage shown).*

GENERAL:
• Check that mint clumps haven't grown outside their allotted area as they can grow rampantly if unchecked. Use a spade to dig out unwanted shoots and runners.
• Trim sage, cotton lavender, bay and rue, to keep plants neat and to encourage fresh, tender shoots.

PLANT HEALTH
Pests and diseases:
▷ Uproot and dispose of old brassica stumps by burning them to avoid a build-up of clubroot. Never compost brassica roots as this can spread it around the garden and seriously reduce the efficacy of rotations.
▷ Check the state of fruit netting and supports and repair if necessary.
▷ Try to avoid using any insect control sprays during flowering as this may affect pollinating insects.
▷ Keep an eye out for pests generally throughout the garden.

Soil and climate:
▷ Early flowering fruits may need protection against frost on cold evenings as this can damage the blossom and result in major crop losses. Drape hessian (burlap) or fleece over the plants in late evening but remove this in the morning to enable pollination to take place.

▷ Give some extra protection to lettuces and outdoor tomatoes on colder nights and don't be tempted to remove cloches prematurely. Drape a bit of extra fleece over them on especially cold nights, but ensure you remove cloches or ventilate freely on warm spring days to prevent scorch.
▷ Hoe to remove all weeds from crops, especially in dry weather, when the sun will aid the weeding process by making the soil looser.

Above: *Drape fleece over vulnerable plants.*

LATE SPRING

The arrival of warmer weather and longer daylight hours, often combined with plenty of gentle late spring showers, can create some of the best growing conditions of the year. This is the time to carry out the essential groundwork to ensure a bumper crop on the allotment in the months to come. Make sure that you get your priorities straight and don't try and be too ambitious; it is better to grow fewer crops properly than too many and not be able to give them proper attention.

Above: *Tart green gooseberries are one of the treats of late spring, and signal the arrival of the soft fruit season in the allotment.*

OVERVIEW

Despite the need to get sowing and planting, late spring still gives us a lot of leeway to work out what we need to do for the rest of the year as the plants are still growing and tend to present few problems compared to what could happen in the months to come.

The warm days may distract us from the fact that there may still be an occasional frost, and these can have devastating results on more tender plants or those not properly hardened off before they were hastily planted out. Where there is even a slight chance of frost you should delay putting tender specimens out until early summer.

Late spring is also the time when the army of pests hell bent upon 'sharing' your crop will start to appear in earnest. Vigilance is the key aspect in your defence against these and you should make regular health checks of the crops to ensure that they are in peak condition. Take swift action if you do spot any pests or diseases.

VEGETABLES

SOWING OUTDOORS NOW:

- Asparagus peas
- Beetroot (beets) (maincrop)
- Calabrese
- Carrots
- Cauliflowers
- Chicory
- Courgettes (zucchini)
- Endives
- Florence fennel
- French (green) beans
- Kale
- Kohlrabi
- Leeks
- Lettuces (short rows in succession)
- Marrows (large zucchini)
- Parsnips
- Peas (maincrop)
- Pumpkins
- Purple sprouting broccoli
- Radishes
- Runner (green) beans
- Salad onions
- Salsify
- Scorzonera
- Sea kale
- Spinach (ordinary and New Zealand)
- Spring cabbages
- Squashes
- Swedes (rutabagas)
- Turnips
- Winter cabbages (early maturing)

SOWING UNDER COVER NOW:

- Cucumbers
- French beans
- Marrows
- Runner beans
- Sweetcorn (corn)

PLANTING OUTDOORS NOW:

- Aubergines (eggplants)
- Brussels sprouts
- Cauliflowers (summer)
- Celeriac
- Celery
- Courgettes
- Jerusalem artichokes
- Peppers
- Pumpkins
- Summer and winter cabbages
- Sweetcorn
- Tomatoes

HARVESTING NOW:

- Broad (fava) beans
- Cauliflowers (spring-heading)
- Celeriac
- Chicory
- Early asparagus
- Endives
- Kohlrabi
- Over-wintered carrots
- Peas (early)
- Radishes
- Salad onions

- Salsify
- Scorzonera
- Spinach (summer and winter)
- Spring cabbages
- Spring lettuces
- Sprouting broccoli (late forms)
- Swiss chard
- Texsel greens
- Turnips

GENERAL:

- Apply dilute liquid manure to cauliflowers and celery.
- Harden off plants that are to be planted out in early summer.
- Keep greenhouses ventilated. Check cold frames, ventilating when necessary. By the end of the month, the frame covers will only be needed if there is a chilly evening.
- Remove side shoots from vine tomatoes growing under glass.
- Water crops as needed.

LAST CHANCE TO:

- Plant out early potatoes and Jerusalem artichokes.
- Sow sprouting broccoli, winter cabbage, autumn cauliflower, kale, carrots, parsnips, salsify, scorzonera, asparagus peas, broad beans, leeks, and New Zealand spinach.

FRUIT

HARVESTING NOW:

- Green gooseberries
- Rhubarb
- Strawberries (under cloches)

GENERAL:

- Apply nitrogen such as hoof and horn to strawberries if growth is poor as this will promote improved growth over several weeks. Commence foliar feeding with seaweed extract at least every two weeks.
- Protect blossoms of late-flowering fruit from frosts. Remove blossom from newly planted trees.
- De-shoot wall-trained peaches and nectarines and remove shoots from wall-trained plums and damsons growing towards or away from a wall.
- Hoe off or pull out raspberry suckers appearing between rows.
- Mow grass around fruit trees.
- On indoor vines, allow only one flower truss to develop on each lateral shoot and remove the others. Pinch out the tips of fruiting laterals two leaves past a flower truss and non-fruiting laterals after five leaves. Stop side-shoots after one leaf.
- Open one side of fruit cage to allow entry for pollinating insects.
- Remove unwanted shoots from raspberries, leaving only strong healthy growth.
- Shorten back leaders and side-shoots on over-vigorous restricted forms of apples and pears (such as cordons, espalier fans etc.).
- Start netting all fruit at the first sign of ripening.
- Water all bushes and trees well (especially stone fruits and those trained against walls) after flowering.

Above: *Net bushes as fruit ripens.*

Above: *Harvest rosemary.*

HERBS

SOWING OUTDOORS NOW:

- Basil
- Borage
- Chervil
- Coriander (cilantro)
- Dill
- Fennel
- Florence fennel (bolt-resistant)
- Nasturtium

HARVESTING NOW:

- Bay
- Rosemary
- Sage

GENERAL:

- Top-dress container-grown herbs with garden compost.
- Lift and divide chives, hyssop, rosemary and sorrel. Replant with a little added compost.

PLANT HEALTH

Pests and diseases:

▷ Ensure good air circulation in the greenhouse to reduce risk of botrytis and downy mildew on grapes and, if needed, start to apply shading to the greenhouse to prevent overheating.

▷ Control slugs and snails and check all plants for pests, diseases and dieback. Be ready to spray against pests as soon as they are noticed, using natural products. Watch for the tell-tale holes of flea beetle attacks on brassica seedlings. Water well to help them grow out of the pest damage.

▷ Pests can be kept off a wide range of crops by covering with a fine woven plastic mesh, such as Enviromesh. Just make sure that the corners are tucked in or buried to prevent the pests breaching this defence.

▷ Put up pheromone traps in the orchard to help reduce codling moth numbers. Biological control (such as *Bacillus thruingiensis*) may be needed if numbers are high.

▷ Set out companion plants (annuals) around all trees and bushes to encourage beneficial predators.

▷ If using spray of natural products, such as neem, citronella or garlic oil against pests, delay applying this until flowering is complete.

▷ Do not be too worried if the leaves on a pear tree start to come up in small pale blisters. This is probably due to

Above: *Put straw around strawberries.*

the pear leaf blister mite and, although there are currently no effective organic controls for this, the damage is not as severe as the plant's appearance may suggest and infested trees can still go on to produce a good crop of pears.

▷ Put dry straw around strawberry plants in order to deter slugs and keep fruit clean. Remove blossom from spring-planted runners of summer-fruiting strawberries.

▷ Weed control is very important at this time of year as they can easily compete with your crops for moisture and nutrients. Hoe between rows during dry weather to maximize the effect of this treatment.

Soil and climate:

▷ Be prepared to drape some fleece over more tender crops if cold weather threatens.

EARLY SUMMER

Early summer is the time that sees the longest day of the year, and the associated extra light and warmth encourages the garden to put on an exuberant burst of growth. As a result, the allotment really starts to become productive around now. Prolonged warm spells will also accelerate the rate at which the soil dries out, however, so new plants must also be watered and greenhouses, frames and cloches will need good ventilation during the daytime to prevent inside temperatures soaring.

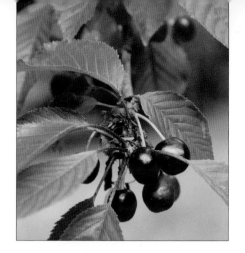

Above: *The flavour of home-grown cherries, far surpasses that of store-bought ones as they should be eaten as fresh as possible.*

OVERVIEW

The ever-strengthening sunshine during the early part of the summer means that gardeners need to keep on top of weeds from now on. Hoe annual weeds off and dig out any persistent perennial ones regularly. Mulching when the ground is wet can help suppress weeds as well as conserving moisture.

Early summer is the prime time to plant out tender crops that have been lovingly raised under cover. If you hardened them off properly in late spring then they should be fine, but be prepared to place a covering of fleece over them if cold nights threaten. This will reward you with stronger plants, which in turn helps improve yields.

Although weeding and watering will be the two most important tasks of the month, pests and diseases can become a real problem. Be vigilant and look out for them, as you will need to act quickly once, and if, you find them. Time spent now is a real investment for ensuring the best results at harvest time.

VEGETABLES

SOWING OUTDOORS NOW:
- Beetroot (beets)
- Cabbages (Chinese)
- Calabrese
- Carrots
- Chicory (Belgian endive)
- Chinese broccoli
- Courgettes (zucchini)
- Endives
- French and runner (green) beans
- Kohlrabi
- Lettuces
- Marrows (large zucchini)
- Oriental greens
- Peas (maincrop)
- Pumpkins and squashes
- Radishes
- Spring onions (scallions)
- Swedes (rutabagas)
- Turnips

PLANTING OUTDOORS NOW:
- Courgettes
- Runner (green) beans
- Sweetcorn (corn)
- Tomatoes (outdoor)

TRANSPLANT:
- Broccoli
- Brussels sprouts
- Kale
- Leeks

Above: *Harvest Swiss chard.*

HARVESTING NOW:
- Asparagus
- Beetroot
- Broad (fava) beans
- Calabrese
- Carrots
- Cauliflowers (spring-heading and early summer)
- Chicory
- Cucumbers (indoor)
- Endives
- French beans
- Kohlrabi
- Lettuces
- Onions (bulb – autumn-sown)
- Peas (early and maincrop)
- Potatoes (early)
- Radishes
- Spring cabbages
- Spring onions

- Spinach (summer)
- Swiss chard
- Turnips

GENERAL:
- Earth up late potatoes.
- Pinch out the top of broad beans once the lowest flowers have set.
- Set up an irrigation system.
- Support climbing French and runner beans with canes.
- Thin rows of vegetables when they become overcrowded.

LAST CHANCE TO:
- Harvest the last asparagus.
- Plant celery and outdoor tomatoes.
- Sow calabrese, swede, courgette, marrow, squash, pumpkin and summer spinach.

Above: *Uproot fresh young carrots.*

FRUIT

PLANTING NOW:
- Melons

PRUNE NOW:
- Begin summer pruning of apples and pears.
- Carefully tie fragile new growths of climbing fruit plants.
- Continue disbudding wall-trained peaches or nectarines and tie-in selected shoots.
- Pinch out the top buds on the young shoots of figs at five leaves.
- Prune out old canes on newly planted raspberries.
- Red and white currants will need to be summer pruned before mid-summer.
- Thin and summer prune gooseberries as mid-summer approaches.

GENERAL:
- Apply nitrogen such as hoof and horn to strawberries if not already done and apply a dilute foliar feed of seaweed extract at least every two weeks.
- Loosely tie in new shoots of raspberries and train in new shoots of blackberries and hybrid berries.
- Mulch raspberries and currants.
- Peg down runners of strawberries for new plants. Transplant these once they have rooted.
- Put straw, black polythene or mats down for strawberries, and remove unwanted runners.
- Remove any fruits from fan-trained cherries and plums that are growing towards a wall or fence.

Above: *Harvest raspberries.*

- Thin apples lightly if fruit set is heavy, waiting until after mid-summer drop for a final thinning.
- Thin fruits on plums in the early part of the month and again toward the end of the month.
- Thin gooseberries toward the end of the month.
- Thin pears if heavily set.
- Ventilate protected strawberry plants and remove cloches when fruiting has finished.
- Water fruit when necessary and spray foliage in evening during hot weather if possible.

HARVESTING NOW:
- Cherries
- Gooseberries
- Raspberries
- Red and white currants
- Rhubarb
- Strawberries

LAST CHANCE TO:
- Prune gooseberries, red and white currants.

HERBS

SOWING OUTDOORS NOW:
- Basil
- Borage
- Chives
- Coriander (cilantro)
- Fennel
- Parsley
- Rocket (arugula)
- Savory (summer and winter)

HARVESTING NOW:
- Bay
- Borage flowers
- Chives
- Nasturtium (leaves and flowers)
- Parsley
- Rosemary
- Sage
- Tarragon
- Thyme

GENERAL:
- Hoe and remove weeds regularly.
- Plant out pots of basil or other tender herbs raised under cover.
- Take softwood cuttings of shrubby herbs.
- Trim shrubby herbs after flowering.

PLANT HEALTH

Pests and diseases:
▷ Hang sticky straps in greenhouses to monitor flying pest numbers, treating all pest outbreaks as they are detected.
▷ Continue to protect fruit against birds and regularly check nets for deterioration or damage.
▷ Check for signs of damage on raspberry canes from raspberry beetle, spraying with derris if it is found.
▷ Continue to watch for the tell-tale holes of flea beetle attacks on brassica seedlings.
▷ Keep alert for gooseberry sawfly damage and the raised red blisters of currant blister aphid.
▷ Keep an eye out for asparagus beetles, which are black, red and yellow, and their creamy-black larvae. Pick them off stems and foliage by hand.
▷ Check for signs of apple and pear canker, bacterial canker, and blossom wilt, removing affected material and burning it immediately.

Soil and climate:
▷ Improve ventilation and shade greenhouses or frames if necessary.
▷ Ventilate greenhouses and conservatories every day, but remember to close the vents on chilly nights to prevent a sudden temperature drop.
▷ Remove cloches from all outdoor crops as the risk of frost disappears.
▷ Hoe between rows during dry weather to remove weeds, which can compete with your crops for moisture and nutrients.

Above: *Shade greenhouses.*

MID-SUMMER

Traditionally the warm mid-summer period is a time when you start to gain a real sense of the harvest to come. These long, balmy summer days also offer a chance to sit back and enjoy the work of the previous months, as the long days and summer evenings ensure that there is time to do this after you have tended your crops. There is still plenty to be done though, and hot, dry days can mean that you will spend much of your time making sure everything is kept fed and watered.

Above: *Runner beans (pictured) and French beans are prolific, and provide a bountiful and reliable crop for relatively little effort.*

OVERVIEW

Mid-summer is usually the hottest and driest part of the year. While it can still be prone to showers and unsettled periods, rain is often a bonus and you should try and save water when you can. Frost is rare now, but not impossible, and gardeners in cold areas still need to keep an eye on the local forecasts.

Weeds grow at a phenomenal rate at this time of year, meaning that plots should be regularly hoed off, preferably weekly or even more frequently to ensure control. Pests and diseases also thrive in the warmth, meaning that you will inevitably need to treat these with chemical or biological controls in order to protect your crops from harm.

A lot of crops will be ready for harvesting this month and many of these will need to be gathered quickly as they can soon be past their best if left out. Even if you have a glut, never leave crops to rot as they can quickly spread disease to their neighbours. Share and swap excess produce with neighbouring plot holders, if you like.

VEGETABLES

SOWING OUTDOORS NOW:
- Beetroot (beets)
- Carrots
- Calabrese
- Chicory (sugar-loaf and red)
- Endives
- Florence fennel
- Kohlrabi
- Lettuces
- Oriental greens
- Peas (maincrop)
- Spring cabbages
- Swiss chard
- Turnips
- Winter radishes

PLANTING OUTDOORS NOW:
- Broccoli
- Kale
- Leeks
- Sprouts
- Winter cabbages

HARVESTING NOW:
- Asparagus peas
- Beetroot
- Cabbages (summer)
- Calabrese
- Capsicums (protected)
- Carrots
- Cauliflowers (early summer)
- Celery (self-blanching)

- Chicory
- Courgettes (zucchini)
- Cucumbers
- Endives
- Florence fennel
- French (green) beans
- Globe artichokes
- Kohlrabi
- Lettuces
- Marrows (large zucchini)
- Onions (bulb and spring)
- Peas
- Potatoes (early)
- Pumpkins
- Radishes (summer)
- Runner (green) beans
- Salad leaves
- Shallots
- Spinach (New Zealand and summer)
- Squashes
- Sweetcorn (corn)
- Swiss chard
- Tomatoes (protected)
- Turnips

GENERAL:
- Apply regular doses of liquid manure to heavy feeders.
- As cauliflowers start to form their curds, break a few leaves over the curd to protect them from the sun and keep them white.
- Dry shallots ready for storing.
- Earth up and stake brassicas.

- Earth up sweetcorn and celery.
- Feed plants when necessary, usually once every 1–2 weeks with a liquid feed.
- Hand-pollinate the female flowers of marrows and courgettes if fruit is failing to set.
- Mulch runner beans after watering.
- Pinch out any remaining side shoots of cordon tomatoes (not bush types).
- Spray the flowers of outdoor tomatoes and runner beans with water to ensure a good set of fruit.
- Thin carrots and beetroot as they start to fill out.
- Water outdoor cucumbers, marrows, courgettes and beans regularly.

LAST CHANCE TO:
- Sow beetroot, Florence fennel, beans (French and runner), maincrop and early peas and lettuces (main outdoor crop).

Above: *Harvest young potatoes.*

FRUIT

PLANTING NOW:

- Continue to peg down strawberry runners if new plants are needed.

PRUNE:

- As soon as raspberries have finished cropping, prune out old canes and tie in new ones.
- Complete the summer pruning of all trained fruit trees and bushes by the end of the month but delay if wet as this can encourage water sprouts near the cut branch tips.
- Protect the surface of wounds on plum trees with an antifungal control.
- Prune fan-trained plum and cherry trees.
- Spur prune gooseberries.

HARVESTING NOW:

- Blackberries
- Blackcurrants
- Blueberries
- Cherries
- Gooseberries
- Loganberries
- Melons
- Peaches
- Raspberries
- Rhubarb
- Strawberries

GENERAL:

- Check tree ties for constriction and loosen appropriately.
- Complete any remaining thinning on apples and plums and support heavily laden branches.
- If you have fruit bushes such as citrus growing under cover, these can go outside until the autumn.
- Train in new canes of blackberries, keeping a couple of longer ones so that tip layering for new plants can be done at the end of the month.
- Water all fruit-laden plants when necessary and protect all remaining fruits against birds. Spray foliage in evenings during hot weather.

LAST CHANCE TO:

- Summer-prune wall-trained fruit trees.

HERBS

SOWING OUTDOORS NOW:

- Basil
- Borage
- Coriander (cilantro)
- Chervil
- Parsley

HARVESTING NOW

- Basil
- Dill
- Hyssop
- Lemon balm
- Marjoram
- Mint
- Parsley
- Sage
- Summer savory
- Tarragon
- Thyme

GENERAL:

- Begin gathering seed of caraway and angelica.
- Dead-head where flowers have faded, unless seed is to be collected.
- Dry any excess pickings for later use.
- Feed plants when necessary, usually once every one to two weeks.
- Hoe and remove weeds regularly.
- Most other herbs can also be sown now, and constant picking will help keep young shoots coming throughout the summer.
- Mulch around the bases of moisture-loving herbs such as mint or parsley.
- Take softwood cuttings.
- Thin seedlings sown outdoors.
- Water any plants that show signs of stress.

Above: *Tarragon is at its best in summer.*

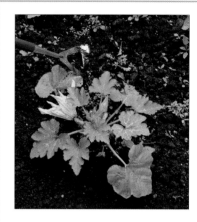

Above: *Hoe weeds regularly.*

PLANT HEALTH

Pests and diseases:

▷ Continue to check plants regularly for pests and diseases and treat them accordingly.

▷ Watch out for potato blight, which can be a problem at this time of year, particularly when damp. Remember that it often also attacks tomatoes. Lift potatoes and harvest tomatoes as soon as it is seen. Burn affected plants.

▷ Remove mouldy or damaged strawberries to prevent the spread of botrytis (grey mould) and, immediately after they have finished cropping, remove foliage, straw, surplus runners and all weeds. Dispose of debris, preferably by burning.

▷ Remove any fallen plant debris, such as leaves or old flowers, as this will prevent potential pest and disease problems later in the year.

▷ Keep an early eye out for the sunken brown patches of blossom end rot on tomatoes, especially if the weather has been dry. It can be a sign of irregular watering.

Soil and climate:

▷ Ventilate glasshouses to their maximum to prevent scorch damage to remaining plants and water crops freely in early morning or late evening to avoid the risk of leaf scorch on hot days.

▷ Damp down greenhouses on very hot days.

▷ Continue to hoe off weeds regularly in dry weather.

LATE SUMMER

Late summer is generally the last of the truly hot months and is often dry and sunny, especially at its start. In some places, however, the late summer can be prone to thunderstorms, and as a consequence it may tend to be humid and dull, providing the perfect conditions for pests and diseases to thrive in. Weeds continue to grow apace and as days begin to shorten, the burdens of weeding, watering, and the increasing numbers of plants ready for harvest can make this one of the busiest times on the allotment.

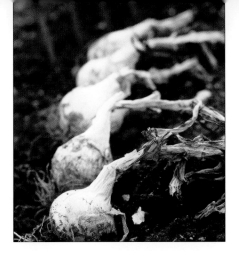

Above: *Choose a sunny day in late summer to dry onions on the surface of the soil, ready for autumn storage.*

OVERVIEW

Many vegetables are ready for harvesting this month and it is important that this is done promptly, as they can soon be past their best. Never leave crops to rot as they can spread disease to their neighbours. Always ensure that rows of crops do not become overcrowded.

Despite the fact that the days are often still hot, evenings are starting to draw in by the end of the summer and it is wise to start to make plans for the coming months. This is a good time to sow and raise seeds for autumn-planted crops. Prepare vacant ground for these future crops by digging deeply, removing any trace of weeds and crop the residue as you go. Work in plenty of garden compost or well-rotted manure as you do this.

You will also need to prepare a plan for how to deal with the crops to be harvested. Ensure your storage areas are clear and clean, and make a timetable for preparing preserves, pickles or for freezing your produce.

VEGETABLES

SOWING OUTDOORS NOW:
- Chicory (sugar-loaf and red)
- Chinese cabbages
- Corn salad
- Endives
- Florence fennel
- Kohlrabi
- Land cress
- Lettuces
- Onions (bulb)
- Oriental greens
- Radishes (summer and winter)
- Scorzonera
- Spring cabbages
- Spring onions (winter scallions)
- Swiss chard
- Turnips
- Winter radishes

PLANTING OUTDOORS NOW
- Cauliflowers
- Late cabbages
- Leeks

HARVESTING NOW:
- Asparagus peas
- Aubergines (eggplants)
- Beetroot (beets)
- Broad (fava) beans
- Cabbages (summer, autumn, Chinese)
- Carrots
- Cauliflowers (summer and early autumn)
- Celery (self-blanching)
- Chicory (sugar-loaf and red)
- Courgettes (zucchini)
- Endives
- Florence fennel
- French (green) beans
- Garlic
- Globe artichokes
- Kohlrabi
- Leeks
- Lettuces
- Marrows (large zucchini)
- Onions (bulbs)
- Oriental greens
- Potatoes (maincrop)
- Pumpkins
- Radishes (summer)
- Runner (green) beans
- Shallots
- Spinach (New Zealand)
- Spring onions
- Squashes
- Sweetcorn (corn)
- Swiss chard
- Tomatoes (outdoor)
- Turnips

GENERAL:
- Earth up and stake brassicas that are to be kept for late autumn, winter or spring cropping.
- Feed plants when necessary, usually once every one to two weeks, with a liquid feed.
- Green manure or winter cover crops.
- Hoe weeds during hot weather.
- If the weather is dry, apply water directly to the soil in mornings or late evening, rather than watering little and often, to prevent leaf scorch.
- Lift and dry onions, preferably in the sun, to fully develop their flavour.
- Pinch out runner beans that have reached the end of their support.
- Remove any foliage from pumpkins and winter squashes and lift them on to a straw mat or a couple of bricks.
- Stake outdoor tomatoes and pinch the growing tip out at four or five trusses.

LAST CHANCE TO:
- Sow Chinese cabbage, spring cabbage, autumn cauliflower, kohlrabi, radish (summer), turnip, onions (autumn-sown) and Swiss chard.

Above: *Raise squashes up on straw.*

FRUIT

PLANTING NOW:

- Rooted runners of summer-fruiting strawberry varieties if beds were prepared last month.

PRUNE:

- Continue pruning restricted forms of apples and pears as well as any over-vigorous trees.
- Prune plums, gages and damsons after fruiting. Cover large wounds with a suitable wound treatment.
- Summer prune cobnuts and filberts by breaking strong lateral growths by hand to about 6–8 leaves from the base and leaving them to hang.
- As soon as wall-trained peaches and nectarines have fruited, cut out the shoots that have borne fruit as well as any dead wood, and tie in replacement shoots.
- Remove dead wood from fan-trained plums, shorten pinched-back shoots and tie in.
- Continue pruning and tying-in new canes of raspberries, blackberries and hybrid berries, cutting out old canes that have finished fruiting.
- Hoe regularly and mulch around the bases of trees and bushes with compost or grass clippings, leaving a gap around the stem to allow air circulation.

HARVESTING NOW:

- Apples (early varieties)
- Apricots
- Blackberries
- Blackcurrants (2nd half of month)
- Currants (last part of month)
- Loganberries

Above: *Harvest blackberries.*

- Peaches
- Pears
- Plums
- Raspberries
- Strawberries (perpetual types)

GENERAL:

- Continue to protect all fruits against birds and water fruit-laden bushes as and when necessary.
- Feed plants when necessary, usually once every one to two weeks with a liquid feed.
- Prepare ground for planting a new rhubarb bed.
- Prepare ground before the end of the summer for summer-fruiting strawberry beds.
- Prepare ground for planting currants, blackberries, peach trees, apricot trees and gooseberries.
- Spray foliage of all fruit in the evening during hot weather.

LAST CHANCE TO:

- Prepare beds for planting summer-fruiting strawberries.

HERBS

SOWING OUTDOORS NOW:

- Parsley (warmer regions)

SOWING UNDER COVER NOW:

- Chives
- Coriander (cilantro)
- Dill
- Parsley (cooler regions)

HARVESTING NOW

- Basil
- Bay
- Chives
- Dill
- Marjoram
- Mint
- Oregano
- Parsley
- Rosemary
- Sage
- Tarragon
- Thyme

GENERAL:

- Take cuttings of rosemary, bay and hyssop.
- Cut back flowered herbs such as marjoram to encourage a second flush of growth.
- Water any plants that may be showing signs of stress and mulch moisture-loving herbs such as mint to prevent them drying out.
- Thin seedlings that have been sown direct in the garden.
- Dead-head herbs with faded flowers, unless seed is to be collected from them.
- Gather seed from angelica, caraway, coriander, cumin, chervil, dill and fennel.

PLANT HEALTH

Pests and diseases:

▷ Remove any fallen plant debris, as this will prevent potential pest and disease problems later in the year.

▷ Check plants for signs of pests, treating these accordingly with a suitable control.

▷ Look out for the caterpillars on peas and brassicas, and spray immediately with derris or the biological control *Bacillus thruingiensis*.

▷ Remove apples, pears and plums affected with brown rot to prevent the disease from spreading and gather scabby leaves from diseased apples and pears. Do not compost any of this.

▷ Remove and burn any outdoor tomatoes and potatoes affected by blight to prevent further infection of the crop. Cut off stems from blighted potatoes and burn them, although the potato tubers can still be harvested.

Soil and climate:

▷ Ventilate greenhouses to their maximum to prevent soaring temperatures. Use shading if necessary.

▷ Water all crops freely when they are in growth and damp down greenhouses on hot days.

▷ Spread mulches over ground that has recently received rain. Rotted-down compost is ideal and will free up space in the heap for next month's waste.

EARLY AUTUMN

The start of autumn is usually a continuation of warm summer weather although inevitably, this gives way to cooler, damper and often rather windier conditions over the ensuing weeks. The other change, which becomes especially noticeable now, is the shortening days. Although conditions remain mostly mild in the day, frosts can occur anytime from now on, meaning you should protect or gather in the last of your tender, summer crops as cold conditions threaten.

Above: *Leeks keep much better in the ground than in storage, so it is best to eat them straight after harvesting.*

OVERVIEW

Despite the advent of cooler, shorter days, the growing season can be extended well into the early autumn, especially in warmer locations, simply by applying a mulch to crops in late summer to help keep the warmth in the soil for longer. Occasional night frosts become common as mid-autumn approaches, particularly in exposed areas, on high ground, and in frost pockets, so have some horticultural fleece handy for the odd nights when it is needed.

Early autumn is the time to reflect upon the success of your labours by reaping the rewards of your hard work, particularly in the vegetable patch. You are likely to have a glut of many crops and so you will need to set about storing it for the winter ahead, when the pickings from your plot can be quite meagre. Towards the end of the month the inevitable clear out must commence as you embark upon the autumn cultivations and soil treatments that will help nourish next year's crop.

VEGETABLES

SOWING OUTDOORS NOW:
- Cauliflowers (for transplanting to a frame in mid-autumn)
- Lettuces
- Spinach

SOWING UNDER COVER NOW:
- Chicory (sugar-loaf)
- Lettuces
- Pak choi
- Salad leaves

Under cloches:
- Broad (fava) beans
- Carrots
- Lettuces
- Spring cabbages

PLANTING OUTDOORS NOW
- Japanese onions (sets)

HARVESTING NOW:
- Aubergines (eggplants)
- Beetroot (beets)
- Brussels sprouts
- Cabbages (autumn)
- Calabrese
- Carrots
- Cauliflowers (summer, early autumn and autumn)
- Celery (self-blanching)
- Chicory (sugar-loaf and red)
- Courgettes (zucchini)
- Cucumbers (outdoor)
- Endives
- Florence fennel
- French (green) beans
- Garlic
- Globe artichokes
- Kohlrabi
- Leeks
- Lettuces
- Marrows (large zucchini)
- Onions (spring and bulb)
- Oriental greens
- Parsnips
- Peas (maincrop)
- Potatoes
- Radishes (summer)
- Runner (green) beans
- Salad leaves
- Spinach (summer and New Zealand)
- Squashes and pumpkins
- Sweetcorn (corn)
- Swiss chard
- Tomatoes (outdoor)
- Turnips

GENERAL:
- Cover leafy vegetable crops with bird-proof netting.
- Cut down asparagus foliage and add to compost heap.
- Earth up celery, leeks and winter greens.
- Give Brussels sprouts a liquid feed.
- Keep up with watering winter squash and pumpkins.
- Leave the roots of pea and bean plants in the soil to increase fertility.
- Lift main crop carrots and cut off the tops. Put aside any with split roots. Store the remainder in layers of sand in seed boxes. Keep in a frost-free shed.
- Lift maincrop potatoes and leave to dry before storing them.
- Lift beetroot when they are the size of cricket balls and store in the same way as carrots.
- Sow a quick-growing green manure such as mustard, on land cleared of crops and dig in before it flowers.
- Stake plants of Brussels sprouts and sprouting broccoli exposed to wind.
- Start new compost heaps. Spread the compost you made this year over vacant ground.

Above: *Pick lettuces and salad leaves.*

FRUIT

PLANTING NOW:
- Strawberries

PRUNE:
- Complete any remaining summer pruning of apples and pears.
- Cut off old canes of blackberries and hybrid berries after fruiting and tie in the new ones ready for next year.
- Finish pruning and tying in summer fruiting gooseberries, cutting off any mildewed tips and burning them.
- Finish pruning wall-trained peaches, and nectarines.
- Prune blackcurrants and take cuttings from healthy plants.
- Prune plums and damsons straight after they finish cropping.
- Remove dead wood from wall-trained cherries. Tie down or cut out strong vertical shoots and complete tying-in.

HARVESTING NOW:
- Blackberries
- Blueberries
- Apples (early and mid-season)
- Apricots
- Cobnuts and filberts
- Damsons
- Figs
- Grapes
- Pears (early and mid-season)
- Plums
- Raspberries (autumn-fruiting)
- Strawberries (perpetual)

GENERAL:
- Clear weeds around fruit bushes and trees as these may seed.
- Cover perpetual varieties of strawberry with cloches.
- Order new fruit trees and bushes.
- Prepare for storage by obtaining or cleaning wooden trays and boxes.
- Protect ripening fruit on outdoor vines by covering them with netting. Fold back leaves away from the fruit trusses. Remove damaged or mouldy grapes.
- Remove mulches from around fruit bushes and trees.

LAST CHANCE TO:
- Plant strawberries.

HERBS

SOWING OUTDOORS NOW:
- Angelica
- Chives
- Coriander (cilantro)

SOWING UNDER COVER:
- Chervil
- Parsley

HARVESTING NOW
- Angelica
- Basil
- Bay
- Borage
- Caraway

Above: *Transplant sage seedlings.*

- Chervil
- Chives
- Coriander
- Dill
- Fennel
- Horseradish
- Hyssop
- Liquorice
- Marjoram
- Mint
- Parsley
- Rosemary
- Sage
- Sweet cicely
- Thyme
- Winter savory

GENERAL:
- Trim parsley to encourage fresh shoots and cut back herbs that have flowered, such as marjoram or oregano, to encourage a second flush.
- Take cuttings of rosemary, lavender, bay and hyssop and divide herbs before they die back in the cold, in order to keep clumps potted up in the greenhouse for use over the winter.
- Plant out spring sown seedlings of sage.

PLANT HEALTH

Pests and diseases:
▷ When bringing tender, pot grown plants under cover, check carefully for any pests and diseases they may have picked up outside, in particular red spider mite, mealybug and scale insect, treating these as they are seen.
▷ Remove nets from soft fruit to allow the birds to clear up pests over the winter. Hoeing around fruit trees and bushes will also expose pests to birds and other predators.
▷ Begin painting or applying grease bands to trunks of fruit trees to protect against pests next spring.
▷ Cut out gooseberry, apple and pear shoots infected with powdery mildew and destroy infected shoots by burning. Never compost them as this will spread the spores around the plot.
▷ Place slug traps around new sowings and plantings, ideally doing this a week or two before sowing or planting.

Soil and climate:
▷ Ventilate greenhouses and frames during the remaining warmer days to prevent soaring temperatures, but reduce ventilation once the cooler autumn weather sets in. Damping down usually becomes unnecessary as the month progresses.
▷ Reduce watering under cover and try to do this in the earlier part of the day, so that conditions are dry by evening.
▷ Make a note of what was growing where for your crop rotation before harvesting.

Above: *Apply grease bands to trees.*

MID-AUTUMN

Mid-autumn sees a distinct chill setting in as days become much shorter. The growing season is all but over and the winter feel is further enhanced at the end of the month as vegetation dies back and trees and bushes lose their leaves. There is much to be done on the allotment, though, in order to prepare for the new season to come, and the ever-shortening days from now until mid-winter mean that time spent on the allotment becomes all the more action-packed as a result.

Above: *It is time to pick apples when the first fruits have begun to fall and the stems separate easily from the branches.*

OVERVIEW

Despite occasional warm days, frosts become increasingly likely as winter approaches. Gales and rain are both to be expected from now on. Having said this, if the summer and autumn have been warm, sheltered locations can still expect reasonable conditions.

Prepare for frost by moving tender plants into the greenhouse. Outdoors, slightly tender specimens will need a covering of fleece, straw, bracken, paper or some other packing material to protect them from the ravages of the winter. A thick layer of mulch over dormant crowns of tender crops will ensure they return strongly next spring.

The wise should remember that it is easy to be tricked by the first mild days of mid-autumn, as with early spring. Warm days are frequently punctuated by sharp, night time frost, particularly under clear skies, and it is these sudden fluctuations in temperature that wreak havoc on any crops that have not yet been harvested.

VEGETABLES

SOWING OUTDOORS NOW:
- Broad (fava) beans (mild areas)
- Carrots
- Garlic
- Peas (early round-seeded types in mild areas)
- Spinach (summer and winter in mild areas)
- Winter lettuce (mild areas)

SOWING UNDER COVER NOW:
Under cloches or cold frames:
- Broad beans
- Carrots
- Cauliflowers (early summer)
- Peas (early)
- Radishes (indoor)
- Salad leaves
- Spinach
- Winter lettuces

PLANTING OUTDOORS NOW
- New potatoes (plant early cultivars in sacks of compost to harvest in early winter)
- Onion sets (winter)
- Spring cabbages
- Winter lettuces (mild areas)

HARVESTING NOW:
- Beetroot (beets)
- Brussels sprouts

Above: *Harvest Florence fennel.*

- Cabbages
- Carrots
- Cauliflowers (autumn)
- Celeriac
- Celery (self-blanching),
- Chicory (red and sugarloaf)
- Chinese artichokes
- Endives
- Florence fennel
- French (green) beans
- Kohlrabi
- Leeks
- Lettuces
- Onions (spring and bulb)
- Oriental greens
- Parsnips
- Peas (maincrop)
- Peppers
- Potatoes (maincrop)
- Pumpkins and squashes

- Radishes (summer)
- Runner (green) beans
- Salsify
- Scorzonera
- Spinach (summer)
- Swedes (rutabagas)
- Swiss chard
- Sweetcorn (corn)
- Turnips

GENERAL:
- Continue to earth up celery and leeks.
- Protect cauliflowers by bending leaves over the white curds.
- Cut down tall stems of Jerusalem artichokes as they yellow and place on the compost heap.

LAST CHANCE TO:
- Plant winter onion sets.

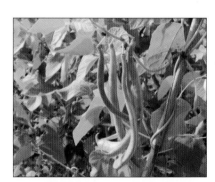

Above: *Harvest runner beans.*

FRUIT

PLANTING NOW:
- Strawberries

PRUNE:
- Finish pruning blackberries and hybrid berries.
- Prune blackcurrants if not already done, but delay the pruning of gooseberries, red and white currants until leaf fall. If bird damage is likely then delay this until spring.
- Remove any broken branches from stone fruit trees and treat the resultant wounds to protect them from fungal infection.
- Root prune excessively vigorous bushes or small trees, waiting a week or so after leaf fall.

HARVESTING NOW:
- Apples
- Cranberries
- Grapes
- Melons
- Pears
- Raspberries

GENERAL:
- Commence planting fruit trees and bushes as soon as leaves fall.
- Do not mix late apples in the store with earlier cultivars.
- Keep apples and pears separate.
- Lift and divide old rhubarb crowns.
- Order new fruit trees early (in advance of the coming planting season) to make sure you get the varieties you want.
- Prepare the ground for planting new fruit bushes and trees from late autumn onward. Give a dressing of rock phosphate a couple of days before planting new stock.
- Provide winter protection for wall-trained outdoor figs to help embryonic green figs overwinter
- Take hardwood cuttings from this year's growth on healthy berry plants.
- Tidy strawberry beds, removing leaves from perpetual types.

LAST CHANCE TO:
- Plant out strawberry plants before spring.

HERBS

SOWING OUTDOORS NOW:
- Angelica
- Lovage
- Scatter the seed of annuals and second year biennials that have finished flowering.

SOWING UNDER COVER:
- Chervil
- Parsley

HARVESTING NOW
- Bay
- Marjoram
- Parsley
- Rosemary
- Sage
- Thyme

GENERAL:
- Lift and divide sections of selected herbs, which can be potted up and transferred to the greenhouse for use as winter crops.

- Parsley and herbs sown outside for late season crops will need to be covered with cloches before the winter.
- Plant evergreen hedge plants such as box if these are to be used to divide your herb plot.
- Plant hardy perennial herbs such as rosemary and sage.
- Tender herbs such as basil will not survive outside during the winter, so bring them under cover.
- Start planning a new herb garden or think about changes you want to make to an existing one.

Above: *Cover outdoor crops with cloches.*

PLANT HEALTH

Pests and diseases:
▷ Put up sticky grease bands on fruit trees to protect them from female winter moths. Tree stakes will also need banding if they provide a route up into the branches.
▷ Collect fallen apples and pears affected with brown rot. Pick off any affected fruit that remains on the tree otherwise the fruits become mummified and form a source of infection for next year.
▷ Remove mulches from around fruit bushes and trees so that overwintering pests will be exposed to birds and other predators.

Above: *Lift all potatoes and dry off.*

▷ Take care not to spread compost used for tomato growing over your potato beds, as these crops can share many pests and diseases.
▷ Always ensure that you do not compost any diseased material.
▷ Always check for slug damage and disease whilst hoeing between rows.

Soil and climate:
▷ Dig the plot over as soon as you have cleared crops, removing all residues except for the roots of peas or beans.
▷ Draw up plans for next year's cropping, paying close attention to crop rotation.
▷ Ground to be left vacant until the spring will benefit from having a green manure sown, such as field beans, winter tares and Italian ryegrass to prevent autumn weeds establishing and to act as a soil improver.
▷ Lift any remaining potatoes before late autumn arrives, as keel slugs become a problem by then and can cause considerable losses. Allow them to dry off and store in hessian or paper sacks to prevent storage rots.

LATE AUTUMN

Winter is drawing ever closer: a fact to which the leaves, which by now are falling rapidly everywhere, will attest. Long, colder nights and frequent rain tend to be the norm, but mild spells are possible and a few crops continue to grow and produce a harvest. The gardener's work is far from over, though, as late autumn sees the commencement of a great deal of pruning and planting, tidying and preparation, not only in readiness for the winter cold and wet that lies ahead, but also for the coming spring.

Above: *To harvest Swiss chard, cut the leaves from the base as they mature. Trim off any older leaves and discard them.*

OVERVIEW

Cold snaps are likely, particularly in the last few days of autumn, and frost, gales, freezing rain or even some early snow can become a distinct possibility, depending on where you live. It is important, therefore, that you and your allotment are prepared in advance for cold weather.

Once leaves have fallen from deciduous (not evergreen) shrubs and trees, these can now be collected and either put on the compost heap, or into plastic sacks with several holes poked into them. These will rot down and make leaf-mould – one of the finest soil conditioners there is. It is important that you use plastic sacks only

for leaves, however, as any other plant material is likely to yield little more than a smelly, slimey, useless mess.

As long as the ground is not waterlogged or frozen, continue digging, especially on clay soils, so frosts can help make them crumbly and easy to work. Sandy soils can be left as late as early spring.

VEGETABLES

SOWING OUTDOORS NOW:

- Broad (fava) beans (mild areas)
- Peas (mild areas on free-draining ground)
N.B. Keep both peas and beans under cloches if a hard winter threatens.

SOWING UNDER COVER NOW:

- Broad beans (in pots in an unheated greenhouse)
- Peas (in pots in an unheated greenhouse)
- Dig up chicory roots to be forced, pot them up and position them in a dark warm place.

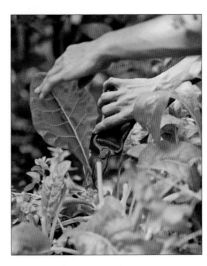

Above: *Harvest leafy greens.*

Under cloches:

- Broad beans
- Peas

PLANTING OUTDOORS NOW

- Garlic

HARVESTING NOW:

- Beetroot (beets)
- Brussels sprouts
- Cabbages (winter)
- Carrots
- Cauliflowers
- Celeriac
- Chicory (red and sugar-loaf)
- Endives
- Jerusalem and Chinese artichokes
- Kohlrabi
- Leeks
- Lettuces (protected winter)
- Oriental greens
- Spinach (summer and winter)
- Swedes
- Swiss chard
- Salad plants
- Turnips

GENERAL:

- Cover endive and sea kale with bins or large flower pots to blanch them.
- Cut down any dead asparagus (if not already done) and cover beds or rows with crumbly compost or well-rotted manure.

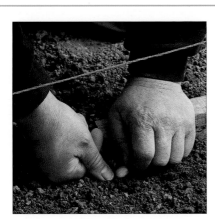

Above: *Plant garlic cloves outdoors.*

- Give protection to globe artichokes in very cold areas.
- Order seed catalogues for next year, if you have not already done so.
- Place cloches over perpetual spinach to protect it.
- Place orders for seed potatoes now to ensure you get the varieties you want, as some are always in short supply due to popular demand.
- Remove yellow and decaying leaves from Brussels sprouts and other brassicas. Place these on the compost heap.

LAST CHANCE TO:

- Plant garlic.
- Sow spinach (winter).

Above: *Finish picking pears.*

FRUIT

PLANTING OUTDOORS NOW:
- Cane, bush and top fruit trees, pruning these immediately after planting.
- Rhubarb crowns

PRUNE:
- All currants and berries not already done in mid-autumn.
- Begin pruning grape vines, immediately after the leaves have fallen. Cut all fruited shoots back to one or two buds from the main stem.
- Continue formative pruning of dwarf pyramid, espalier, fans and other restricted forms.
- Prune established apples and pears immediately after leaf fall, but do not prune plum trees.
- Root prune over-vigorous trees only after leaf fall.
- Summer-pruned trees should be pruned back to mature wood where secondary shoots have been produced.

HARVESTING NOW:
- Complete picking of all but the very late apples and pears.

GENERAL:
- If the plot is not ready when bare-root plants arrive, heel them into a spare piece of ground to keep the roots from drying out.
- Regularly check stored fruits, removing any rotting or mouldy specimens promptly so the rot doesn't spread.
- Take hardwood cuttings of gooseberries, redcurrants, white currants and blackcurrants.
- Check supports and wires for raspberries and blackberries and ensure that canes are securely tied. Loosely bundle new canes together and tie to a wire for winter protection.
- Check tree ties, stakes and rabbit guards on young fruit trees before any winter gales.
- Order any new fruit trees and bushes, if you didn't do this last month.

LAST CHANCE TO:
- Plant cane fruits (before early spring) on wet or heavy soils.
- Repair fruit cages to protect buds from birds during the winter.

HERBS

SOWING OUTDOORS NOW:
- Angelica
- Sweet cicely

SOWING UNDER COVER:
- Chervil
- Chives
- Parsley

HARVESTING NOW:
- Bay
- Chives (under cover)
- Hyssop
- Mint (under cover)
- Parsley (under cover)
- Rosemary
- Sage

GENERAL:
- Place cloches over tender herbs or those sensitive to excess rain, to protect them against winter wet and cold.
- Divide and pot up plants of chive or mint, and grow them under cover for winter use.
- In wet areas, apply gravel mulch and/or a well ventilated cloche to help prevent botrytis (grey mould) and fungal leaf spots on Mediterranean herbs, such as rosemary, sage and thyme.

PLANT HEALTH

Pests and diseases:
▷ Cover all brassicas with netting if pigeons are a problem.
▷ Watch out for pests, such as aphids, on over-wintering plants or glasshouse crops.
▷ Ventilate glasshouses, frames and cloches well on mild days and remove any yellow or dead leaves and plant debris to reduce the chances of fungal spread.
▷ As the days shorten, reduce watering to a minimum for specimens growing under cover in pots, in order to keep roots healthy and reduce the spread of soil-borne pests.
▷ Collect and dispose of any apples and pears affected with brown rot.
▷ Ensure fruit cages are closed and netting is in good order, as this will help prevent bud damage from birds.
▷ Trap winter moths by placing grease bands around fruit trees.

Soil and climate:
▷ Late autumn is a good time to check soil pH and to add lime if needed to bring it to the ideal conditions for next year's crop.
▷ Remove or clean off shading in glasshouses or frames and wash down glass.
▷ Remove all remaining plant debris from the allotment. Do not compost any diseased material; burn or bin it.

Above: *Remove greenhouse shading.*

EARLY WINTER

Although a few mild days are still likely, early winter marks the time where it begins to get much colder. The approach of the shortest day is enhanced by increasingly cloudy conditions, meaning that light levels are significantly reduced. This, combined with cold winds and the ever-present risk of snow or icy conditions, eventually brings crop growth to a virtual standstill. It is not a period of total rest though, and you should use the time wisely to make plans for the growing season to come.

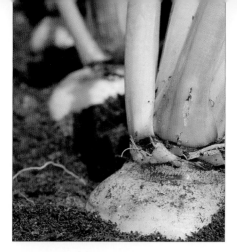

Above: *You should try to lift any turnips by the beginning of winter or they may become woody and inedible.*

OVERVIEW
In all but the very mildest areas, or those within the shelter and stored heat of cities, night frosts should be expected from now until spring. Even in relatively mild spells, gales, wind and rain can make it feel colder than temperatures would suggest and it can be a tough time for any remaining winter crops.

Frosts are not all bad news, however, as they improve the flavour of winter vegetables. Sprouts, winter cabbages and parsnips are all considerably sweetened by frost, meaning that they are at their best from now until spring. Frost also helps to improve the crumb structure of previously dug soil, and may kill off some pests and diseases.

The hiatus in growth can be a welcome break, and one in which you can do plenty of planning for the growing season ahead. Review what you grew over the last season and spend some time reading the seed and plant catalogues you ordered in the autumn to see what is on offer and perhaps plan to grow something different.

VEGETABLES
SOWING OUTDOORS NOW:
• Nothing

SOWING UNDER COVER NOW:
• Carrots (round varieties)
• Cauliflowers
• Lettuces
• Onions
• Salad onions
• Spinach
• Summer cabbages
• Turnips

Under cloches:
• Onions (if they can be kept frost free)

PLANTING OUTDOORS NOW:
• Shallots (the shortest day of the year is the traditional time to plant them)

HARVESTING NOW:
• Beetroot (beets)
• Brussels sprouts
• Cabbages (winter)
• Carrots
• Kale
• Leeks
• Lettuces (protected)
• Salad leaves (protected)
• Parsnips
• Perpetual spinach (protected)
• Swedes (rutabagas)
• Turnips

GENERAL:
• Dig up chicory roots to be forced, potting them up and positioning them in a dark warm place.
• Firm the roots of all winter brassica crops that may have been lifted by frosts and net them against pigeons.
• Force sea kale outside using a light-proof upturned pot.
• Lift a few leeks at a time and heel them in to freshly dug soil, which will not freeze solid, to make harvesting easier.

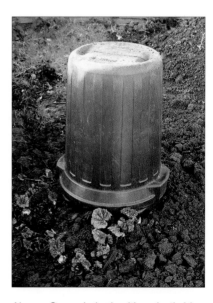

Above: *Cover rhubarb with a plastic bin.*

Above: Dig a slit trench for beans.

• Lift winter root crops such as parsnips and swedes before the ground becomes frozen, in very cold areas.
• Mature rhubarb crowns can be covered with a large forcing pot or an upturned, tall, plastic bin.
• Prepare a bean trench.
• Stake tall Brussels sprouts by placing a short stake on the windward side and tying the plant to it.

LAST CHANCE TO:
• Harvest late trench-grown celery that has been protected from frost.
• Harvest the last of the kohl rabi before the end of the month.

FRUIT

PLANTING NOW:

- Apples
- Pears
- Soft fruit

PRUNE:

- Apples (in frost-free periods)
- Autumn-fruiting raspberries (to ground level)
- Finish any root pruning
- Gooseberries
- Pears (in frost-free periods)
- Redcurrants
- White currants

HARVESTING NOW:

- Gather any very late-maturing apples.

GENERAL:

- Feed all fruit trees with slow-release fertilizers and apply a thick layer of compost or well-rotted manure.
- Lift and divide overgrown crowns of rhubarb, bringing small sections into a cool greenhouse for forcing.
- Take hardwood cuttings of soft fruit gooseberries, redcurrants, white currants and black currants.
- Trees that cannot be planted directly should be heeled in at a 45° degree angle.

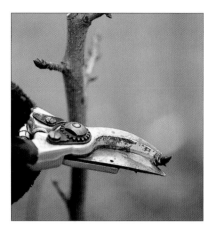

Above: *Prune pear trees.*

HERBS

SOWING OUTDOORS NOW:

- None

SOWING UNDER COVER NOW:

- None

HARVESTING NOW:

- Bay
- Chervil
- Marjoram
- Parsley (protected)
- Rosemary
- Sage
- Thyme

GENERAL:

- Place cloches over tender herbs or those sensitive to excess rain (if not done already), and protect them from the winter wet and cold.
- Mulch the crowns of herbs that have died down for the winter – this will improve drainage and provide some frost protection.
- In cold areas, either bring bay trees under cover for the winter, or place them in a sheltered position.
- Bring mint, chives and other herbs into a greenhouse or sheltered frame to 'force' them for winter use.

PLANT HEALTH

Pests and diseases:

- ▷ Apply fatty acid-based winter washes to dormant fruit trees to control over-wintering pest problems, such as aphids, apple suckers and scale insects.
- ▷ Ensure that crops remaining in the ground, such as Brussels sprouts, cabbage and other brassicas as well as new sowings under cloches, are protected with adequate netting from pests such as mice and pigeons.

Soil and climate:

- ▷ Even at this time of year, a little winter sun can raise the heat in cold frames to quite high levels, so give ventilation when required.
- ▷ Reduce watering and feeding of all indoor crops as the days shorten.
- ▷ Clear leaves and twigs from greenhouse and shed gutters.
- ▷ Check all stakes and ties on fruit trees and bushes, 'firming in' any loose plants and loosening ties if constricted.
- ▷ Do not apply fertilizer to freshly dug ground, left rough to allow the frost to break the soil down, as without any crops, it will leach away quickly.
- ▷ Cover part of the vegetable plot with polythene to warm up the soil if you want to make early sowings in late winter.
- ▷ Top up compost and leafmould bins.

Above: *Leeks and brassicas such as cabbages are winter mainstays on the allotment.*

MID-WINTER

Mid-winter remains cold, and although the days gradually begin to lengthen, much of your plot will remain dormant. This makes it the perfect time to finalize plans for your allotment and firm your resolve in preparation for the coming season. Long winter nights present an ideal opportunity to brush up your garden knowledge by giving your gardening books a really good read and, on any fine days, you can catch up on a whole host of jobs before crops start to grow in earnest.

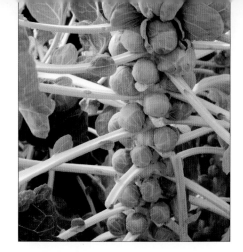

Above: *Brussels sprouts are plentiful in mid-winter. Their distinctive flavour often improves following a frost.*

OVERVIEW

As mid-winter progresses, it's soon time to make the first sowings of seeds under cover. As late winter approaches, take the opportunity to clean out your frames and greenhouses. Good hygiene will be important over the coming season as it will help to prevent fungal diseases that may devastate seedlings and tender plants later in the spring. Clear out all of the old plant debris and wash down the glass to increase the light transmission.

Take some time to thoroughly clean and oil all your garden tools to ensure that they are fit for action in the season ahead. Start by giving them a good wash, preferably with hot soapy water, but do not soak wooden handles as this can lift the grain. Leave them to dry thoroughly before wiping over with an oily rag to stop them going rusty.

If you did not finish your winter digging before Christmas all is not lost as heavy soils can still benefit from frost action in the cold of mid-winter.

VEGETABLES

SOWING OUTDOORS NOW:
- None

SOWING UNDER COVER NOW:
- Broad (fava) beans
- Cabbages (summer)
- Carrots (round varieties)
- Cauliflowers (summer)
- Leeks
- Lettuce
- Onions (early)
- Peas (early)
- Radishes
- Salad onions
- Spinach
- Turnips
- Winter salad leaves

On a heated bench or propagator:
- Aubergines (eggplants)
- Chillies
- Peppers
- Tomatoes

Under cloches:
- Broad beans
- Garlic
- Lettuces
- Peas (early)

PLANTING OUTDOORS NOW:
- None

Above: *Work from a plank of wood.*

HARVESTING NOW:
- Beetroot (beets)
- Brussels sprouts
- Cabbages (winter)
- Cauliflowers (protected)
- Carrots
- Chinese and Jerusalem artichokes
- Celeriac
- Endive
- Jerusalem artichokes
- Kale
- Leeks
- Lettuces (protected)
- Salad leaves (protected)
- Salsify
- Scorzonera
- Parsnips
- Perpetual spinach (protected)
- Radishes (winter)
- Sprouting broccoli
- Swedes
- Swiss chard
- Turnips

GENERAL:
- Continue preparing ground as long as it is not waterlogged or frozen. When working on wet soils, try to do so from a plank of wood, rather than treading directly on a bed, to avoid soil compaction.
- Force sea kale and chicory outside in milder areas. Chicory can also be forced indoors.
- Start the sprouts on early seed potatoes. Set the tubers to chit (produce shoots) as soon as they arrive.

LAST CHANCE TO:
- Order seed potatoes if not already done.

Above: *Sow early onion seed under cover.*

Above: *Mulch fruit trees.*

FRUIT

PLANTING NOW:
- Apples
- Pears
- Soft fruits

PRUNE:
- Apples
- Established and newly planted bush fruit
- Pears
- Raspberries (summer-fruiting)

HARVESTING NOW:
- None

GENERAL:
- Apply a balanced fertilizer such as fish blood and bone to cobnuts and filberts.
- Apply a potassium-rich fertilizer such as wood ash to strawberries, gooseberries, red and white currants to help them through cold spells.
- Mulch fruit trees, bushes and canes with organic matter.
- Place cloches over existing rows of strawberries to ensure an early crop. Remove covers on fine days to allow pollinators in.
- Prepare a bed for strawberries. Ensure that this is done at least one month before planting.
- Rhubarb can be divided and crown sections brought indoors for forcing.
- Sow alpine strawberry seeds under cover.
- Trees that arrive and cannot be planted directly should be heeled in, in a sheltered spot at a 45° degree angle away from the wind.

LAST CHANCE TO:
- Order bare-root trees and bushes for winter planting.

HERBS

SOWING OUTDOORS NOW:
- None

SOWING UNDER COVER:
- Chervil (glasshouse or frame)
- Chives (glasshouse or frame)
- Parsley (glasshouse or frame)
- Summer savory (heated propagator)

HARVESTING NOW:
- Bay
- Chervil
- Marjoram
- Parsley (protected)
- Rosemary
- Sage
- Thyme

GENERAL:
- As late winter approaches some undercover sowings of herbs can commence. Prepare the ground by placing cloches over the soil to warm it up before planting them out under these in early spring.

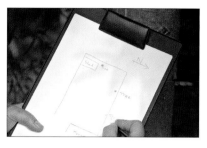

Above: *Make a plan for next year.*

- In mild spells, some plants will make new growth. Protect these with cloches to enable an early harvest.
- Review what has done well this year and spend some time planning new ideas and plantings for next year.
- There is relatively little to do in the herb patch at this time of the year. Most plants are dormant, surviving the winter on stored energy made during the growing season.
- Tidy the patch and prepare the ground where new plants are to be planted by digging well-rotted organic matter into the soil.

PLANT HEALTH

Pests and diseases:
▷ Remove big buds on blackcurrants and burn them to control the mite that causes this condition.
▷ Inspect apples and pears for canker, removing infected material and destroying by burning if possible.

Soil and climate:
▷ Check all tree stakes and ties on newly planted specimens for firmness, especially after gales.
▷ Move any stacks of pots, bundles of old canes, etc, outside to sit in the frost for a couple of weeks as this will help to kill off any over-wintering pests.
▷ Watch out for winter germinating ephemeral weeds such as chickweed or bitter-cress, which can soon overwhelm winter salads and other plants, particularly on rich soils.
▷ Avoid pruning fruit trees and bushes during periods of hard frost as the newly cut wound may be damaged by this.
▷ Net crops if not already done so to reduce pigeon damage.

▷ Regularly check stored fruit and vegetables and remove any rotting or mouldy specimens.
▷ Wash canes and supports in storage.
▷ Ventilate cold frames when possible to help prevent build-ups of mildew. Leave them open on mild days but remember to close them at night or if the weather changes.
▷ Continue turning compost heaps to increase decomposition. Leave freshly dug ground for frost to break down, as this will make final cultivation easier in the spring.
▷ When digging soils that are on the acidic side, apply lime to the surface at 70g/m² (2oz/yd²). This is especially important if brassicas were grown in the plot the year before.
▷ Clear spent crop residue and compost. Burn items such as cabbage roots that could spread clubroot.
▷ Make a cropping plan of the plot and set out a rotation system for vegetable plots to ensure the same ones are not grown in the same beds year after year. This will help prevent disease build up.

LATE WINTER

Despite gradually lengthening days and the promise of spring to come, late winter often gives us the coldest conditions of the year, and this can limit the work you can do, particularly when frost or a covering of snow keeps you off the land. Despite this, however, it is also a time of promise as the new green shoots of spring begin to appear above the soil. It's a time to start raising new stock, and often represents the last chance you will get to finish planning and preparing for the coming season.

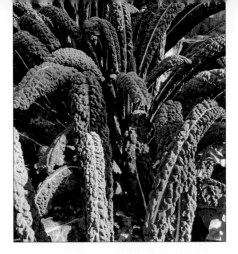

Above: *Kale is a fabulous winter vegetable, packed with flavour and beneficial nutrients, so it is well worth growing on an allotment.*

OVERVIEW

Despite the cold, late winter is a time to get out and check over-wintering crops. Although the winter takes its toll on the allotment, at the first sign of any warmth, those gradually lengthening days soon start to bring a return to growth for some crops and, with this, a fresh harvest.

It is still a little early for outdoor sowing, although seeds can now be sown under cover and it is time to plant some hardier varieties of crops as spring approaches. The real urgency now, however, is that late winter is the last chance to finish off all of those important jobs that help to pave the way for the season ahead.

Ground preparation can continue apace, as you begin to break down the rough dug earth that you left for the winter frosts to work on. Late winter is also the perfect time to apply a dressing of bonemeal to perennial or over-wintering crops. It takes a few weeks before it starts to break down in the soil, providing a ready source of plant food.

VEGETABLES

SOWING OUTDOORS NOW:
- Cabbages (summer)
- Carrots (early)
- Fennel
- Parsnips

SOWING UNDER COVER NOW:
- Brussels sprouts (for early picking)
- Bulb onions
- Cabbages (summer)
- Cauliflowers
- Celery
- Celeriac
- Kohlrabi
- Leeks
- Lettuces
- Spring onions (scallions)

On a heated bench or propagator:
- Aubergines (eggplants)
- Cucumbers
- French (green) beans
- Peppers
- Tomatoes

Under cloches:
- Beetroot (beets) (early)
- Bulb onions
- Carrots
- Parsnips
- Peas (mangetouts or sugar snaps)
- Potatoes (compact early varieties)

- Radishes
- Spinach
- Spring onions (scallions)
- Turnips

PLANTING OUTDOORS NOW:
- Broad (fava) beans
- Early potatoes
- Garlic
- Jerusalem artichokes
- Lettuces (autumn-sown)
- Onions (sets)
- Peas (early and snap)
- Shallots
- Spinach

HARVESTING NOW:
- Celery
- Celeriac
- Chicory
- Chinese and Jerusalem artichokes
- Early purple sprouting broccoli
- Endives
- Kale
- Leeks
- Oriental greens
- Parsnips
- Radishes
- Salad plants (protected)
- Salsify (forced)
- Scorzonera
- Sea kale
- Swiss chard

- Winter brassicas
- Winter spinach

GENERAL:
- Draw up earth to the hearts of young spring cabbages and apply a fertilizer such as bone-meal.
- Dress asparagus beds with a general fertilizer such as fish blood and bone.
- Salsify and sea kale can be forced outdoors in mild areas.
- Start potatoes into growth now (if not already done), in trays in a cool frost-free place with plenty of light for around four weeks before planting.
- Start to dig in over-wintered green manures prior to planting.

LAST CHANCE TO:
- Dig, lime or manure beds in time for spring planting.

Above: *Plant out early potatoes.*

FRUIT

PLANTING OUTDOORS NOW:

- Rhubarb
- Strawberries
- Trees and bushes

PRUNE:

- Apple and pear trees
- Blackcurrants
- Cobnuts and filberts (if weather is mild)
- Gooseberries
- Newly planted and established stone fruits as growth begins
- Outdoor and indoor vines
- Raspberries (autumn-fruiting, to 15cm (6in) from ground
- Raspberries (tip-pruned, summer-fruiting)

Above: *Prune apple trees.*

HARVESTING NOW:

- Rhubarb (forced)

GENERAL:

- Apply nitrogen-rich fertilizer and mulch to young trees, bushes and cane fruit with manure or compost as early spring approaches.
- Apply potassium-rich fertilizer to apples, pears and plums.
- Check all stored fruit and remove any that show signs of rotting or shrivelling.
- Check all tree stakes and ties on newly planted specimens for firmness, especially after gales. Do not let bush fruit or fruit trees crop in the first year.
- Cover wall-trained trees with draped hessian or the equivalent.
- Divide rhubarb crowns into sections, replanting some and forcing the remainder under cover.
- Place cloches over strawberries early in the month for an early crop.
- Sow melon seeds under cover in a heated propagator to extend the cropping season.

LAST CHANCE TO:

- Plant bare-rooted trees and shrubs.
- Prune apple and pear trees.

PLANT HEALTH

Pests and diseases:

▷ Peaches and nectarines can be protected against peach leaf curl if not sheeted over by spraying them with Bordeaux mixture.
▷ Apply sticky bands to apple trees.
▷ Check apples and pears for canker and treat if necessary, pruning out infection if possible.

Above: *Tidy up plant debris.*

▷ Net cabbages and other crops to reduce pigeon damage.
▷ Dig up any 'volunteer' potato plants growing from tubers left in last year, as soon as you see them. They could be carrying potato blight.
▷ Clear up any plant debris, and remove diseased leaves from overwintered crops; put them on the compost heap.

Soil and climate:

▷ Ground left rough for winter frosts to penetrate can now be broken down if not too wet.
▷ Place protective covering over soil in areas where you are going to plant or sow seeds to warm up of the earth so that sowing can take place earlier.
▷ Elsewhere, complete all digging, liming and manuring by the end of the winter, if possible, as time is now running out for this.

Above: *Harvest hyssop.*

HERBS

SOWING OUTDOORS NOW:

- Chervil (under cloches in mild areas)
- Chives (under cloches in mild areas)
- Dill (under cloches in mild areas)
- Parsley (under cloches in mild areas)
- Sage (under cloches in mild areas)

SOWING UNDER COVER:

- Chervil
- Chives
- Dill
- Parsley
- Rocket (arugula)
- Sage

HARVESTING NOW:

- Horseradish
- Hyssop
- Parsley
- Sage
- Thyme
- Winter savory

GENERAL:

- Clear away any dead twigs and remains of fallen leaves from perennial herbs, especially if they are lying on top of the plants, and mulch them with a 2–5cm (1–2in) thick layer of garden compost.
- Lift, divide and pot up plants of chives for growing indoors.
- Protect tender shoots that have emerged during mild spells against hard frosts with fleece or hessian. Remove the protection on warmer days to allow air to circulate around the plants.
- Repair any paths and bed edgings as necessary before growth recommences.

INDEX